Empires of Trust

EMPIRES OF TRUST

How Rome Built—and America Is Building—

a New World

THOMAS F. MADDEN

DUTTON

DUTTON
Published by Penguin Group (USA) Inc.
375 Hudson Street, New York, New York 10014, U.S.A.
Penguin Group (Canada), 90 Eglinton Avenue East, Suite 700, Toronto, Ontario M4P 2Y3, Canada (a division of Pearson Penguin Canada Inc.) • Penguin Books Ltd, 80 Strand, London WC2R 0RL, England • Penguin Ireland, 25 St Stephen's Green, Dublin 2, Ireland (a division of Penguin Books Ltd) • Penguin Group (Australia), 250 Camberwell Road, Camberwell, Victoria 3124, Australia (a division of Pearson Australia Group Pty Ltd) • Penguin Books India Pvt Ltd, 11 Community Centre, Panchsheel Park, New Delhi – 110 017, India • Penguin Group (NZ), 67 Apollo Drive, Rosedale, North Shore 0632, New Zealand (a division of Pearson New Zealand Ltd) • Penguin Books (South Africa) (Pty) Ltd, 24 Sturdee Avenue, Rosebank, Johannesburg 2196, South Africa

Penguin Books Ltd, Registered Offices: 80 Strand, London WC2R 0RL, England

Published by Dutton, a member of Penguin Group (USA) Inc.

First printing, July 2008

10   9   8   7   6   5   4   3   2   1

Ⓡ REGISTERED TRADEMARK—MARCA REGISTRADA

LIBRARY OF CONGRESS CATALOGING-IN-PUBLICATION DATA
Madden, Thomas F.
    Empires of trust : how Rome built—and America is building—a new world / by Thomas F. Madden.—1st ed.
        p.   cm.
    Includes bibliographical references.
    ISBN 978-0-525-95074-5
    1. Rome—History—Republic, 510–30 B.C. 2. United States—History—20th century. 3. United States—History—21st century. 4. United States—Public opinion. 5. United States—Foreign public opinion. 6. Comparative civilization. I. Title.
    DG231.M23 2008
    937—dc22   2008006646

Printed in the United States of America

Designed by Carla Bolte • Set in Granjon

For Helena and Melinda

CONTENTS

PREFACE

There is an exceptionally beneficial and fruitful advantage to be derived from the study of the past. There you see, set in the clear light of historical truth, examples of every possible type. From these you can select for yourself and your country what to imitate, and also what, as being mischievous in its inception and disastrous in its consequences, you should avoid.

—Titus Livius (Livy), *Ab urbe condita,* preface

By historical standards, the United States is a young country. We shouldn't be surprised, then, if Americans tend to view the great expanse of human history as stretching not too far beyond the past generation or two. And they do. Don't believe me? If you have a television handy, try turning on the History Channel right now. Then wait for the end of the commercial. There, see? Odds are that you are watching a show about something that occurred less than one hundred years ago—probably a documentary on World War II. The people at the History Channel know what sells. And Nazis sell.

As a history professor, I see this all the time in my undergraduate students. Like many Americans, they consider the historical period from World War II until the present to be modern history. Anything between the Declaration of Independence and Pearl Harbor is lumped into a foggy world of early history. Before 1776 brings us to ancient history, which is, well, ancient history. It doesn't matter. As a specialist in the premodern world, that naturally irritates me. But if I'm honest, I also have to say that it provides a nice measure of safety and security too. Historians of the twentieth century are forever caught up in modern politics, always scrutinized for their political leanings and the effect those have on their histories. Medieval historians, on the other hand, are free to research and tell their stories without a thought about controversy. After all, no one cares anymore if you are a Guelf or a Ghibelline. For that reason, premodern historians like me are among the most sheltered of the ivory tower academics. Although most people think that we should have them, premodern historians are often thought of as odd antiquarians—like an old uncle who is forever leafing through dusty scrapbooks in the attic. He's harmless and his stories are good. But you certainly wouldn't ask him for anything serious, like a job or investment advice.

I have spent some time in that happy, quiet attic and I can tell you that it is nice. (If you like that sort of thing.) I thoroughly expected to spend the rest of my life examining big questions like the reception of ecclesiastical reform in high medieval Venice or the sources of Pope Urban II's information on Turkish-held Palestine. These studies would allow us (and by "us" I mean other interested professional historians with the training and interest to read my scholarship) to better understand these aspects of medieval civilization. Studies such as these are very important. Really. It is this kind of specialized research that forms the building blocks of history. Sure, only a handful of people will read those journal articles, but among them some will write specialized books incorporating my research, and then others will use those books to write broader texts that might be assigned in classrooms or even find a general audience. At least that's the way it's supposed to work.

Then came the knock on my attic door. It seems that a group of Islamist terrorists had flown planes into the World Trade Center and the Pentagon. Their organization, al-Qaeda, had a host of grievances against the West, only a few of which occurred after World War II. When Americans asked the question "Why do they hate us?" the answer they got back was a swirl of events including the fall of the Ottoman Empire, the Reconquest of Spain, and the Crusades. Suddenly, "ancient history" was no longer so ancient. Opening the creaky attic door, I was surprised to see a throng of reporters with microphones, notebooks, and cameras. They had a lot of questions.

Before 9/11 the media and I were strangers. No longer. In the hundreds of interviews that I have given since then I've learned a lot about reporters and the press. Although approval ratings for journalists have now sunk to lawyer levels, I have found most interviewers to be pleasant people. They remind me very much of my undergraduates. Like most Americans, they tend to have limited exposure to history before the last century. And what they do know comes disproportionately from television and movies. Many reporters that I talked to swallowed whole the terrorists' contention that the Crusades marked the beginning of the West's long war against Islam—a war that continues to this day. They were genuinely surprised to learn that the Crusades had nothing at all to do with modern events in the Middle East or the development of Islamist extremism. I have seen more than one incredulous face stare at me in amazement as I explained that the Crusades began as a response to Muslim attacks on Christians. That's not what they had heard.

During those years I learned some lessons about the importance of "ancient history." Simply put, ignorance of the past is dangerous. We are in large part defined by our culture and our civilization. If we fail to learn its history, then we have no defense against those who would warp it or corrupt it. In other words, we leave to others, including our enemies, the task of defining us.

Ignorance of the past is dangerous in another way too. It is natural for human beings to look to the past in order to make decisions about the future. We do it all the time in our personal lives. But because so many Americans consider modern (and therefore relevant) history to begin with World War II, we are drastically reducing the lessons and experiences that we can draw from when charting our future course. American schoolchildren today are not trained in Latin or Greek or the Classics or even the history of the medieval world. Instead, they get a smattering of U.S. history sprinkled over the top of a relatively vapid social studies curriculum. Naturally enough, when they grow up and begin making important decisions they will not look to Plato, Cicero, or Dante for guidance. Instead, every challenge will be forcibly jammed into the mold of the last century's events.

It is already happening. Simply look at approaches toward recent American conflicts, including the current occupation of Iraq. For those on the political left, every war is another Vietnam. American intervention overseas, therefore, is usually wrong and must always be short. If it continues longer than a few months, it's a quagmire. The answer, then, is to retreat and avert one's eyes from the aftermath. For conservatives, on the other hand, every conflict is World War II. A clear evil has moved against the United States and it must be defeated, no matter the cost. Appeasement only emboldens the enemy. If your historical horizon extends just sixty years, those are the sorts of lessons you are likely to draw. It is a safe bet, though, that few American policy makers or politicians are looking at Iraq in terms of British colonial wars, or the Mongol invasions, or the campaigns of Trajan, or the conquests of Alexander. Those, after all, are ancient history.

My experiences in the wake of 9/11 led me to reevaluate my role as a scholar and an educator. Although I remain devoted to my research, I see now that it is equally important to speak about history to someone other than my colleagues. History belongs to everyone. Sure, it can be complex. But that doesn't mean that historians shouldn't try to explain it. And if historians don't do it, then we have no right to complain when journalists, novelists, and freelance writers try their hands at it. (And, trust me, we complain.) In short, although I still enjoy my attic, I'm resolved to spend part of my time downstairs telling the family just what I've found. I hope they don't mind the dust.

Which brings us back to the present book. The Crusades are not the only nugget from the distant past that has made an appearance in modern political discourse. Since the fall of the Soviet Union and the emergence of the United States as the only remaining superpower, many commentators have suggested parallels between American hegemony in the modern world and Roman hegemony in the ancient world. These comparisons grew in number after the American invasion of Iraq, which was viewed by some as an act of unprovoked aggression. (Cullen Murphy has even written a recent book entitled *Are We Rome?*) Some have argued that the United States is following in the footsteps of the Romans, building an empire through hard-nosed conquest. That got my attention.

When I began this project my plan was simply to demonstrate that the parallels being drawn between the United States and Rome were either misleading or false. And, for the most part, they are. But the more I looked into the question, the more I began to see that in some very important respects the dynamics that led the Romans toward hegemony seem also to be at work in the growth of American power today. More importantly, I saw that the confluence of those dynamics is exceedingly rare in human history—so much so that they have escaped our notice. This book is about those dynamics and the histories that they caused and are still causing.

What this book is *not* is another political screed that yanks bloody bits of Roman history out of context in order to make hackneyed partisan points. We have enough of those already. Instead, I have tried as much as possible to set the stage as it was in the ancient world, based always on the original sources and modern scholarship. This book, therefore, does not seek to chain the United States to the Roman example and then watch it sink beneath the waves of its "decline and fall." Anyone with even a passing acquaintance with the history of the late Roman Empire knows that it bears almost no similarities with the modern United States. There are, for example, no deified American emperors who must regularly put down rebellious American generals across the world. The Rome that fell, it should be remembered, was over two thousand years old. We should be so lucky. No, the young United States has nothing at all in common with the aged imperial Rome, but it has some important things in common with the youthful Roman Republic. That is what we will explore here.

Let me be clear at the outset: It is not my contention that the United States is a new Rome or that it is precisely following in the course of Roman history. It is not. But, the similarities in culture, self-image, national character, and a host of other factors between the two "empires" is striking and worth examining. What I am arguing is that it was those factors that pushed the Romans into an empire they never wanted—just as they are doing to Americans today. By studying Rome we can learn a lot about ourselves. We can discern opportunities and pitfalls up ahead and learn how the Romans dealt with them or failed to do so. That's important. That's what history—all of it—offers to us.

Throughout this book we will see the word *empire* quite a bit. It's a problematic word, so let me explain what I mean. The English word refers to two sorts of states. The first is one that is governed by an emperor. It doesn't matter if the state is big or small—if it has an emperor then it's an empire. The Holy Roman Empire, the Bulgarian Empire, the Empire of Trebizond ... these are all examples of relatively weak states that are called empires because of the person on the throne. We are not going to worry about those in this book. The other form of empire is a state that has extended its reach beyond its borders and thereby controls other peoples or countries or colonies. It doesn't matter if that state has an emperor or not. It is an empire because of its expansionism—its policy of acquiring foreign lands. This would include states such as the Soviet Empire, the British Empire, the Spanish Empire, and, of course, the Roman Empire. By that definition, the United States has an empire too.

Now, here is the mildly confusing part. Rome was an empire in the geographic, expansionistic sense by 250 BC, but it did not have emperors until 27 BC. Before that time, like the United States, it was a republic. Therefore, when speaking about the Roman government before 27 BC I will refer to the Republic, but when speaking of the expanding Roman world, I will refer to its empire. To avoid confusion, this book will refer to geographic empires according to three different types: Empires of Conquest, Empires of Commerce, and Empires of Trust.

An increasing number of books are being written today on the question of American Empire. All make some appeal to the lessons of history. Those lessons, though, are frequently drawn by those with both feet planted firmly in the modern world. As a historian of the ancient and medieval world, I approach this subject from a different perspective, but one that I think is crucial to understanding our present and future. This book finds its touchstone in the ancient past, looking forward from the marble columns of Rome to the marble columns of Washington, D.C. From that perspective I cannot help but hold some optimism about the future of the United States and the world. Although it is certainly more fashionable to predict a coming collapse, the lessons of Rome suggest that the American Empire is both vigorous and young.

The ancients believed that history was a great teacher. They were right. But history's lessons do not expire after a few decades. In this book we will listen to some of them.

_____

Chapter 1

Empires of Trust ... and the Other Ones

Now Judas heard of the fame of the Romans, that they were very strong
and were well-disposed toward all who made an alliance with them, that
they pledged friendship to those who came to them and that they were very
strong. But with their friends and those who rely on them they have kept
friendship.

—1 Maccabees 8: 1–2, 12.

In 204 BC the mood in the Roman Senate was good, almost jubilant. After
fourteen years of brutal and dangerous war with the African power Carthage—a war fought largely on Italian soil—the tide had finally begun
to turn in Rome's favor. Spain, the rich storehouse supplying the Carthaginian invasion forces, had two years earlier fallen to the daring young
Roman general Publius Cornelius Scipio. A charismatic man of action,
Scipio was loved by the people of Rome, although only tolerated by the
older senators who dismissed him as both rash and reckless. Upon his
return to Rome, Scipio had argued for a bold new tactic: a direct assault
on Carthage itself. After a contentious debate in the Senate, in which the
conservative senator Quintus Fabius Maximus led the opposition, Scipio
got his way. He received command of several Roman legions with a mandate to bring the war to the enemy's homeland—across the sea to Africa
itself. Scipio hoped his plan would draw the Carthaginian general Hannibal out of Italy once and for all. The Roman leader and his soldiers
marched south to the toe of the Italian boot, crossed over to Sicily, and
prepared to sail to Africa.

On his way, Scipio conquered several Italian city-states that had years
earlier broken their oaths of alliance to Rome by joining Hannibal. One

of the turncoat cities was Locri, an exquisite jewel on the Italian coast that Plato himself had once called the "flower of Italy." After capturing Locri and expelling the Carthaginians, Scipio left behind one of his lieutenants, Pleminius, and a contingent of Roman troops to maintain order in the city. It would be up to the Senate to decide what to do with these Locrians, who had so treacherously betrayed the Roman people and their allies.

And so it was, on a pleasant summer morning in 204 BC, while the senators were still considering how best to win the war in Italy, that Locrian ambassadors arrived in Rome with an urgent request to address the Senate. The request was granted. As the senators assembled and took their seats, they naturally expected the Locrians to serve up a rich rhetorical feast of elaborate excuses and appeals for mercy. After all, for more than a decade the Locrians had been actively working with Hannibal to destroy Rome. Surely an apology and a bit of groveling was in order. But the senators were disappointed, for the ambassadors had come with a very different purpose in mind.

To the amazement of the room, the Locrians strode angrily into the Senate chambers, gazing almost contemptuously at the Roman assembly. After a perfunctory greeting, the Locrians announced that they would not be discussing the matter of their own treachery against the Roman people, putting that matter off until a more convenient time. Instead, they had come to speak to the senators about the deplorable conditions in Locri since its conquest by the Romans. They claimed that Pleminius and his soldiers had behaved horribly toward the Locrians, treating them as if they were a conquered people. The chief ambassador exclaimed:

> In this officer of yours—the extremity of misery gives me courage to speak freely—there is nothing human except his face and appearance, there is no trace of the Roman except in his clothing and speech.... It is difficult to decide which is the worst misfortune for a city: to be captured by an enemy in war, or to be crushed by force and violence by a bloody tyrant. All the horrors which attend the capture of a city we have suffered and are still suffering to the utmost; all the tortures

which ruthless and cruel tyrants inflict on their down-trodden subjects Pleminius has inflicted on us, our children, and our wives.

And if this sort of treatment were not bad enough, the ambassadors complained, Pleminius had also looted the most sacred shrine of Locri, the famous Temple of Proserpine. In loud and angry voices, the Locrians demanded that the Senate recall Pleminius immediately, try him, and punish him for his outrageous crimes against the people of Locri.

For a long moment the Senate chamber was filled with stunned silence. Then the Locrians were politely thanked for their report and asked to wait outside while the Senate deliberated on this matter. Fabius, the venerable leader of the Senate, rose to address his colleagues. One might imagine that the bold demands of those who had so recently betrayed Rome would not be given the highest priority in the Roman Senate. But Fabius took the words of the Locrians very seriously indeed. And he was not alone. Fabius gave a blistering speech in which, after excoriating the general lack of discipline among Scipio's soldiers, he insisted that the Senate take immediate action to rectify the situation at Locri:

> I move that Pleminius be brought to Rome to plead his case in chains, and if the charges which the Locrians have brought against him are substantiated, that he be put to death in prison and his property confiscated. With regard to Publius Scipio, as he has left his province without orders, I move that he be recalled, and that it be referred to the tribunes of the plebs to bring in a bill before the Assembly to relieve him of his command. As to the Locrians, I move that they be brought back into the [Senate] House, and that we assure them in reply to their complaint that the Senate and people of Rome in no way approve of what has been done, and that we recognize them as good and trustworthy allies and friends. And, further, that their wives and children and all that has been taken away from them should be restored, and all the money taken from Proserpine's treasury should be collected, and double the amount put back.

3

There is no doubt that partisanship played a role in Fabius' remarks. He and his party had strongly opposed Scipio and the war in Africa, so it is not surprising that they would use the Locrian report as a way of discrediting both. Yet, although Scipio's own party attempted to minimize damage to the general and the war, they nevertheless agreed wholeheartedly that the conduct of the Roman soldiers at Locri was disgraceful. In the end, rather than recalling Scipio the senators agreed to send a delegation to investigate the charges against him. All the rest of Fabius' proposals were enacted by the Senate. In other words, every one of the Locrian demands were met.

Although this type of episode is not unusual in Roman history, it is extraordinarily rare in human history. Consider this for a moment. Rome was a militarily powerful state in a death struggle with an equally powerful enemy, Carthage. One of its trusted allies, Locri, had not only refused to honor its sworn commitments but had actually joined Carthage and actively sought to vanquish Rome. Virtually every powerful (and even not so powerful) state in history would have responded to this kind of treachery with punishment and retribution. In other words, it would have responded much the way that the Roman general Pleminius and his men did—by looting the city and taking advantage of the people. And by the standards of most societies it would have been perfectly justified in doing so. After all, the Locrians were conquered enemies. Why should they not be treated as such?

What is startling about this particular case is that the Locrians obviously did not expect that kind of treatment at all. Indeed, they expected their lives, their property, and their honor to be respected by the Romans—and complained bitterly when they were not. Because of his actions, they claimed, Pleminius had "no trace of the Roman" in him. He had visited upon them "all the horrors which attend the capture of a city." Of course, that is exactly what Locri was: a captured city. Indeed, it had been captured after treacherously allying with Rome's worst enemy. Yet the people of Locri were so certain that the Romans would use their power responsibly, prudently, and even mercifully, that when their expectations were not met, they sent a delegation to Rome to chastise the

4

Romans and issue demands. In other words, they trusted the Romans to act responsibly, and even when that trust was violated, they trusted the Romans to make it right. And that, of course, is exactly what the Romans did.

This type of trust is among history's rarest treasures. The vast majority of empires, kingdoms, and states that have ever existed have sought to build their power in whatever way they can, making war on their neighbors when it seems advantageous and continuing to do so until stopped. They are trusted only to use power for their own benefit and to treat those they conquer as, well, conquered. Across the grand sweep of human history, one can select an empire almost at random and observe just this standard operating procedure: Hittites, Assyrians, Persians, Greeks, Arabs, Turks, Mongols, French, Germans, and on and on. All of these and hundreds more built standard, garden-variety empires—what I call Empires of Conquest—bent on absorbing their neighbors' territories through military invasions.

The Romans, however, built something quite different and exceedingly rare: an *Empire of Trust*. By that I mean that they were not only trusted by friends and foes alike with a responsible use of power, *but that their empire itself came about as a direct result of that trust*. This may seem surprising at first glance. Many people have an image of the Romans as lords of a brutal Empire of Conquest, built by marching legions crushing all opposition before them. That is wrong. As numerous scholarly histories of Roman expansion have made clear, the image of the Romans as brutal conquerors does not reflect the actual dynamics at work at all. The simple fact is that the Romans acquired their empire slowly and with great reluctance. As the Roman historian Ernst Badian once remarked, conquest is history's norm and requires no explanation. "What does call for an explanation, when it appears in history, is that relatively high level of sophistication that *rejects* opportunities for the extension of power." It was actually that rejection that made the Romans seem trustworthy to others, that formed the basis of their Empire of Trust. The Romans did not want an empire, which is precisely why they got one.

Roman history is interesting in its own right. But the means by which the Roman people came to rule an empire is particularly important today. That is because, as I will argue, similar dynamics are once again at work in the rise of what some commentators now call the "American Empire." Like the Romans more than two thousand years ago, Americans are acting in an ad hoc fashion, doing what they think best for themselves and their allies, and finding themselves pulled reluctantly into an empire. Like Rome, the United States is building that historical rarity, an Empire of Trust. But to see it we must look at the United States and its growing power within the framework of millennia, that is, within the context of hundreds of generations, not simply the last one.

Compare the Roman response to the actions of a few of their victorious soldiers at Locri with the American response to the actions of a few of their victorious soldiers in Iraq. In April 2004 *The New Yorker* and *60 Minutes II* reported that American soldiers were torturing Iraqi prisoners at Abu Ghraib prison. The accompanying pictures of prisoner humiliation shocked the country and the world. Abu Ghraib was already infamous. According to Amnesty International, it had been Saddam Hussein's preferred site for the torture, mutilation, and execution of many thousands of prisoners. In 1984 alone more than four thousand prisoners were executed there. Shortly before the American invasion of Iraq, Saddam Hussein had ordered the expansion of Abu Ghraib in order to increase its capacity. The facility was empty when the American troops arrived in 2003, having been looted by its former prisoners. It was subsequently converted into a detention facility for Saddam loyalists and others targeting American and coalition forces. The shocking pictures were taken during apparent attempts by some soldiers to extract information from those prisoners.

From the perspective of human history, the American response to the Abu Ghraib incident was just as unusual as that of the Roman response to Locri. Imagine for a moment that some other great power in modern history had been in a similar situation. If, for example, Soviet forces under Stalin, or German forces under Hitler, or Japanese forces under Tojo, or French forces under Napoleon, had rounded up insurrectionists the *expectation* would be that they would be tortured for information and/or executed. After all, these prisoners were actively seeking to kill or expel the conquering soldiers. Citizens in any Empire of Conquest (like the German, Japanese, and French empires) would surely note that most of the prisoners at Abu Ghraib were fighting to restore Saddam Hussein or his party to power. In other words, they were seeking to put Abu Ghraib back in the business of mass torture and execution of the Iraqi people. Why should torture not be used on them?

That, however, was not the American response to the reports of Abu Ghraib. Just as importantly, everyone around the world *knew* that it would not be the American response. Like the traitorous Locrians who bitterly accused the Romans of a betrayal of trust, Arab leaders, who use torture daily in their own countries, excoriated the United States for prisoner abuse. Those Arab leaders so trusted the United States to use power responsibly that on an occasion when that trust was violated, they also trusted that the Americans would make it right. And so they did—or tried to.

When American senators came together to discuss Resolution 356 condemning the abuse of Iraqi prisoners there was never any doubt that it would pass. Democrats who opposed President George W. Bush and the war in Iraq naturally sought to use the reports to discredit both. Republicans tried to minimize the damage but agreed wholeheartedly with the other party that the actions of those American soldiers were disgraceful. The resolution passed 92–0. No excuses were offered. The Senate condemned "in the strongest possible terms the despicable acts at Abu Ghraib prison and joins with the President in expressing apology for the humiliation suffered by the prisoners in Iraq and their families." The subsequent debate was in many ways a perfect echo of that held in the Roman Senate more than two millennia before. Senator Orrin Hatch, a Republican from Utah, rose to say:

> I strongly support the resolution that is before the Senate. It adds our apology to those offered by the President and the Secretary of Defense; it rightly commends the vast majority of service members who are serving nobly abroad to support liberty; and it reiterates our

commitment to bring to justice those who broke the law. It is a beginning to set things right.

Senator Dianne Feinstein, a Democrat from California, agreed, saying:

> … as Americans we are defined not just by the way in which we deal with our friends but by how we treat our enemies. I know that in many countries around the world, abuse of prisoners is commonplace and brutal interrogation is the norm, rather than the exception. But America, a Nation that was founded on the idea of liberty and justice for all, must hold itself to a higher standard. We liberate, not torture, and we free, not oppress.

An observer who watched the proceedings in the Roman Senate in 204 BC and the American Senate in AD 2004 could not help but be struck by the similarities. A partisan subtext hung in the air in both bodies as parties jostled for position. That is the nature of republics. But the unanimous reaction of both Senates was one of outrage and a determination to correct the problem, punish the guilty, and make the necessary reparations. Not a word was said against the victims. As far as we know, no Roman senator rose to condemn the Locrians as treacherous enemies who deserved to be treated as vanquished foes. Neither did any American senator even hint at the activities of the prisoners at Abu Ghraib that caused them to be there in the first place. In other words, the focus was not on the enemy or his actions at all, but solely on the actions of the soldiers of the Empire of Trust. The moral yardstick for both the Romans and the Americans was unrelated to the actions of their enemies. It is instead part of an internalized self-image unconnected, indeed even opposed, to the concept of acquiring imperial power.

To understand why the United States seems to share this rare characteristic with another empire so far removed from it in time and space we will need to look more closely at the histories of both Rome and the United States, for it is there that we can begin to see the foundational elements that shaped their view of themselves and the rest of the world.

The most startling of these shared elements is an abiding and sincere desire simply *to be left alone*. It's true. The extraordinary irony of both the Roman and American empires is that they were not the result of expansionistic impulses to dominate the world, but of an isolationism woven deeply into both societies. That is the crucial yet overlooked key to understanding America's present and future place in the world. Americans do not want an empire, which is one big reason that they are getting one.

Comparing the United States to the Roman Empire has become somewhat of a cliché of late. The problem is that the comparisons are often marred by fundamental misunderstandings about Rome. For many people, ancient Rome was a tyrannical and cruel empire of conquering legions, barbaric gladiator games, and slavery. The United States, with its widely deployed military, mass market entertainment, and history of slavery fits that mold well enough. With the parallel thus established, the United States is then accused of trying to build a similar kind of empire—an Empire of Conquest. The comparison is generally accompanied by a warning to America's swaggering triumphalists that the Roman Empire did, after all, fall. For example, the French writer Emmanuel Todd in his book *After the Empire: The Breakdown of the American Order* (2003) assures his readers that "Roman history is the history of the acquisition of territory. The genetic code of that city-state seems to have included the principle of expansion by force of arms. Everything else—internal politics, economics, art—was secondary." The United States, which Todd sees as a declining power in the face of European resurgence, will thus meet the same fate as Rome. Not quite as dramatic, but arguing along the same lines, is Charles A. Kupchan, a professor of international relations, who tells us in his book *The End of the American Era* (2002) that the United States is at a stage in its history very like the last days of the Roman Empire. Exhausted and doomed to oblivion, the United States will pass the mantle of imperial greatness on to the European Union, with Brussels becoming the great capital of the world just as Constantinople did in the aftermath of Rome's fall.

Not every observer who compares America with ancient Rome believes that the end is nigh. Many simply believe that the end of the republic is nigh. In this construction of events the villain is the imperial presidency (and whoever happens to occupy it), which is turning America into a military dictatorship. For example, Chalmers Johnson in his book *The Sorrows of Empire: Militarism, Secrecy, and the End of the Republic* (2004) warns that "the main lesson for the United States ought to be how the Roman Republic evolved into an empire.... Rome ruled all the known world except for China, but in the process Roman democracy was supplanted by dictatorship, and eventually the Romans were overwhelmed by the world of enemies they had created." Although Johnson accuses American leaders of knowing little about Roman history, he might want to bone up a bit on it himself. Rome was a republic, not a democracy—a Greek form of popular rule that the Romans considered dangerous. Nor was Rome conquered by any enemies that it created. It is not even clear what enemies Johnson has in mind.

Similarly, Robert Harris, who writes novels about ancient Rome, in *The New York Times* and National Public Radio claimed that a pirate raid on Ostia in 68 BC was used by the Roman general Pompey to subvert the pristine constitution of Rome, whipping the people into a frenzy of fear and thereby winning for himself unprecedented powers to wage a "war on terror." "Those of us who are not Americans," he continues, "can only look on in wonder at the similar ease with which the ancient rights and liberties of the individual are being surrendered in the United States in the wake of 9/11." Charitably, one might assume that Harris is just not well-versed in Roman history. The truth is that Rome's constitution was already in shambles long before 68 BC. More than a decade earlier the Roman military leader Sulla had marched his troops to Rome, taken over the government, and reformed the constitution according to his liking. Pompey himself had led troops against Rome. If George W. Bush had come to power by commanding American military forces to threaten Washington, D.C., and if he was the second such politician to have done so, then one might reasonably conclude that some parallels could be drawn. But equating the administration's policy toward terrorism as the "end of the Republic" is to indulge in a fiction as gross as in Harris's books. It is not reasoned historical analysis.

Authors who think that the extension of American power is generally a good thing have tended to run as far away from the Roman comparison as possible. Martin Walker, for example, writes that "Rome's empire was the real thing, held down by brutal force and occupation.... It had no allies, only satellites and client states that were required to reward their protectors with the tribute that symbolized dependence. And Rome showed no magnanimity to its defeated enemies; it organized no Marshall Plans or International Monetary Fund bailouts to help them recover and join the ranks of the civilized world." The example of the Locrians speaks against this view. Clearly the Romans did believe that defeated enemies should be treated with respect and dignity. More than that, as we shall see, the Romans, like Americans, were famous for making friends out of enemies, rebuilding and restoring them after militarily defeating them. As the Roman statesman Cicero once noted, "By defending our allies our people have gained the whole world."

It is not surprising that so many people view the ancient Romans as aggressive and immoral conquerors, given that they are rarely portrayed as anything else in the media. In the HBO/BBC series *Rome*, the city and empire are fetid pools of perverted sex, horrifying violence, and appalling treachery—traits that coincidentally make for smashingly good ratings. According to writer and creator Bruno Heller, ancient Romans "had no prosaic God telling them right from wrong and how to behave. It was a strictly personal morality, and whether or not an action is wrong would depend on whether people more powerful than you would approve. You were allowed to murder your neighbor or covet his wife if it didn't piss off the wrong person. Mercy was a weakness, cruelty a virtue, and all that mattered was personal honor, loyalty to yourself and your family." One is left wondering how such a dysfunctional society could have avoided complete collapse, let alone built an empire that lasted more than two thousand years. The truth, of course, is that neither HBO nor the BBC is a particularly reliable source of historical information. The Romans, as we will see, were intensely religious people—so much so that they considered atheism to be both disordered and dangerous. Although affluence injected many of the same sorts of excesses, abuses, and absurdities into post–Punic Wars Roman culture that today infect post–World War II American culture, the Romans, like the Americans, held fast to an internalized moral compass that continued to guide them through the centuries.

But is Rome perhaps the wrong example? A few observers have argued that it is profitable to compare the United States as lone superpower with the British Empire. Writers like Niall Ferguson and Deepak Lal make a strong case for that comparison, and both authors generally consider the development to be a good thing. A liberal American empire in the mold of Great Britain, they contend, could bring widespread peace and prosperity across the globe. Other authors, like Patrick Buchanan, point to the relatively short life-span of the British Empire and urge the United States to avoid heading down a historical dead end. The comparison is a useful one—particularly when explored by a historian of Ferguson's caliber. However, as with any comparison, it has some problems. The developmental histories of the United States (an Enlightenment-era republic) and Britain (a medieval feudal kingdom) have less in common than one might suppose—indeed, the former is the child of the latter. Britain actively sought to build an empire, while the United States has actively sought to avoid one. To put it a different way, British expansionism was decidedly proactive, while American expansionism has been largely reactive. The British established colonies and colonial governments that reported directly to London. Those elements of traditional imperial control play little part in the projection of American authority in the world today. There are important differences in degree as well. Although the British were militarily powerful, they were never in a position of uncontested supremacy. During the Victorian era, for example, the Royal Navy was the largest in the world—slightly larger than the second and third largest navies combined. Today, the United States Navy is also the largest in the world, but it is larger than *all* of the other navies in the world combined. Americans currently spend almost as much on their military as the combined expenditures of *all of the other countries on the planet*. Military analysts today do not evaluate whether the United States has sufficient power to defeat any given foreign country, but rather how many such wars the United States could conceivably fight and win *simultaneously*.

Nevertheless, it would be wrong to lump the British Empire into the basket of history's garden-variety Empires of Conquest. It was something different. I would classify it as a third sort of empire—an Empire of Commerce. Like that of similar empires such as ancient Athens, medieval Venice, or early modern Holland and Portugal, its expansion was largely driven by a desire for profit. As such, the British Empire took the form of colonies founded or conquered either to establish trade with the natives or to exploit foreign raw materials directly. Such empires tend to be very far-flung, scattering colonies that share direct connections to the mother country. This was not the Roman model of expansion, nor is it the American one.

In three important areas—developmental history, motives and means of expansion, and military supremacy—the United States and Rome bear remarkable similarities. Both states had their roots in colonialism. The first Americans were British subjects who rebelled against their king and declared a new and independent country. So it was with the Romans, who were ruled by Etruscan kings before their own war of independence. These early experiences led both peoples to craft new governments without kings and without rulers—governments of the people. The Romans called theirs the *res publica*, literally "the public business," from which we get our word *republic*. Above all Roman government cherished the individual liberty of its citizens and the rule of law. Romans, like Americans, had an abiding distrust of concentrated power. They purposefully fashioned a constitution of checks and balances that strictly regulated the authority of generals, magistrates, and representatives. Throughout their long history the Romans would continue to hold fast to an attitude toward royalty that is remarkably similar to that of Americans: They loved to hear about royalty, read about royalty, revel in the culture of royalty—provided it was someone else's royalty. The idea of a king of Rome was just as repugnant to ancient Romans as a king of the United States would be to modern Americans.

Like the fledgling United States, ancient Rome was situated on the periphery of the civilized world. Since they were small and relatively weak, the Romans did not attract the attention of the great powers of the eastern Mediterranean. Although Rome was not far from the sea, the early Romans had no real navy, focusing instead on the rich soils of the plains of Latium. Roman values sprang from the earth, turned by the till of the family farmer. Above all they valued piety, hard work, self-reliance, and patriotism. Like early Americans, early Romans knew well enough that there was a larger world beyond their horizon, but they had little interest in it. In order to defend themselves against Etruscans or other powers, the Romans made alliances with their nearest neighbors—residents of city-states that spoke the same Latin tongue. Even this the Romans did with reluctance, as a concession to the demands of a dangerous world. At its beginning, then, Roman foreign policy was fixated on the acquisition of allies who might aid in their defense. Although this effort was limited to central Italy in the early years, the Romans soon learned that the more prosperous they became, the more attractive a target they presented for conquest. This, in turn, led to the extension of their efforts to secure additional allies, which, in a nutshell, is a fundamental dynamic behind Rome's empire building. A Roman in the second century BC would have objected strenuously to the concept of "empire," much preferring the idea of Rome as a state with many, many friends and allies. Modern Americans are the same.

The motives of Roman expansion find a remarkably clear echo in American expansion. Aside from the unusual "Old World" colonial venture of the Spanish-American War, the United States has traditionally avoided the outright conquest and subjugation of foreign lands. Instead, American foreign policy has consistently focused on securing allies when possible in order to maintain an isolationist defense of the country. Both the Roman and American empires repeatedly responded to their defeated enemies by rebuilding their cities, restoring their wealth, and reconciling with them as friends—what Ferguson has called the "imperialism of anti-imperialism." The overriding dynamic behind Roman and American expansionism was not to build an empire of the vanquished, but a community of allies—in other words, an Empire of Trust.

Yet how does a desire to surround oneself with allies to ward off external threats culminate in a vast empire like that of Rome? Well, that has everything to do with the nature and severity of the threats. For a long time the ancient Romans were content with their regional alliances. These were sufficient protection against renegades or an all-out assault by the Etruscans. That was before 390 BC. In that year a powerful army of Gauls—Celtic warriors from the forests of what is today France—poured over the Alps into northern Italy. These were not the forces of an invading empire, but disorganized bands of barbarians out for a good time. Their objective was simple: take all that could be taken, destroy the rest, and move on. At first the Romans paid little attention to the invasion, assuming that the Etruscans, who were directly in the path of the marauding armies, would deal with it. But the Gauls made short work of the Etruscans and continued to press southward, leaving a trail of chaos and destruction in their wake. The Roman leaders snapped to action, calling up their legions and activating their alliances. It was too little and too late. The Gallic warriors broke through the Roman defenses, captured Rome, and brutally sacked it.

The Gallic Sack had a profound impact on the Romans, for it was in that carnage that they learned a sad truth: Ignoring the world does not mean that the world will return the favor. The response of the Roman people was a major reform of their military as well as the structure of their alliances. In order to defend against attacks by powerful enemies from distant lands, it was clearly necessary that they organize not just an alliance of central Italians, but of all Italians. They believed that for the security of Rome it was crucial to have a wide network of friends—even if that meant going to war to convert enemies into friends. The Roman determination to vigorously win and faithfully honor defensive friendships gained them a reputation for fair-dealing and trustworthiness across the known world. It also made them more powerful, for each new ally added further to their strength. It is not surprising, then, that when the Jews in 161 BC sought allies against the Greeks they turned to the Romans. Even across the Mediterranean the reputation of Rome as a faithful ally was firmly established.

The United States had much the same sort of education as early Rome. Americans strove ardently to avoid "foreign entanglements" until 1941, when the outside world intruded at Pearl Harbor. It was then that Americans came to the same realization: that the outside world simply could not be safely ignored. In the aftermath of World War II, Americans, like the Romans, were determined to build larger alliance structures in order to keep such an attack from happening again. They, again like the Romans, were determined to transform their former enemies into fast friends. In the case of Germany and Japan their efforts bore rich fruit.

Both Rome and the United States eventually came to a difficult realization. Acquiring more and more friends may indeed make one more secure. But it also commits one to defending those friends. Ironically, more friends actually translates into more wars, albeit smaller wars far from home and therefore of less danger to the citizens or the state. Each such war brought new victories and new vanquished, whom the Romans invariably attempted to convert into allies or friends. This in itself had the effect of expanding Rome's horizon of friendship, continually bringing it into potential conflict with even more distant enemies. It was this persistent attempt to "secure the horizon" that led directly to Rome's vast empire. The projection of Roman power continued to widen until the second century AD, when it simply reached the limits of ancient transportation and communication technologies.

The American Empire has grown similarly. Each new friend brings additional enemies, whether they be the North Koreans, Chinese, or Soviets. When the United States conquered Iraq in 2003, true to form its leaders were toppled and the government was transformed into an ally. Now this new ally, situated in the middle of the Muslim Middle East, requires defense from potential external enemies, such as Syria or Iran, and a host of internal enemies. The horizons of the American Empire again expanded. And they will expand again, for the technological limitations that bedeviled Rome no longer exist. Indeed, new technologies allow for rapid communication and transportation that the ancient Romans could never have imagined. Despite these changes, the expansion of both of these Empires of Trust rests on the same two foundations: the imperial power's desire for peace and security, and the allies' trust in the responsible use of the imperial power's overwhelming military might.

Like the ancient Romans, the United States has now achieved a military hegemony that is unquestioned. But military hegemony is nothing new in human history. All great Empires of Conquest seek it and some have even achieved it—usually by crushing their opponents. But the Romans did not do that and neither have the Americans. Why? In the first place it was impossible. Even at its peak, Rome had no more than about 200,000 men under arms across its empire. That was far too few to hold down an empire stretching from Scotland to the Persian Gulf. The United States has approximately 1.5 million troops, which is likewise far too few to dominate a world of 6.5 billion people, should the world not wish it. Yet both powers had (and have) sufficient military power to respond to numerous local threats or even several major threats to security among their allies. That is all that is needed. That, and trust. For without trust, everything else falls apart. Without trust, other powers will arm themselves, leading inevitably to insecurity, war, and collapse.

The response to Roman military hegemony was the eventual disarmament of allied states. Indeed, for the first time in Western history new cities were founded with no fortifications and no thought at all of defensive geography. Those under Roman protection, although they were generally free to have armies and navies if they wished, discovered that they simply had no need of them. Why pay to outfit an army if Rome will provide for your defense? Ironically, then, Roman military supremacy actually led to an overall decline in the size of militaries in the Mediterranean world. Precisely the same thing is happening today—indeed, has been happening for decades. America's NATO allies, for example, spend only a tiny portion of their GDPs on their militaries. In fact, all of them have smaller militaries today than at any other time in their modern histories. Most are incapable of defending themselves against an attack by a well-armed power. Since their neighbors have also largely disarmed, this is not a major concern. But the reason for the disarmament is just as clear today as it was during the ancient Roman Empire. NATO allies trust the United States not only to refrain from attacking them but also to come to their rescue should they themselves be attacked.

Drawing parallels between one's own state and the glory of ancient Rome is hardly novel. Indeed, one would be hard-pressed to find any Western state in the past fifteen hundred years that did not make some claim to Roman descent or rebirth. Even the Germanic barbarians, who invaded and destroyed the empire in the West, legitimized their authority through Roman titles, commissions, and regalia. Rome for them was the very definition of civilization and government—and it would remain so in Europe for centuries upon centuries. The ghost of Rome has long haunted Western civilization. With regularity the Roman Empire is "reborn" seemingly in full vigor, yet each time it is merely the same shade, with no substance. In AD 800 Pope Leo III crowned the Frankish king, Charlemagne, "Emperor of the Romans." This, Leo insisted, was the restoration of the Roman Empire in Europe. Charlemagne embraced the title, referring to himself as "ever August Emperor," and waged war against the real Roman emperor in Constantinople in an effort to gain his recognition. Thus began the famed Holy Roman Empire, which would endure in one form or another until the nineteenth century. There was, of course, nothing Roman at all about a loose coalition of German and Italian principalities. But that did not stop "emperors" from the Ottonians to the Hapsburgs from proudly donning the imperial insignia of Rome and styling themselves as successors of the Caesars. Voltaire was quite correct when he quipped that the Holy Roman Empire was "neither Holy, nor Roman, nor an Empire." Yet, the concept of Romanness, or *Romanitas*, remained important for medieval Europeans.

Napoleon attacked the Holy Roman Empire, yet the specter of Rome remained just as vigorous for him as it had been for his predecessors a millennium earlier. The French Revolution itself was draped in a Roman toga. Indeed, the revolutionaries actually considered making the toga the national dress for French citizens! Fortunately, they settled instead on the *sans-culottes* trousers, which the rest of the men in the Western world also quickly adopted. (Real togas are exceptionally difficult to put on, requiring the assistance of several servants.) By 1799 the French government was rife with Roman allusions. It had a tribunate, a Senate, and consuls. Napoleon himself became first consul and in 1802 was elected consul for life. He made no bones about his belief that the Roman Empire had been reborn in France. Indeed, he followed the example of Caesar Augustus by becoming the ruler without taking the title of king. Instead, by popular vote he was proclaimed emperor of France. To complete the picture, he emulated Charlemagne by having Pope Pius VII personally anoint him at the coronation. One need not look far to see how seriously Napoleon and the French took this association with Rome. Simply stroll through Paris and admire the Arc de Triomphe and the Louvre, or visit the imperial palaces of Fontainebleau or Malmaison. This is, after all, the period of "empire style." If Rome truly had been born again in France, then it stood to reason that it should look like it.

France was not alone in claiming Roman descent. Many other Western states at the time began to style themselves along Roman models, implicitly or explicitly claiming the ancient inheritance. British imperial administration buildings in London and abroad were frequently taken directly from Roman models. The same is true in the United States. A visitor walking down the Mall or past the Supreme Court in Washington, D.C., might easily imagine that he has been transported back in time to ancient Rome. The very architecture of Rome instills in those of us from the West a feeling of authority, stability, and strength—which is precisely what government leaders wish to instill in their citizens. As we will see, the American Founders consciously sought to re-create those aspects of Roman government and culture that they believed worked well, while avoiding those that had led to Rome's problems.

It is not my contention, however, that the United States in any way constitutes a rebirth of the Roman Empire, or that Roman history has a deterministic hold on America's future. As the distinguished American historian Charles A. Beard long ago argued, "America is not to be Rome or Britain. It is to be America." The truth is that, although there are remarkable similarities between ancient Rome and modern America, there are numerous and important differences as well. To give an example, although some Americans may glance at their horoscopes in the daily newspaper, very few would alter their day based on something they find next to the crossword puzzle. Yet ancient Romans lived by oracles, portents, and omens. Sacred chickens, lightning patterns, flocks of birds, animal livers—all were closely observed before any important decisions were made. The Romans had no scientific or industrial revolutions. They lived in a premodern world in many ways very different from our own. But there is enough that is similar between Americans and Romans to command our attention. Here we will explore those similarities and, in so doing, uncover some important aspects of the American Empire, past, present, and future.

Chapter 2

Distrusting Kings

On a warm night in 510 BC a group of Roman military leaders decided to have a party. The army had been besieging the town of Ardea for several weeks, and since that was likely to continue for a while, a half dozen or so officers got together for dinner and, of course, plenty of wine. After the meal the men relaxed in the flickering torchlight and conversation drifted from subject to subject, finally settling on the relative merits of their wives. All married men, the leaders began boasting about the beauty, loyalty, and chastity of their own spouses. Among the boasters was Sextus Tarquinius, the son of Tarquinius Superbus, who was the king of Rome. In these early days, the city of Rome was ruled by kings from Etruria, a land of wealth and power in northern Italy. The people of Etruria, known as Etruscans, were a proud and cultured people who had spread their influence and power southward into central and southern Italy. Rome had been ruled by Etruscan kings for many years. As a prince and the heir to the throne of Rome, Sextus naturally insisted that his wife was superior to everyone else's, although the other revelers good-naturedly disagreed. Finally, someone suggested that the surest way of settling the matter was for all of them to mount their horses and ride back home. Showing up unexpectedly, they would find out just what their wives were up to while they were away. A road trip seemed a good way to break the monotony and so, fortified with more wine, the group headed out to investigate the situation.

There were plenty of surprised women in Rome that night. In house after house the crew rushed in only to find their wives doing pretty fair imitations of their husbands—drinking, banqueting, and generally having a good time. All of the leaders who found their wives thus occupied were deeply embarrassed, for no good and chaste Roman wife would ever engage in that sort of revelry. It was only at one of the homes, that of Collatinus, that the leaders found a dedicated and true Roman wife. Although it was late, Collatinus' wife, Lucretia, was hard at work spinning wool. (Spinning wool was what Roman wives were *supposed* to be doing in the evening.) She received the drunken men graciously, inviting them to the table for refreshment, and proceeded to dote on her husband. Collatinus basked in his victory.

But Prince Sextus did not like to lose. He was, after all, an Etruscan, ruling over these base Romans. How was it that Collatinus had a wife superior to his in every way? Surely, as their leader, anything that belonged to them also belonged to him. Or so Sextus reasoned. Proceeding on this assumption, a few days later, after the men had returned to the siege, Sextus went back to Collatinus' house alone. Lucretia cordially welcomed him for dinner and then provided a guest room for him for the night. But sleep was not what Sextus had in mind. He waited until the whole house—servants, slaves, everyone—was asleep. Then, he quietly entered into Lucretia's bedroom, where she lay sleeping. All at once, Sextus was upon her, covering her mouth with one hand and holding a sword to her breast with the other. He grunted out his love for her and when she reacted violently to his advance he threatened to kill her. Lucretia continued to struggle mightily. Finally, Sextus told her that if she did not submit, he would kill his slave and lay him in her bedroom with her own dead body. He would then claim that he had found the two of them committing adultery and killed them both. Lucretia stopped struggling and Sextus raped her. Satisfied, the prince left Collatinus' house, "exulting in his conquest of the woman's honor."

When Lucretia finally pulled herself together she immediately sent for her father and husband, saying nothing about what had happened. Collatinus came quickly, bringing with him another Roman officer, Lucius Brutus Junius, whom he happened to meet on the way back home. When the three men arrived at Collatinus' house they found Lucretia no longer spinning, but sitting quietly in a chair.

"Is all well?" Collatinus asked.

"Far from it," she replied coldly, "for what can be well with a woman when she has lost her honor? The print of a strange man, Collatinus, is in your bed! Yet my body only has been violated; my heart is guiltless, as death shall be my witness. But pledge your right hands and your words that the adulterer shall not go unpunished." Then she told them of Sextus' crime.

The startled men swore to exact punishment for the deed. They tried to console Lucretia, but she would have none of it. She insisted that she would never live to be an example for an unchaste woman. Suddenly, to the horror of the men, Lucretia drew a knife from the folds of her dress and plunged it into her own heart. The men's cries of alarm soon turned into tears and wailing. Lucretia's father and husband both collapsed in grief. But not Brutus. He walked solemnly toward the slumped body of Lucretia, the pure Roman woman defiled by the polluted violence of the Etruscan prince. Brutus removed the blood-soaked dagger from Lucretia's breast, holding it aloft and exclaiming in a loud voice, "By this blood, most chaste until a prince wronged it, I swear, and I call you gods to witness, that I will pursue Lucius Tarquinius Superbus and his wicked wife and all his children, with sword, with fire, aye, with whatsoever violence I can; and that I will suffer neither them nor any other to be king in Rome!" The dagger, still dripping with the blood of Lucretia, was passed to the others, each in turn swearing his life to free Rome from the curse of foreign kings. And so began the revolution.

A good story, one that the Romans held dear for many centuries. But is it true? Probably not—at least not all of it. There was indeed a king named Tarquinius and the Romans did rebel against Etruria, forming a new government without kings. But the story of Lucretia and the bloody dagger probably belongs to the realm of folklore. That doesn't mean that it isn't true in other ways, though. Most Americans know that George Washington cut down a cherry tree and that he had wooden teeth. Neither is true. But it is true that cherry trees grow in Virginia where George Washington lived and it is also true that the general wore dentures, although not made of wood. More importantly, the story of the cherry tree conveys the truth of Washington's honesty and good character. It also says much about what Americans want in their leaders—whether they actually get it or not.

The same is true with Lucretia. Perhaps there really was an evil prince who preyed upon a good Roman woman. Perhaps that was even the last straw that led to rebellion against the foreign kings. Who knows? The important thing is that later Romans believed the story and that they did so because it described something fundamental about their view of themselves. Lucretia, the morally upright, hardworking woman of Rome, was defiled by a foreign monarch. She would become a symbol of Rome. Like Brutus, Romans were determined that their country would never again be so polluted. They would be free—free of foreign control and free of royal power. They would build a new country, pure and good, one that, like Lucretia, would rather die than live with the embrace of tyrants. Just as every New Hampshire license plate proclaims, the Romans would "live free or die."

The rejection of kings is an extremely rare idea in human history. Most governments that have been formed on this planet are monarchies of some sort. Those that are not are mostly oligarchies, in which a small group of elites share all the power. Democracy, or rule by the people, developed in ancient Athens and spread to various other cities in Greece and beyond, yet even the Athenians thought it right and proper for them to be under the rule of a tyrant periodically. For the Romans, however, the rejection of kings was total. Throughout ancient Roman history this rejection remained a constant. The Romans understood and expected that foreigners would have kings, and they certainly enjoyed welcoming them to Rome and hobnobbing with them at posh parties. But no Roman would ever want one for himself. It was unthinkable.

This rejection of kings is important, not simply because it sets Rome apart from most other civilizations, but because within that rejection lies one of the dynamics behind the subsequent expansion of Roman power.

The Roman revolution, whether it involved Lucretia or not, represented a profound rejection of the outside world and a determined resolve to build a new state in which Romans could be secure and free. The twin desires for freedom and security were the building blocks of Roman isolationism—and, paradoxically, Roman expansion.

A rather obvious parallel can be seen in American history. Americans, like Romans, strongly rejected the foreign kings (in this case, English), who had ruled over them for several centuries. The American Revolution, though, was not simply a rejection of England, but also a rejection of the very idea of monarchy. It was or would become intensely distasteful to both the Romans and the Americans. This was not simply a rejection of concentrated power—although it was that too. Neither the Etruscan king Tarquinius nor the English king George III was an absolute monarch. Both had legislative bodies that curtailed their powers. But the Americans and the Romans rebelled because they had come to recognize the kings as symbols of a corrupt world that must be thrown off. One need only glance at the Declaration of Independence, which lays at the feet of King George all of the actions of Parliament: "The history of the present King of Great Britain is a history of repeated injuries and usurpations, all having in direct object the establishment of an absolute Tyranny over these States. To prove this, let Facts be submitted to a candid world." Two dozen such facts, all of them ascribed to the king, are then listed. Although most people remember the Declaration only for its first few lines, the bulk of the document is a complaint against a king.

When the Declaration was written, monarchy was the norm in the world, just as it was in the sixth century BC. The rejection of monarchy was itself a rejection of the ways of the outside world. But the antipathy for kings woven into the fabric of Roman and American civilizations would have important repercussions when those powers began to interact with that world. The Romans quickly gained a reputation as the enemies of monarchs and the champions of freedom. Even the Jewish writer of 1 Maccabees knew that the Romans "subdued kings far and near, and as many as have heard of their fame have feared them. Yet for all this not one of them has put on a crown or worn purple as a mark of pride."

American attitudes toward foreign kings was equally hostile. Anyone who has read Mark Twain's *A Connecticut Yankee in King Arthur's Court* or laughed at the Duke and Dauphin in his *Adventures of Huckleberry Finn* will have a pretty clear idea of American attitudes toward such things. When the United States entered World War I in 1917, Americans viewed themselves as the bearers of freedom to a world weighed down by monarchs. Woodrow Wilson made that crystal-clear, proclaiming that the purpose of the United States was to "make the world safe for democracy." Indeed, he refused to make peace with the rulers of the German and Austrian empires simply because they were monarchs.

Nowadays, Americans do not get too worked up over kings, although now and then one will hear criticism of the United States' relationship with the "unelected rulers" of Kuwait and Saudi Arabia. American distaste for kingship, though, is just as strong as ever. Referring to President Bush as "King George," for example, was not meant as a compliment. The fact is that there are just not enough kings left in the world worth the name. Those in Europe are merely figureheads, and the rest are either weak themselves or ruling over weak countries. Royalty has become the stuff of tabloid journalism, and as such, Americans are more than willing to read all about it. They are not, however, willing to have their own.

With the removal of the kings both the Romans more than two millennia ago and the Americans more than two centuries ago were faced with the task of crafting a new constitution. Building a new government takes time. Both nations made false starts and mistakes. In the end, though, they produced systems that would last for centuries. The overriding idea in both cases was to have a government that remained in the hands of the people, but which had built-in safeguards against absolute rule by the mobs, an elite oligarchy, or one man. The Romans, like Americans, distrusted concentrated power intensely. For that reason they divided it up into smaller and smaller portions, making certain that no one man or one faction could ever usurp their freedom. How did they do it?

Slowly. At the core of the Roman system was the Senate—a term familiar enough to Americans, since the framers of the American Constitution borrowed it from Rome. But there was more than just a toga's worth of difference between the Roman and American Senates. The earliest Roman Senate was a council of elders. (The Latin word for *elder* is *senex*, where we get words such as *senior* and *senile*.) Over time, though, it became a body of the most respected men in Rome. These were the men who had served Rome well at home and in the field. They knew what worked and what didn't and had more than once proven themselves as men of probity, constancy, and strength. As such, the Senate was repository of wisdom, know-how, and raw political power. It held what Romans called the *mos maiorum*, roughly translated as "the way of the ancestors." One did not get elected to the Senate; at least not directly. One was enrolled for life. The kings had a Senate that advised them and probably kept them in check. The Senate survived the revolution. Since its role was advisory, it only made sense to keep it.

The old king's job was broken up into different magistrate positions, each one elected regularly. For example, the king's authority to wield deadly force was divided up between the office of consul, which could command troops outside the *pomerium* or city limits, and the Assembly of the people, which alone had that authority within the city. This made pragmatic sense. The people of Rome could not command the troops in the field. They needed commanders to do that. But the power to command, to wield that deadly force, belonged solely to the people, and although they might give it to consuls during their term of office, they would not let them use it within the city where they could threaten the Republic.

Yet even that was too much power for one consul to have. The people put strict time limits on their terms of office and then limited the number of times they could hold them. In other words, they had term limits. If that were not enough, the Romans made double certain to restrain the consuls by electing them in pairs. Each year they would elect two consuls, both of whom had equal powers. More importantly, both of them had the legal right to stop the other from taking any action by simply saying,

President John F. Kennedy, State of the Union Address, January 14, 1963.
(Courtesy of the John F. Kennedy Library.)

"I forbid." In Latin, "Veto." If a consul, therefore, thought it was a good idea to march his legion north, his colleague consul could stop it with a single word.

In the days of the monarchy, when a king wanted to take a stroll down the street he would be accompanied by twelve men called lictors. Lictors were attendants who each carried the symbols of political power in Rome, fasces, wherever the king went. A single fasces consisted of a bunch of rods bundled and tied around an imposing-looking axe. It represented the king's authority to beat (the rods) or kill (the axe). If the symbol of the fasces seems familiar, that's because it is. Have a look at the chamber of the House of Representatives. There, on either side of the Speaker's chair, are the fasces. Really big bronze ones.

They can also be seen beneath both arms of the seated Abraham Lincoln in the famous Lincoln Memorial. Why? Because the fasces became the Roman symbol of legitimate political authority. After the kings were run out of Rome, the consuls got the lictors, twelve each. Yet, when they walked through the city, the axes were carefully removed.

Like all new things, the new Roman government had plenty of critics, and truth be told, it did have some rough spots. The same could be said of the American experiment. It would take more than a decade of debate, rancor, and mistakes before Americans would finally settle on the current Constitution. In the Roman case, the people came to the conclusion that they needed some form of written law. A convention of sorts was cobbled together with ten men who were charged with investigating the constitutions of other cities and nations to find out what worked and what didn't. They completed their work in 450 BC with the publication of the Twelve Tables. These collections of laws were ratified by the popular assembly (the Comitia Centuriata) and placed on public display in the Forum.

The Twelve Tables were not a constitution—at least not the way that Americans think of one. Instead, they were the foundational laws of an entirely new form of government—a republic. By modern standards the laws are a bit harsh. For example, Table 8 states that "a person who has been found guilty of giving false witness shall be hurled down from the Tarpeian Rock." Others are simply matters of common sense, such as "a child born ten months after his father's death will not be admitted into legal inheritance." Behind all of these laws, though, are concepts that are crucial to understanding the Roman character and approach to power. Above all the Romans wanted a rule of laws, not men. No one, no matter how wealthy or privileged, was to be above the law. Today we take the idea of equality before the law for granted, but in the fifth century BC it was unusual, to say the least. Like the American Constitution, the Tables not only restricted what individuals could do, but more interestingly what government could do. So, for example, Table 9 forbade the government from executing anyone without a fair trial and a clear conviction.

For the Romans, all political power resided with the people. The people of Rome chose their representatives to serve in popular assemblies. Over the centuries various assemblies rose and fell in importance, but all of them were the legal means by which the people exerted their authority. It was only there that the power to legislate or wage war rested. The legal power to command troops—what the Romans called *imperium*—flowed from the people and was given to commanders only for specific periods of time and in specific places. In order to do the business of Rome, magistrates were elected, but they, too, had their powers strictly defined and were hemmed in by colleagues and laws. The whole system was unwieldy by design. The Romans preferred a system that moved slowly and with deliberation if it meant that power always remained in the people's hands.

Times change, though, and the Romans recognized that. That is why they never produced a written constitution. Instead, their constitution (much like that of modern Britain) remained unwritten. It was the sum total of all laws, all judicial decisions, all Senate deliberations, all customs, of the Romans. It was the *mos maiorum*, or put another way, it was the way that they had always done things in the past. The Romans were an inherently conservative people, resistant to change. If given a choice, a Roman would always stick with the customs, rituals, and laws of the past. But sometimes he was not given that choice. Sometimes events occurred that simply demanded change. In those cases, the Romans would make the smallest possible changes to their system—and even those changes would entail not much more than a tweaking of the existing constitution. For example, only consuls had the authority to command troops and there were only two of them at any one time. That worked well enough when Rome was a city-state, but what about when it projected power across the Mediterranean Sea? How could Rome fight on numerous fronts simultaneously with only two consuls with limited terms? No problem, just tweak things a bit. The Romans created proconsuls, men who were given power to command troops in specific areas by the consuls themselves. In that way, although many men would be exercising consular authority, all of it would still be funneled legally through those same two consuls. This might not seem efficient, but it satisfied the Roman desire to keep to tradition and to keep a firm handle on imperium.

Fittingly, the Roman constitution was not the work of a few men. It was a composite creature, made up of many different parts of many different governments and then conservatively modified by generations. The Romans took great pride in this fact. The great Roman senator Cato the Elder once noted that "the reason for the superiority of the constitution of our city to that of other states is that the latter almost always had their laws and institutions from one legislator. But our Republic was not made by the genius of one man, but of many, nor in the life of one, but through many centuries and generations." Polybius, a Greek observer who knew Rome well, wrote that the Romans did not create their constitution "by any process of reasoning, but by the discipline of many struggles and troubles, and always choosing the best by the light of their experience." The Roman system succeeded because it was at once traditional and adaptable. It took what worked elsewhere and threw away the rest. As Polybius noted, the Romans had successfully blended together monarchy (the consuls), oligarchy (the Senate), and democracy (the assemblies) into one government.

So, let's try winding up the Roman system and see how it works. How, for example, did a bill become a law in ancient Rome? Laws, as I mentioned, could only be made in the popular assemblies. That is where all power theoretically resided. They were introduced by tribunes, who were elected leaders of the people. Before that happened, however, everything went first to the Senate. There the senators would discuss, debate, and issue a judgment on the bill—or anything else that was currently important, for that matter. Although the Senate was no longer a council of elders, it remained the repository of all that Romans saw as good. The men in the Senate were from the patrician families—those clans that had distinguished themselves by service to the state over many generations. Senators were usually ex-magistrates with solid experience in civilian government and military tactics. What they said, therefore, carried enormous weight. In fact, for most of the history of the Roman Republic it was unthinkable for the assemblies to do anything without the nod of the Senate. That is why it often seemed to outsiders that it was the Senate that ruled Rome. But it did not, for the Senate itself was subject to the will of the people. Since the magistrates were elected, many senators were thus indirectly elected to their seats. And the fact that their power was only advisory meant that the senators could never stray too far from popular sentiment. For centuries that was never an issue. What the Senate decided, the popular assemblies happily endorsed. The partnership was so harmonious that the Romans referred to their state as *Senatus Populusque Romanus* (SPQR), "The Senate and People of Rome."

Unlike the Roman constitution, the American Constitution was written down. Nevertheless, the process of amendment allows it also to be changed when situations demand. It is no easy thing to amend the American constitution, which is why it is done so rarely. In that way it retains the same elements of continuity with the past and adaptability that made the Roman constitution work so well. There are other similarities too. Both constitutions have separate branches of government with some checks and balances. Above all, both constitutions were crafted with the firm belief that concentrated power was the enemy of freedom. Both constitute a maze of interconnected authority designed to diffuse power and to thwart tyranny.

The similarity is no coincidence. Although modern Americans tend to rely on television and movies for their image of Rome, two hundred years ago ancient authors like Polybius and Livy filled that need. Education in the eighteenth century was not at all what it is today. Although students missed out on Internet navigation classes, they consoled themselves with Latin. Yes, Latin. Schoolboys (girls were educated differently, I'm afraid) in colonial America were trained almost exclusively in the language of the Roman Empire. After wading through Caesar, they perfected their Latin by reading Cicero, Ovid, Virgil, and Sallust—every one of them a Roman. Once they had mastered Latin they started in on Greek, reading Polybius, who, while not a Roman, was writing about them. The minimum entrance requirement for all American colleges was reading proficiency in Latin and some level of competence in Greek. That was the requirement *to get in*. Few American college students today can even correctly decipher *E pluribus unum* when they *graduate*. But Thomas Jefferson found it deeply embarrassing when he learned that

William and Mary College was having to help some of its students to catch up on their Latin and Greek.

Now, not every American was a college man, of course. Indeed, not even every American who signed the Declaration of Independence or helped frame the Constitution had gone to college. But most had, and even those who had not still had a primary education in the classics. That fact alone represents a vast pedagogical gulf between the days of the founding of the United States and our own. The framers of the Constitution were men steeped in the languages and history of antiquity. For them it was not "ancient history," but something that was very much alive. Ancient authors boldly asserted that they were writing for the benefit of future generations, and those young Americans who sweated over their Latin believed them. It is only natural, then, that Americans who were throwing off the rule of a foreign king and creating a new government would see in themselves an echo of ancient Rome.

The symbols and mottoes that the new Americans chose to represent themselves and their government were overwhelmingly Roman and the words, Latin. The first federal currency bills were covered in Roman symbols, particularly the goddess Justicia carrying her scales and sword and Libertas sporting her cap and rod. They included the words *Sic floret res publica*, "Thus shall flourish the republic." Before 1776 minting coins was treason against the throne, which meant that states took to it with relish soon afterward. Rather than the image of the British monarch, the new coins included Roman images and words. Early American coinage had on it the head of a Roman—a Roman!—with the words *Non vi virtute vici*, "I triumph by virtue, not force." They also included the eagle, itself an ancient symbol of Rome. All of the thirteen original state seals included Roman imagery, Latin, or both. The seals of Virginia and Georgia, for example, included a phrase from Virgil's *First Eclogue, Deus nobis haec otia fecit*, "God has made this tranquility for us."

The stamp of Roman imagery on the foundation of the new republic can perhaps be seen nowhere better than in the Great Seal of the United States of America, adopted by the Continental Congress in 1792. You

The Great Seal of the United States of America
From Gaillard Hunt, *History of the Seal of the United States*
(Washington, D.C.: Dept. of State, 1909)

may be carrying one in your pocket right now, since it appears on every
dollar bill.

On the front is the American (and Roman) eagle holding in its right
talon an olive branch, the traditional Roman symbol of peace, and thirteen arrows in the left talon, which represent the ability to make war. In
his beak, the eagle carries a scroll with the Latin motto *E pluribus unum*,
"Out of many, one" (as any freshman would have known in Jefferson's
day). This not only described the union of states, but it also had the virtue
of containing exactly thirteen letters. On the reverse is the rather startling
image of an unfinished pyramid with an eye on top. There is nothing
Roman about that. It is a Masonic image, although precisely how it found
its way onto the Great Seal remains a point of debate. The rest of the reverse, though, is Roman. Over the eye are the words *Annuit coeptis*, "He
approves of the undertaking," which is taken from Virgil's *Aeneid*, in
which Ascanius prays for and receives the support of Jupiter. Below the
pyramid steps are the words *Novus ordo seclorum*, meaning "A new order
of the ages." This is also from Virgil, this time from the *Fourth Eclogue*.
On the base of the pyramid is "1776" in Roman numerals, of course.

But it was not simply the symbolism of the United States that was adorned in a toga, but the Constitution itself. Like the early Romans, the framers of the American Constitution looked across the seas and across history for models on which to build. No one reads it much nowadays, but John Adams wrote a three-volume work entitled *A Defence of the Constitutions of Government of the United States of America*. He wrote it in 1787, when he was himself overseas, serving as the American ambassador to England. At that time the states were busy creating their own constitutions, all greatly influenced by Adams's ideas that he had earlier spelled out in *Thoughts on Government*, published in 1776. Several European intellectuals found much to criticize in those ideas, and so it was that Adams put quill to ink in London and wrote his much larger work, one that would exert a strong influence over the American Constitution itself. *Defence of the Constitutions* is an amazing book that demonstrates the extraordinary erudition behind the American experiment. For Adams the great man of government was Cicero, the Roman senator and jurist. Adams believed that the United States government must emulate the Roman, for the "Roman Constitution formed the noblest people and the greatest power that has ever existed." The genius of the Roman system, Adams argued, was its extraordinary balance, which kept any one group from acquiring too much power. He rejected modern governments like those of England and France that called themselves "republics" but in reality apportioned supreme authority to one body or another. The Roman Republic "by the splendor of its actions, the extent of its empire, the wisdom of its councils, the talents, integrity, and courage of a multitude of characters, exhibits the fairest prospect of our species." Of all of the governments in history, that was what Adams and his associates sought to copy.

Yet Rome fell. Adams knew that well enough and he was determined that the same thing would not happen to the United States. More specifically, he worried about the fall of the Republic in the first century BC, when the rise of military strongmen led to the creation of the Principate, wherein one man ruled. Through the eyes of Polybius, Sallust, Livy, and Cicero, Adams and his generation had watched the freedom and moral virtue of the Roman Republic turn into the tyranny and excess of the

Roman Empire. And they had a pretty good idea what had led to it. Even while the Republic was still in good shape, Polybius had predicted that it would collapse as a result of its own successes. More wealth would make the people less willing to serve and more demanding of their government. Politicians would then step in to give them what they wanted, pitting one group against another for their own political benefit. In the end, Polybius predicted, the constitution would be overturned in the name of freedom and democracy, which was simply another way of saying mob rule.

Adams had no doubt that Polybius was right. The problem with the Roman constitution, Adams believed, was that the various branches of government were not equal in power. The consuls, as chief executives, had no way of checking the assemblies. The Senate had no legal power at all and so no means to assert its wisdom. The flaw in the Roman system, he concluded, was that all of the power lay with the people. That, Adams insisted, was its own form of tyranny, for it gave one body, in this case the popular assemblies, all authority. If, however, the Roman consuls and Senate had had some means to check the assemblies, things would have been different. Very different. Adams wrote, "If the consuls had been possessed of a negative in the legislature, and of all the executive authority, and the senate and people had been made equal and independent in the first establishment of the commonwealth, it is impossible for any man to prove that the [Roman] republic would not have remained in vigour and in glory at this hour."

What Adams and the other framers of the Constitution wanted was a government based on the Roman Republic, but without its fatal flaws. Like the Roman Republic, the American republic would be fashioned as one of laws, not men. If it were to remain that way, though, it was crucial that the three branches have power to check and balance one another. "There can be no government of laws without a balance," Adams insisted, "and ... no balance without three orders; and that even three orders can never balance each other, unless each in its department is independent and absolute." Thus, from the pages of ancient history would arise the Constitution of the United States.

Although few could see it, within the republican beginnings of both

Rome and the United States was an important seed that would lead directly to their subsequent growth into world empires. Both states were born in a violent rejection of monarchy that forever marked them with a deep and abiding suspicion of concentrated power of any kind. Americans and Romans were convinced that, as the saying goes, power corrupts and absolute power corrupts absolutely. That is true not just for people, but for states. Throughout their respective foreign policies, both republics would insist that no state should have absolute power, that all states should work together as equals. It was that determination, that worldview, which would lead foreign states, little by little, to trust them with precisely that absolute power. And it is what would lead both republics, the American and the Roman, to deny they had it or wanted it at all.

But we will come to that later. For now, let's look one last time at the emerging Constitution of the United States of America. When the Convention of 1787 finished with its work the document was sent to the states for ratification. A spirited debate played out in the statehouses, newspapers, and market squares of the young country. Federalists, like Adams, believed that only by adopting a constitution that gave greater power to the federal government could the new republic survive. Anti-Federalists were just as enamored of republican freedom, but feared that a stronger central government would itself become a new tyrant. Much of the debate appeared in publications and pamphlets in which the authors used pseudonyms. What sort of pseudonyms did they choose? Some were English, some Greek, some Biblical. But the majority of them, including those of the most important authors, were Roman—all heroes of the Republic. They included "Marcus," "Cato," "Publius," "Cicero," and many others. They also included "Lucius," "Junius," and "Brutus," the noble Roman who drew the bloody dagger from the breast of Lucretia and began a revolution.

The references to early Rome may be lost on us today, but they were vibrantly alive to the first Americans.

Chapter 3

Family Values

Modern Americans and ancient Romans shared a common distrust of concentrated power—a distrust they acquired through their own national experiences with foreign kings. But that is not enough to explain the other similarities to be seen in the growth of the two empires. In the Roman and American cultures there are values that would help form their national characters. The origins of those values are found in the earliest days of the two republics and would continue to animate centuries of their respective histories. The essential building blocks in the formation of that rare species, an Empire of Trust, are those core values.

When someone refers to "homespun American values" most Americans—and even many non-Americans—have a pretty good idea what that means. The very phrase evokes an image of a self-sufficient family (home spinning, after all), hardworking, honest, courageous, friendly, and pious. One can't help but envision the American frontier family that clears the land, tills the fields, tends the animals, and worships on Sundays at the little whitewashed church down the road. It is an idealized vision, one familiar enough to anyone who has read novels such as James Fenimore Cooper's Leatherstocking series or watched television shows such as *Little House on the Prairie*. It is the American pioneer/farmer typified by the term "rugged individual." And just because it is an idealized image does not mean that it does not represent a fundamental truth. The history of American culture begins on the frontier and the family farm, and despite modern affluence, wealth, and power, those agrarian values are still held up as quintessentially American. No American today, no matter how rich or cultured, wants to be called "an elite." Yet, conversely, describing someone as "down-to-earth" is always considered to be quite a compliment.

It may not seem readily apparent, but those same values that early on became part of American culture and self-image would later lead to important dynamics behind the Empire of Trust. A farming family was by its nature independent and reasonably isolated. Knowing your neighbors was important, because you might very well need their help one day. But the distances involved meant that every family needed to be able to take care of itself. No one liked excessively needy or noisy neighbors. Freedom from external control was especially prized. Americans also tended to approach foreign countries in the same way. Even today, although Americans are willing to help those in need and band together with others for a common defense, they expect that each country will remain independent, free, honest, and not troublesome. Like the ideal family farmer, Americans have no desire to take their neighbors' property, because they like what they have just fine.

The Romans formed their cultural values and national character in a similar fashion. The earliest Romans were farmers, living in a frontier world in which each family looked after its own interests and well-being. As in America, many of those Roman farms were small affairs, although some were larger, worked with the help of slaves. But they were all family owned and operated. The later Roman statesman and senator Cato the Elder (234–149 BC) looked back on those simpler days, reminding his countrymen that then the greatest compliment one could give to a Roman was not to praise his wealth or status, but simply to say that he was "a good husbandman, a good farmer." "It is from the farmers," he continued, "that the bravest men and the sturdiest soldiers come ... their calling is most highly respected, their livelihood is most assured."

Like early Americans, the early Romans were not just farmers, but soldiers and patriots. Consider the famous story of Lucius Quinctius Cincinnatus. In the earliest days of the Roman Republic, sometime in the fifth century BC, the Roman army suffered a serious defeat at the hands of the nearby Sabine people. Rome itself was in danger and the citizens were in a panic. To deal with cases like this the Roman constitution had an interesting component that provided for quick action in times of national emergency. The Senate could convene and appoint one man to be dictator, a legal office with full powers to rule and command the army for a period of six months. It was a bit like returning to the monarchy, except that the dictator's authority had an expiration date. In this dire situation the senators deliberated and decided to give the office to Cincinnatus, a Roman who had distinguished himself in his earlier services to the state.

A delegation of the Senate, adorned in their formal togas, crossed over the Tiber River and made their way to Cincinnatus' small family farm. There they found him busy plowing his fields. Cincinnatus greeted the senators cordially, but could see that they had not come to exchange pleasantries. They ominously told him that they bore a decision of the Senate and that he should put on his toga so that he could hear it. The Roman historian Livy picks up the story:

> He asked them, in surprise, if all was well, and told his wife, Racilia, to bring him his toga quickly from the cottage. Wiping off the dust and perspiration, he put it on and came forward, at which the deputation saluted him as Dictator and congratulated him, invited him to the City and explained the state of apprehension of the army.

Leaving his plow in the furrow, Cincinnatus went back with them to Rome, where he was hailed by the people. Cincinnatus was a can-do, no-nonsense son of Rome. He immediately took command of the army, restored their courage, and dealt the Sabines a serious defeat. He then returned to Rome, where he received a triumph—a massive parade reserved exclusively for victorious generals. That was week one. During week two he busied himself with restoring order to the city. At the end of the second week he was finished. Although Cincinnatus still had more than twenty weeks left to wield ultimate power, he returned his authority to the Senate and People of Rome. He then crossed the Tiber, returned to his home, took off his toga, grabbed his plow, and got back to work.

Cincinnatus was a real person, although we can't be certain that everything, or even very much, in this story is true. It doesn't matter. The Romans believed it was true—and that does matter. Every Roman knew the story of Cincinnatus, the family farmer who busied himself with his own affairs until his country called him into service. It was only then that he wiped the sweat and dirt from his brow, put on his toga, and transformed himself from a farmer into a leader. Yet he did not covet the power, the pomp, or the acclaim. What he wanted was to return to his farm. While he loved his country, he also loved the independence and relative isolation of his farm. This one story, true or not, summed up for Romans what it meant to be the perfect Roman—strong, patriotic, efficient, hardworking, and down-to-earth (literally). It was a clear reminder that a Roman was first and foremost a good man, and only reluctantly a good statesman or politician.

This same image would become part of the American character. It is no compliment in the United States to call someone a "career politician," although they are as numerous today as they were in ancient Rome. One must always retain the image of someone who is only temporarily transplanted to the halls of power, wielding it for the benefit of those back home, and looking forward to returning. American senators and congressmen conspicuously keep their houses back home, even if they spend only a few days a year there. Although they live in Washington, D.C., the fiction is maintained that their real home is, well, back home. And in some cases they really do return there, although after years, not weeks, of service. The image, though, is important because Americans, like Romans, believe that politicians really *should* be reluctant servants of the people, even when they know it to be rarely true.

Although they lived on frontiers, early American and Roman farmers were well aware that there was a wider and more sophisticated world beyond their horizons. Americans knew all about Europe and the cultural achievements and opulent wealth of its kingdoms and empires. But most of them wanted nothing to do with all that. In fact, they had come to America precisely to get away from it. As for the Romans, they knew all about the great civilizations of the eastern Mediterranean, so powerful and ancient. The Greeks with their great cities of marble, filled with theaters, baths, and great temples, were the cultural parents of Rome, just as the Europeans are for Americans. Early Romans admired the Greeks, but they had no wish to emulate them. The state was the center of life for ancient Greeks, just as it was with eighteenth-century Europeans. Greek governments raised their children, infusing into them the values of Hellenism, and thereby forming them into good citizens. The Romans, like Americans, wanted the state to keep its hands off their children. They would see to their formation themselves.

For early Romans the family, living in its traditional round hutlike house, was the place to raise children, to make a living, and to worship. Hard work and calloused hands were not shameful things, as they were in the sophisticated eastern cultures, but badges of honor for Romans. Every family was led by the father, who had final say in everything. *Patria potestas,* the Romans called it. The father's word—and not the state's—was law in those days. Fathers could reward and punish as they saw fit. They even had the right to kill family members, although this was rarely exercised. Romans believed that the father's guiding spirit, called a genius, was responsible for watching over the household. Everyone had an interest in keeping that spirit happy, which naturally entailed keeping father happy.

Powerful Roman fathers did not, however, mean weak and subservient Roman mothers. Quite the contrary. While in Greece women were sheltered in their households, rarely venturing out alone, the Roman wife, like Lucretia, whom we have already met, was a sturdy and hardworking woman. She was responsible for looking after the young children, going to local markets, taking care of the house, baking, and, of course, spinning wool, sewing, and other crafts. Roman women could pursue their own interests and could even own property—a rarity in ancient societies. All in all they were rugged and independent, much like their husbands.

It is not too difficult for us to imagine life on an early Roman family farm, because it was so much like life on American family farms, particularly in the eighteenth through the early twentieth centuries. Father worked outside plowing the fields, sowing the seeds, harvesting the crops, and taking care of the animals. Mother worked in the home, cooking, washing, making and repairing clothes. Both parents educated the children, paying close attention to the formation of their moral character. Roman boys learned basic reading and writing in the home. It was there that they also learned the most important Roman traits of *gravitas* (dignity), *continentia* (self-control), *industria* (diligence), *benevolentia* (goodwill), *pietas* (loyalty and a sense of duty), *simplicitas* (candor), and above all *virtus* (courageous manliness). There were no schools in Rome until the mid-third century BC, and even then they were attended only by the children of the wealthiest families. For the Romans, home schooling was the norm. Although the sophisticated Greeks sniffed at such a system, the Romans proudly held to it, insisting that it suited them just fine.

Like industry and education, the family was also the foundation for Roman religion. When we think about Roman worship today we tend to conjure up images of great pillared temples devoted to a pantheon of various gods and goddesses, or perhaps wild orgies of drinking and sex. For the early Roman Republic, though, these are the wrong images. In later centuries, Rome would have its share of great temples and wild parties (we will deal with those in time), yet these were imports from the Greek world. Roman religion was much less flashy.

The family farm was at the center of Roman religious belief. Romans believed that the house and fields had various spirits associated with them. It was the job of the father (with the help of his family) to make certain that those spirits remained happy. Happy spirits made for a happy and prosperous family. The Romans called this the *pax deorum*, peace of the gods. And there were a fair number of those spirits to keep peaceful. Vesta, the spirit of fire, was particularly important because it watched over the hearth—the source of warmth and energy for the family. Every day the Roman farming family would prepare a small salt cake, which would be placed into a sacrificial dish. After a few prayers, the cake was tossed into the fire for Vesta's breakfast. No one wanted an unhappy

Vesta, lest the all-important hearth fire go out. The door to the family's house had its own spirit, Janus, who, if kept happy, would ward off evil spirits. Other areas of the house, like the bedroom or pantry, had their own spirits too. The fields had spirits, and they could make or break a crop. Each spirit had its own specific rituals and prayers that were necessary if a family wanted to maintain the crucial *pax deorum*.

Sharing a house with a dozen or so needy spirits might seem a bit onerous, but in practice not too much was required. Every morning the Roman family would pray together, asking all of the spirits, but especially the genius of the father, to give them a good, safe, and productive day. Aside from a few other minor rituals (including Vesta's little cake), that was about it. On special days, like first plantings, births, deaths, or marriages, additional rituals were performed. But they were all pretty low-key. Most Romans believed in an afterlife of some sort in which they would be rewarded or punished, but they were not too fussy about the details, which naturally tended to vary from family to family. They recognized that there was a powerful god of some sort, usually referred to as Mars (not yet the god of war) or later Jupiter, but they didn't worry a great deal about him. They figured that he was too important to care much about their little farms.

Compared to the religions of the ancient eastern empires, Roman beliefs were downright primitive. Romans spent their time appeasing a handful of spirits who had not even graduated to the level of gods, since their domain extended not much beyond the family. Greek deities like Zeus, Artemis, or Hera wouldn't have given the time of day to these Roman houselings. Apollo had numerous temples across the Mediterranean with batteries of priests and holy soothsayers. Roman spirits had Dad. Yet, while the Roman religion may have been a bit backward, it was also a mirror of Roman agrarian culture. Above all it was independent, with each family worshipping as they saw fit. There was no priesthood connected to a faraway empire. It was a belief system that put the focus on the family, not the state or the wider world. In that way it fit perfectly with a people who cherished their freedom, independence, and relative isolation.

At first glance, a Roman farming family praying to a houseful of spirits might not seem to have much in common with the religion of early America. Let's face it, a Bible-loving Christian would not go in much for pitching cakes to fire spirits. Yet, insofar as the religions contributed important elements to the later development of an Empire of Trust, the two have much more in common than one might think. First of all, both religions were practiced primarily in the home. The large majority of American family farmers at the beginning of the republic were Protestant Christians. It is still true today that rural American religion is dominated by Protestantism, particularly various forms of evangelical Christianity. For the typical family farmer in the eighteenth or nineteenth century, all one needed was a Bible. The father would lead the family in prayer, at least before the evening meal, and many families would also read the Bible together. Whether they read it or not, though, they had a Bible and it was kept in a prominent place. Where possible, families would get dressed up on Sundays to go to church, but only to say communal prayers and hear the local preacher comment on the Bible. It was nice, but not necessary. In the cities, of course, it was much easier to make it to church, which is why regular churchgoing was more common in the North than in the South. At the time of the American Revolution about 80 percent of Americans attended church regularly in the North, while 56 percent did so in the South.

The traditional Christianity of the American family farmer, therefore, was decidedly independent. Americans knew that in the sophisticated and wealthy East (i.e., Europe) there were magnificent churches in which priests performed elaborate rituals (i.e., Catholics), but most weren't overly interested in all that. They eschewed any such connection, holding instead to their own local beliefs. And they were local. One could hear a preacher in one county interpret a Biblical passage one way, and another do it quite a different way in the next. Like the concept of the Roman household spirits, the commonality of the rural American religion was (and still largely is) the King James Version of the Bible. Who was King James? Who cares? It became the American Bible and that is all that mattered. Of course that brand of Christianity was decidedly primitive when compared to European Catholic theology, itself the product of centuries of university scholarship. But it fit perfectly with an American character that cherished freedom, independence, and relative isolation. In this respect, the similarity to ancient Roman religion is evident.

It is worth remembering that we are talking here about broad cultural trends, because that is ultimately what creates a national character. Not all Americans at the birth of the republic were farmers—some lived in the small but growing cities. And not all family farmers were evangelical Christians. Thomas Jefferson, a family farmer who extolled the virtues of agriculture, was a Deist. George Washington, another famous family farmer, was an Episcopalian, itself a branch of the Church of England. There were some Catholics in the new republic as well, most notably in Maryland and Pennsylvania. But even in those cases the character of American religion remained focused on the family and the local community.

When the Roman state started to grow, the city of Rome naturally grew as well. The creation of a larger and larger urban area posed a problem for Roman religion, since it removed the independent family farm from the equation. How, for example, could an urban father perform the ritual of plowing the *pomerium* (the boundaries of the family's property) when he lived in an apartment complex? The solution was simply to adapt the old religion to the new circumstances. Rather than each household observing the rituals, Rome itself became the household. So, for example, a temple was built for Vesta in the shape of a traditional family farm hut. There Rome's hearth fire burned eternally, watched over by a professional class of priestesses, the Vestal Virgins. Just a few doors down a temple to Janus was built, this one with enormous doors symbolizing the gateway of the Roman state. When the Romans were at war, the doors of Janus were kept open, since it would be necessary for the Roman "family" to leave and go to foreign lands. Yet when peace was again restored, the doors were ceremoniously closed—a dramatic reminder that the outside world was once again outside. And from the Roman perspective, that was a very good thing indeed.

The transformation of the Roman family-based religion to a large urban environment occurred slowly and was adopted in a very utilitarian manner. It was clear to everyone that the *pax deorum* must be maintained, whether in a small farmhouse or a large city. Rather than the family patriarch leading the rituals, though, the city simply appointed its own patriarchs, priests referred to as "fathers," who saw to the various rituals and were themselves overseen by a *pontifex maximus*, who made certain that all was in order. The Romans kept meticulous records of every ritual. Even acts of state were recorded, since those, too, required the proper rituals, just as they had when they were undertaken by a single family.

In some cases the Romans adopted the rituals of their former rulers, the Etruscans. For example, Roman priests followed the Etruscan practices of discerning the future or divine will through omens and portents. The Etruscans had made a science of figuring out such things by watching lightning or gazing at flocks of birds or slicing up sheeps' livers. Since it was better to be safe than sorry, the Romans followed the same practice, even hiring professional augurs whose job it was to provide divine feedback on proposed state actions. There was no sense in starting something, they reasoned, if the gods were against it.

The important point here is that the Roman state religion was an entirely pragmatic sort of thing. It grew directly from the simple religion of the family farm, adapting it as necessary for the needs of a large city and empire. In that way it provided a public service by keeping the spirits, which were increasingly viewed as gods in their own right, happy. Like picking up the garbage or lighting the streets, the Roman state religion provided a maintenance service that insured the continued prosperity and health of the citizens. This was not a religion that one could "join." It required nothing from the average Roman, who was free to deal with his own household spirits, geniuses of ancestors, or whatever else he chose to worship. The Roman state provided for the *pax deorum* for the Roman state, but it was up to individual Romans to come to terms with their own religions on their own.

In this way, Roman state religion very much resembles the religious state rituals that would be practiced in the United States. Prayers, for example, are still said to open the Congress of the United States and the various state assemblies. Those prayers ask God to bless the political body and the country. No one is required to take part in the prayers, but by the same token no one would be allowed to disrupt them either. Every day in America people place their hand on a King James Version of the Bible, still a potent symbol of American religious belief, and swear to tell the whole truth and nothing but the truth. The oath is not more legally binding because of the Bible, nor is it taken for granted that the one swearing the oath could say with any accuracy just what is in that book. But it is used all the same. By U.S. law the first Thursday of May is the National Day of Prayer, yet failing to pray on that day is neither a crime nor particularly remarkable. Every American president ends his speeches with the words "May God bless the United States of America," and every piece of American currency bears the motto "In God We Trust." For many Americans these are deeply meaningful phrases and rituals, because they invoke God's favor on the country. But they do not constitute a state-sponsored religion nor are citizens required to believe them or even take notice of them. In other words, in both the American and Roman religious experiences, individual freedom remained paramount, provided that it did not inhibit the state seeking its own divine blessings.

As the centuries passed for the Romans, new religions and new gods appeared in their growing city and were generally welcomed. Small temples of Apollo and Demeter could be found there as early as the fifth century BC, although the real heyday of foreign cults was still off in the future. As Rome became a big and bustling city it naturally attracted people from across its expanding empire who brought with them their own religious beliefs. Just as the American government made no attempt to stop Catholics, Jews, or Muslims from settling in the United States and practicing their religions, so the Romans were willing to add to the religious diversity of their culture, although they naturally favored their own religious heritage in public events. Religion for Romans, as for Americans, remained a personal choice—one of many that the state should stay out of. But in both cases the transplanted or new religions remained largely an urban phenomenon. Still today one can drive a very long way in rural America and never come across a synagogue, mosque, or even a

Catholic church. But as for local Protestant churches, that's another story.

This is not to say that Romans welcomed every new religion into their society with open arms. In the earlier centuries of the republic the Senate would occasionally take action to protect public morality or avoid giving offense to the state gods. It was a fine line to draw. No one would deny that a priest of an ancient cult, say of Athena or Apollo, was not a valid representative of a legitimate religion. The Romans could read, after all (despite what some Greeks thought), and they were well aware of the vast Greek literature describing the activities of those ancient gods. But what about traveling prophets or preachers who simply made up new religions or falsely claimed to represent old ones? Or what about religious rituals from beyond Greece like Egypt, Persia, or Mesopotamia? Those naturally received greater scrutiny from Roman authorities and were sometimes expelled. In general the Romans were welcoming to other religions provided that they could be certain that the adherents were praying to a real deity for the benefit of Rome. If, on the other hand, the religion worshipped a false god, allowing that to continue would simply upset the real ones. By the same token, atheism, which denied that the gods existed at all, was just begging for trouble. Since the purpose of Rome's policy toward religion was to preserve the *pax deorum*, it made no sense to tolerate those who were certain to break that peace.

That said, the Roman government rarely took action against religions. Even when it did, it was careful to avoid upsetting any gods in the process. Take, for example, the case of the cult of Dionysus, the Greek god of wine. It was a popular enough devotion in Greece as well as southern Italy, which was settled by Greeks. Sometime shortly after 200 BC, a priestess of Dionysus (or Bacchus, as the Romans called him) introduced the religion to Rome and began initiating people into the "mysteries," which is just another way of saying the secret rituals meant only for members. The Bacchus cult was a little unusual in that it did not allow men to join, being led by older women priests. Three times a year they would hold their ceremonies, known as Bacchanalia, which occurred during the daytime. Things went swimmingly for the new cult for several years until one priestess, Paculla Annia, decided to let in some men, beginning with her own sons. Suddenly, the mysteries went from nice afternoon wine-tasting parties into all-night drunken orgies. Interest in the cult skyrocketed. Soon the faithful could be numbered in the thousands and the frequency of rituals increased from three times a year to five times a month.

Rome was a big city by this time, so it wasn't too hard at first for the Bacchanalia to blend into the background noise. But as the cult grew it became increasingly hard to ignore it. For one thing, the rituals began with the members parading through the streets, banging drums, crashing cymbals, and otherwise making an incredible racket. They would then go to a secluded hall or grove, but the noise would continue well into the night. It was also noticed that the elderly leaders of the cult were no longer interested in accepting new members older than twenty. Rumors started to spread and finally the consuls were given authority to investigate. At first it was difficult to crack the cult's vow of secrecy, since all the members feared not only divine retribution, but violent reprisals from their fellow worshippers. Then one person turned state's evidence and the floodgate opened.

The government investigation of the Bacchanalia reveals the limits of Rome's tolerance for religious innovation. The investigating consul could hardly believe it when he heard what happened in the nocturnal gatherings. He reported to the Senate that:

> there was no crime, no deed of shame, wanting. More uncleanness was committed by men with men than with women. Whoever would not submit to defilement, or shrank from violating others, was sacrificed as a victim. To regard nothing as impious or criminal was the sum and total of their religion. The men, as though seized with madness and with frenzied distortions of their bodies, shrieked out prophecies; the matrons, dressed as Bacchae, their hair disheveled, rushed down to the Tiber River with burning torches, plunged them into the water, and drew them out again, the flame undiminished because they were made of sulfur mixed with lime. Men were fastened to a machine and hur-

ried off to hidden caves, and they were said to have been taken away by the gods. These were the men who refused to join their conspiracy or take a part in their crimes or submit to their pollution.

That was enough for the Senate. They gave authority to the consuls to arrest the priests, priestesses, and any members of the religion that they could identify. After the initial roundups, the consuls convened the popular assemblies to explain the situation.

They had a difficult task. Remember, the Romans generally believed that a person's religion was his or her own business and not the state's. There was no way that the consuls could argue that Dionysus did not exist, since his cult had flourished in the Greek world for centuries. Instead, they focused on the danger that the cult posed to the health of the Roman Republic. All of the assemblymen were familiar enough with the Bacchanalia—it made so much noise it was difficult to miss. To the stunned body, the consuls now told the rest of the story:

> Have you any idea what these nocturnal gatherings, these promiscuous associations of men and women are? If you knew at what age those males are initiated, you would feel not only compassion for them, but shame as well. Do you consider, fellow citizens, that young men who have taken this unholy oath should be made into soldiers? That after the training they have received in that shrine of obscenity they should be entrusted with arms? Shall these men, having engaged in sexual perversions themselves and with others around them, wield their swords in defense of the chastity of your wives and children?

This was not a religion, they argued, it was a conspiracy—a dark conspiracy aimed at overturning the Republic.

> So far, their impious association confines itself to individual crimes; it has not yet strength enough to destroy the Republic. But the evil is creeping stealthily on, and growing day by day. It is already too great to limit its action to individual citizens; it seeks to control the State.

Unless, fellow citizens, you take precautions, this Assembly, legally convened by a consul in the daylight, will be followed by another very different assembly gathered together in the darkness of the night. Now they, disunited, fear you, a united Assembly. But when you are dispersed to your homes and your farms they will hold their assembly and plot their own safety and your ruin. Then it will be your turn, scattered as you will be, to fear them in their united strength.

The consuls knew, however, that despite these arguments the Roman people would still have a natural aversion to persecuting a religion. What of the god that they would invariably anger? The consuls addressed this point, admitting that "where crimes are sheltered under the name of religion, there is fear that in punishing the hypocrisy of men we are doing violence to something holy which is mixed up with it." But they assured the assembled that the Senate had already cleared their decision with the Roman pontiffs and augurs, who gave it a green light.

I thought I ought to tell you this beforehand, so that none of you may be distressed by fears with regard to religion when you see us demolishing the meeting places of the Bacchanalia and dispersing their impious gatherings. All that we shall do will be done with the sanction of the gods and in obedience to their will. To show their displeasure at the insult offered to their majesty by these lusts and crimes they have dragged them out of their dark hiding-places into the light of day, and they have willed that they shall be exposed not to enjoy impunity, but to be punished and put an end to.

So there you have it—the gods are on board with our plan. Not only is the Bacchanalia a danger to the Republic, but it is seriously upsetting the *pax deorum*.

What is amazing throughout this story is the extent to which the Romans were willing to be tolerant of a religious practice. No American city would allow weekly parades of drunken revelers to march through the streets collecting teenagers and children for orgies. Revelers who insisted they were performing a religious ritual would be answered with derisive laughter and a trip downtown. If a Church of Child Pornography were established in the United States, claims that they were practicing their religion would not keep the members from being arrested and their materials confiscated. Yet the Romans were only willing to move against the Bacchanalia when it became crystal clear that it was both unholy and unhealthy for the survival of the Republic. The important point here is that the Romans held fast to the idea of maximum personal freedom—an idea born on their family farms and transmitted directly to their empire.

The history of religion and personal freedom in the United States follows a very similar course. While it is true that the U.S. government would never recognize a Bacchanalia as a religious practice, from the beginning of the republic the concept of freedom of religion was paramount. In its ritualized prayers, inscriptions, and invocations the American government takes care of asking God to bless the republic. The people are free to join in, perhaps by singing "God Bless America" or saying the Pledge of Allegiance, but it is not required.

As was the case for the Romans, the foundational American belief was that the health of the republic necessitated that the citizens believe in God and that God, in turn, believed in the republic. This is plain enough in the speeches and writings of the American Founding Fathers. John Adams, for example, wrote:

> We have no government armed with power capable of contending with human passions unbridled by morality and religion. Avarice, ambition, revenge, or gallantry, would break the strongest cords of our Constitution as a whale goes through a net. Our Constitution was made only for a moral and religious people. It is wholly inadequate to the government of any other.

Benjamin Franklin likewise insisted that:

> God governs in the affairs of man. And if a sparrow cannot fall to the ground without His notice, is it probable that an empire can rise

without His aid? We have been assured in the Sacred Writings that except the Lord build the house, they labor in vain that build it. I firmly believe this. I also believe that, without His concurring aid, we shall succeed in this political building no better than the builders of Babel.

Thomas Jefferson maintained:

God who gave us life gave us liberty. And can the liberties of a nation be thought secure when we have removed their only firm basis, a conviction in the minds of the people that these liberties are a gift from God? That they are not to be violated but with His wrath?

Perhaps the most famous such remark was that of George Washington, who in his Farewell Address asserted that "reason and experience both forbid us to expect that national morality can prevail in exclusion of religious principle."

This "national morality" based on religious principle would, the Founders believed, ensure that Americans remained honest, hardworking, civic-minded, and trustworthy. And, looking at the American people as a whole, they were right. Still today, most Americans believe that it is absolutely necessary for a person to believe in God in order to be moral. Most Americans also maintain that it is especially important for children to learn religious faith at home. The Romans felt the same way. This can rub outside observers the wrong way. Few French, for example, agree that religion should be taught in the home. Europeans in general worry that the high rate of churchgoing in the United States is leading to policies that rely on religious convictions rather than intelligent analysis. As an editorial in *The Economist* noted, "To Europeans religion is the strangest and most disturbing feature of American exceptionalism.... They find it extraordinary that three times as many Americans believe in the virgin birth as in evolution ..." Many Europeans today are convinced that American foreign policy, particularly with regard to Israel and the War on Terror, is dictated largely by irrational religious beliefs.

Of course, not all Europeans believe that the United States has become a theocracy or that it develops its policies in a tent-revival-like atmosphere. The French author and commentator Jean-François Revel, for example, regards the United States and its people to be a force for good in the world precisely because of their unique national character. The situation was remarkably similar for the Romans. Most Greeks—Eastern sophisticates who were the cultural forbears of Rome—considered Roman approaches to religion (and everything else, for that matter) to be barbaric. Although the Greeks had long revered the ancient gods, by the second century very few Greeks took them seriously. They were, like many modern Europeans, living in a postreligious world. Yet one Greek writer, Polybius, who lived in Rome after 167 BC, argued that Rome's religiosity was, in fact, the source of its strength:

> The quality in which the Roman republic is most distinctly superior is in my opinion the nature of its religious convictions. I believe that it is the very thing which among other peoples is an object of reproach, I mean superstition, which maintains the cohesion of the Roman state.... For this reason I think, not that the ancients acted rashly and haphazardly in introducing among the people notions concerning the gods and beliefs in the terrors of hell, but that modern people are most rash and foolish in banishing such beliefs. The consequence is that among the Greeks, apart from other things, if members of the government are entrusted with no more than a talent, though they have ten copyists and as many seals and twice as many witnesses, they cannot remain honest. Whereas among the Romans those who as magistrates and legates are dealing with large sums of money maintain correct conduct just because they have pledged their faith by oath. Whereas elsewhere it is a rare thing to find a man who keeps his hands off public money, and whose record is clean, among the Romans one rarely comes across a man who has been discovered in such conduct.

This internal moral compass, built on a sincere (if simple) belief in the divine not only formed the American and Roman characters, but directly contributed to their successes.

For all this insistence that their citizens have *some* religious beliefs, Roman and American societies also insisted that the specifics of those beliefs remain a personal choice. The government, both societies believed, should stay out of that choice unless it somehow presented a real danger to the republic. The Romans moved against the Bacchanalia for that reason and similar arguments have been made at different points in American history. Indeed, almost every "foreign" religion that has come to the United States has sparked at least a few fears of dark conspiracies, not unlike those that the consuls warned the Roman people about so many centuries ago.

For example, although Catholics existed and flourished in America at the founding of the republic, they did not become a sizable minority until the flood of Irish and German Catholic immigrants arrived in the 1830s. It was then that some Americans began to claim that the immigration was, in fact, a well-planned invasion ordered by the pope in order to add the United States to his worldwide empire. In his book *Foreign Conspiracy Against the Liberties of the United States* (1835), Samuel F. B. Morse (the inventor of the telegraph), argued that the pope was sending droves of Catholics to overturn the free republic of America and replace it with the tyranny of (ironically) Rome. The same year Lyman Beecher (the father of Harriet Beecher Stowe) published *A Plea for the West*, in which he laid bare the secret plans of the pope to send nuns, priests, and bishops to the American West to establish schools and churches so as to pollute and destroy the freedom and true Christianity of the United States. These fears remained strong in America for many decades. In 1855, Beecher's son, Edward Beecher, wrote *The Papal Conspiracy Exposed*, which again claimed to lay bare the pope's plans for world domination.

Just as importantly, these books and others like them claimed that American Catholics were actively working, both secretly and in the open, to subvert the republic. One could pop into any bookstore in America and find such titles as *Dangers of Jesuit Instruction* (1846), *Pope or President? Startling Discoveries of Romanism as Revealed by its Own Writers* (1859), and *Washington in the Lap of Rome* (1888). In 1871 the popular magazine *Harper's Weekly* published an editorial cartoon called "The

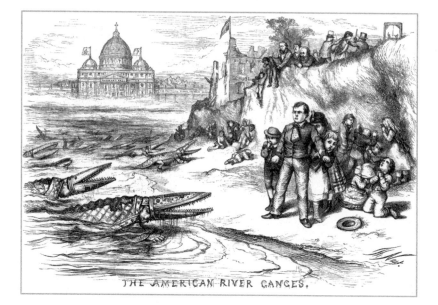

The American River Ganges
From *Harper's Weekly,* 1871 (Courtesy of HarpWeek., LLC)

American River Ganges," in which Catholic politicians, having destroyed American public schools, were shown dumping American children into waters infested with bishops in the guise of alligators. In the distance can be seen the guiding hand of St. Peter's Basilica.

There was an especially good market for books that claimed to describe the secret (and diabolical) rituals of the Catholics. These included such exposés as *Awful Disclosures of the Hotel Dieu Nunnery* (1836) and *The Testimony of an Escaped Novice from the Sisterhood of St. Joseph* (1855). All of this even led to the creation of a political party, the Know-Nothings, who in the 1850s won major elections across the country and swept the legislative and gubernatorial elections in Massachusetts!

Fears of a Catholic conspiracy to overturn the American republic subsided in the twentieth century, although they did not die altogether. When the Democratic Party nominated Alfred E. Smith in 1928 and John F. Kennedy in 1960, both men, who were Catholic, had to answer tough questions about their willingness to take orders from Rome. Other "Old World" religions have elicited similar concerns among Americans. In the 1920s Henry Ford, the great automaker, used his newspaper *The Dearborn Independent* to "expose" an international conspiracy of Jews that he believed was active in the United States. Even in the twenty-first century fears of Jewish conspiracies continue. More than one recent observer has claimed that American policy toward the Middle East is manipulated by secretive Jews or "New York money people." Similarly, in the wake of 9/11 some Americans worry that Muslims—any Muslims—are working to either promote terrorism or turn the United States into an Islamic state. Criticism of Muslim schools in America frequently sounds like that leveled against Catholic schools more than a century ago. The fear that is enunciated in rows of popular books is that Western civilization is declining in the wake of Islam's gains and that the United States had better do something about it.

Both societies, the Roman and the American, put a high premium on two sometimes conflicting necessities: religious piety and personal freedom. The religious piety was believed to be crucial not only for the formation of honest citizens, but also to maintain divine blessings. The personal freedom was also crucial because it is what led to the creation of the republic, and its preservation was the core purpose of the government. Neither state could have one without the other. And so, they would have to shoulder the continuing problem of balancing them.

The national characters of the Romans and the Americans were born and raised on the family farm. Citizens of both empires valued hard work, self-reliance, personal freedom, and religious conviction. Their suspicion of foreign "Old World" powers led them to question and even persecute some religions. Yet even in those cases the rationale was the preservation of the secular state, not an attempt to define heresy or enforce doctrinal uniformity. The ideal citizen in both societies was "down-to-earth," and that in itself is unusual. Most great states or empires afford the highest praise and status to those people with, well, the highest status. Nobility in most societies do not hesitate to celebrate their lofty lineage, wisdom, and distance from the common people. Leaders in most human societies—from tribal to imperial—claim origins from either the divine or the extraordinary. They do not claim to be common.

Yet that was the claim made by leaders in ancient Rome and modern America. The image of the ideal leader in both cultures, forged on the family farm, is of an independent, hardworking, no-nonsense man from a humble (or at least agrarian) background who reluctantly agrees to lead the people for a time. Although both states regularly elevated blue-bloods of one sort or another to positions of power, those same leaders made a point of portraying themselves as the basest commoners, while casting their opponents as privileged elites. Cato the Elder, for example, was one of the most powerful and wealthy men in Rome. Yet he regularly pined for his farm and the simple pleasures of agriculture, even writing a widely used manual on agriculture.

And there is the example of Marius, a Roman who wielded extraordinary power in the years around 100 BC. Despite his position, when he addressed the Roman people he cast his opponents in the Senate as privileged elites in thrall to sophisticated Greek culture:

My words are not carefully chosen. I attach no importance to such artifices, of which true merit stands in no need, since it is plainly visible to all. It is my adversaries who require oratorical skill to help them cover up their turpitude. Nor have I studied Greek literature; I had no interest in a branch of learning which did nothing to improve the characters of its professors. The lessons I have learnt are such as best enable me to serve my country—to strike down an enemy, to mount guard, to fear nothing but disgrace, to endure winter's cold and summer's heat with equal patience, to sleep on the bare ground, and to work hard on an empty stomach.... They call me vulgar and unpolished, because I do not know how to put on an elegant dinner and do not have actors at my table or keep a cook who has cost me more than my farm overseer. All this, my fellow citizens, I am proud to admit. For I was taught by my father and other men of blameless life that while elegant graces befit a woman, a man's duty is to labor; that every good man should live for honor rather than for riches; that the weapons he carries in his hands, and not the furniture he keeps in his house, are ornaments most worth having. Well, then, let them continue to do what pleases them—the love-making and drinking that they set such store by; let them spend their old age as they spent their youth, in the pleasure of the table, the slaves of gluttony and lust. Let them leave the sweat, the dust, and the rest of it to us, to whom such things are better than a feast.

Marius boasts of his vulgarity and general ignorance of high culture. There are very few civilizations in which that would constitute a résumé enhancer—particularly for those vying for the pinnacle of political authority.

But, of course, we see the same thing in American culture and for the same reasons. The United States has certainly elected plenty of presidents from the most elite families in America. Yet in all cases these men downplayed every aspect of their aristocratic background, focusing instead on whatever common-man credentials they could scrape together. Consider, for example, the 2004 election. Both candidates, John F. Kerry and George W. Bush, came from privileged backgrounds and went to the very best schools. Yet both did their best to convince the electorate that they were, after all, just regular Joes. At the same time they made a point of describing their opponents as members of the highest elite. Think about that for a moment. The president of the United States *is* the highest elite. He (or she) is the most powerful person in the known universe. If that's not elite, then nothing is.

Yet American candidates race for the bottom, each attempting to demonstrate that he or she is the least elite of the field. In 2004 Kerry put his military combat experience in Vietnam front and center in his campaign, while implying that Bush's powerful father pulled strings to keep him out of the war. Kerry toted a hunting rifle and dug into a Philly cheesesteak (neither very well), while his campaign cast Bush as a rich frat boy, irresponsible and pampered. For his part, Bush stressed his Texas ranching roots. There were plenty of photo ops of the president clearing brush back home, something that he insisted he really enjoys. (By all accounts, that is true.) Bush's campaign avoided talking about military service, instead casting Kerry as an elite Massachusetts liberal who had protested against the Vietnam War and testified against the military. When Kerry was praised in Europe for (among other things) his ability to speak French, Bush supporters immediately dubbed him "Jean-François Kerry." The fact that public opinion polls in Europe overwhelming supported Kerry for president allowed Republicans to characterize him as the candidate of the elite and sophisticated Old World, and simultaneously to portray Bush as the plainspoken man from Texas. This is precisely the same tactic that was used in the third century BC by the political enemies of the Roman leader Scipio Africanus, who "taunted his style of dress as being un-Roman and even unsoldierly. It was asserted that he walked about the gymnasium in a Greek mantle and Greek slippers and spent his time amongst rhetoricians and athletes and that the whole of his staff were enjoying the attractions of [Greek] Syracuse and living a life of similar self-indulgence and effeminacy."

These campaign tactics are not only nothing new—they are ancient. American candidates in all races are regularly tested on their common-man credentials. In 1992 George H. W. Bush was gravely harmed by pictures of him gawking at a grocery store scanner. So was Michael Dukakis in 1988, when he looked grossly out of place dressed up in military gear and riding in a tank. It is almost routine now for reporters to ask candidates if they know the price of milk or bread—as though that proved that they really were frequent grocery shoppers. Ronald Reagan, a Hollywood actor and former head of the Screen Actors Guild, donned a cowboy hat and, like Cato the Elder, went back to his ranch every chance he got. Jimmy Carter said little about his training in nuclear physics, but a great deal about his peanut farm. John F. Kennedy downplayed his patrician background and Harvard education, focusing instead on his military service aboard the PT-109. And on and on. In all cases, these men sought power by conforming their image to that of the American ideal— an ideal that one might be hard-pressed to describe fully, but which most people know when they see it.

The poster child of that ideal is Cincinnatus. Whether his story is completely true or not, the memory of Cincinnatus passed down through the centuries was of a man who worked hard, and was honest, forthright, pious, and effective. He was a straight shooter who loved his country and was willing to come when duty called, but accepted power only reluctantly, longing to return to his farm. This image of the farmer/patriot was very strong during the early days of the American republic. One can still see it, for example, on the Great Seal of the state of Delaware, created in 1776, which depicts a single man as both farmer and soldier. It was also evoked in 1783 when America's first veterans' organization was formed—called, appropriately enough, the Society of the Cincinnati. Created to provide recognition and support for officers who served until the end of the Revolutionary War, the Society was so named because each member was thought to be a Cincinnatus unto himself. Each was a common man who came to serve as a military leader when his country called, but who now eagerly returned to his previous occupation. The first president of the Society, a farmer who gladly returned to his fields by the Potomac after serving his country, was none other than George Washington.

Today if you visit the Virginia State Capitol Building you will find there under the main rotunda a magnificent life-size marble statue of George Washington, sculpted in the 1790s by the French artist Jean-Antoine Houdon. In this striking composition Washington stands resolutely, still dressed in his revolutionary uniform yet having already taken off his hat. In his right hand is a walking stick, signifying his return to civilian life. But it is his left side that is more interesting. There his arm rests on a Roman fasces, the symbol of political power that accompanied the ancient Cincinnatus as he entered Rome. And behind George Washington, waiting for the victorious general's return, is his plow.

Chapter 4

Building an Empire While Trying Not To

Building an empire is not too difficult. Plenty of people have done it. First, get a large army. Second, select a target—preferably something that you want or just generally dislike. Third, defeat said target with said army and conquer territory. Repeat until satisfied or stopped. That's it. It's empire building, after all, not rocket science. It has been successfully undertaken countless times across the ages by such luminaries as Alexander the Great, Charlemagne, Genghis Khan, Suleiman the Magnificent, Louis XIV, Napoleon, and on and on. The nice thing about this system is that with each new conquest the ruler becomes more powerful and better able to reward his troops and (sometimes) his people. As every conqueror knows, nothing succeeds like success. With enough of that success, the leader will have a large empire of subject peoples that can be exploited to his or her heart's content. Easy.

There is a downside, though, to this traditional style of empire. By its nature it is built upon conquered subjects, who, in most cases, did not ask to be conquered. That means that they will support the imperial power only insofar as they are forced to do so. The first time a rebellion seems possible or another would-be emperor comes over the horizon, those conquered territories will move fast to regain their freedom. For example, when Hitler was defeated in Europe no one had to convince the French, Belgians, or others in liberated areas that they should sever their ties with Nazi Germany. When the Soviet Union fell, no arms were twisted in East Germany, Hungary, the Baltic states or any of the other Eastern Bloc countries to declare their independence from Russian control. They had longed for it for generations and eagerly grasped it when it became available. An Empire of Conquest, therefore, is certainly the simplest and quickest sort to build, but it does have the disadvantage of disintegrating in an equally simple and rapid fashion.

The ancient Romans built an altogether different sort of empire—an Empire of Trust. That unusual sort of empire has the advantage of a very long life, but it is extremely difficult to build. In order to do so one will need all of the basic components of an empire—a strong military, sound economy, et cetera—and one more extremely rare component: a fervent desire *not* to have an empire. Put another way, what you need to build an Empire of Trust is a solid, stable, and peaceful civilization that wants the rest of the world to leave it alone. We will see later how this isolationist attitude can lead, ironically enough, to the creation of a vast empire. For the moment, however, we need to establish that it actually existed both in ancient Rome and modern America.

Isolationism flows directly out of those unusual characteristics we examined in the last chapter—characteristics that both Rome and the United States shared. They were both frontier societies that developed their national character on the family farm. They valued hard work, honesty, piety, and virtue. They were a people who minded their own business and believed that others should do the same. Their experiences with foreign kings also led them to distrust concentrated power and generally look with suspicion on foreigners. All of this made them isolationist.

A distinction needs to be made from the outset. Both Romans and Americans were isolationist in their approach to other "civilized powers" as they understood them. This isolationism did not extend, however, to primitive societies, which both states considered to be a hindrance to be assimilated, moved, or destroyed. The Roman approach to the refined Greeks, for example, was worlds away from their attitude toward the tribal peoples of Spain or Gaul. By the same token, nineteenth-century Americans avoided intervention in European affairs, but quite dramatically intervened in the affairs of American Indians.

The tradition of American isolationism (or, as it is sometimes called, noninterventionism) can be seen from the earliest days of the American republic. In his farewell address, George Washington pointedly told his countrymen:

> The great rule of conduct for us, in regard to foreign nations, is in extending our commercial relations, to have with them as little political connection as possible. Europe has a set of primary interests, which to us have none, or a very remote relation. Hence she must be engaged in frequent controversies the causes of which are essentially foreign to our concerns. Hence, therefore, it must be unwise in us to implicate ourselves, by artificial ties, in the ordinary vicissitudes of her politics, or the ordinary combinations and collisions of her friendships or enmities.

Twenty-five years later President John Quincy Adams could confidently tell the House of Representatives that America "goes not abroad, in search of monsters to destroy. She is the well-wisher to the freedom and independence of all. She is the champion and vindicator only of her own." By necessity, therefore, this meant that Americans were uninterested in building an empire. No other state had anything to fear from them. As Thomas Jefferson wrote in 1791, "If there be one principle more deeply rooted than any other in the mind of every American, it is, that we should have nothing to do with conquest."

In the nineteenth century, Americans were expanding across North America. This brought them in contact with Spanish and French territories. However, Americans had come to see the Western Hemisphere as their own unique sphere of influence, a new world to be kept free from the problems of the old. The result in 1823 was the Monroe Doctrine, in which the United States made clear that it would no longer tolerate further European colonization or interference in the Americas. As President James Monroe insisted, "In the wars of the European powers, in matters relating to themselves, we have never taken part, nor does it comport with our policy, so to do. It is only when our rights are invaded, or seriously menaced that we resent injuries, or make preparations for our defense." Americans were so uninterested in projecting power beyond their shores that from the 1860s through the 1890s the country of Chile had a larger navy than that of the United States.

At first glance the Spanish-American War of 1898 might seem like a change in American isolationism. But in large measure it was a reaction to instability in Cuba under Spanish rule. The original impetus of the war was to remove Old World control over an American territory very close to the United States. By the end of hostilities, the United States would find itself with control over the former Spanish colonies of Puerto Rico, Guam, and the Philippines, thus extending American power beyond the hemisphere for the first time. In Europe, these were the glory days of nationalism, when it was taken as a matter of course that great nations should have great empires. France, Britain, Italy, Germany, even little Belgium, were quickly gobbling up colonies in Africa and Asia. There were Americans who agreed with this line of reasoning, but just as importantly there were plenty who did not. Many Americans continued to insist that the United States should stay out of "foreign entanglements." Mark Twain ridiculed those who prayed for American victories overseas, since those prayers naturally sought ruin for those who were attacked by U.S. soldiers. In his short story "The War Prayer," he included the flip side of those prayers for victory:

> For our sakes who adore Thee, Lord, blast their [the enemies'] hopes, blight their lives, protract their bitter pilgrimage, make heavy their steps, water their way with their tears, stain the white snow with the blood of their wounded feet! We ask it, in the spirit of love, of Him Who is the Source of Love, and Who is the ever-faithful refuge and friend of all that are sore beset and seek His aid with humble and contrite hearts. Amen.

Although the United States would become much more involved in foreign wars and international diplomacy in the twentieth century, the isolationist nature of the American character remained fairly constant.

Americans were determined to stay out of World War I, entering it only near the end and only because the Germans targeted American vessels. When the war ended, President Woodrow Wilson spearheaded the creation of the League of Nations, which he believed would stop future wars in Europe and the world. Joining the League of Nations, though, would require the United States to make a legal commitment to engaging in foreign interventions whenever the peace was disturbed. Attaching American foreign policy to the problems of the Old World was too much for most Americans. Supporters of the League of Nations were derisively called "internationalists." As Senator Henry Cabot Lodge famously said, "The United States is the world's best hope, but if you fetter her in the interests and quarrels of other nations, if you tangle her in the intrigues of Europe, you will destroy her powerful good, and endanger her very existence." The United States Senate refused to ratify President Wilson's treaty and so the United States never entered the League.

American isolationism was just as strong in the years leading up to World War II. With the rise of Nazism and Fascism, it was plain enough that the European powers were once again heading toward war. Americans were determined to stay out of it. Even after Hitler had conquered France and begun his attacks on Britain, there was virtually no popular support for American involvement in the war. President Franklin Delano Roosevelt had to content himself with supporting Britain through the Lend-Lease Program, arguing to his fellow Americans that if your neighbor's house was on fire you would at least lend him a hose. Americans only grudgingly agreed. It was the Japanese attack on Pearl Harbor that prompted Americans to join the war and fundamentally altered the nature of their isolationism.

This isolationism, woven into the DNA of the American character, would eventually lead to the development of an American empire. Before exploring that strand of history, we must first have a look at similar dynamics at work in ancient Rome. When we think of Roman power, we frequently conjure up images of marching legions subjecting the known world to their control. From that perspective, the rise of Rome seems pretty straightforward, well in line with the creation of an Empire of

Conquest. All that was needed was for the Senate (or later the emperors) to point the legions at someone they did not like or something they desired, and after a bit of bloodshed, the empire expanded.

Yet that is not at all how Rome grew. From what we have seen when looking at the development of the Roman national character, we might expect that Romans were as isolationist as Americans, desiring peace, stability, and independence above all. We might even expect that the Romans, like Americans, would actively avoid projecting power except when necessary. And we'd be right.

Like Americans, Romans strongly believed that conquest must never be a reason for war. That concept, which seems self-evident to modern Americans, is one that they share with very few people in history. Yet war, even for them, was sometimes necessary. To deal with matters regarding foreigners, the early kings of Rome had established a guild of priests, known as the *fetiales*. It was their job to oversee all treaties, embassies, and declarations of war. They were priests because it was important to the Romans that when dealing with foreigners all of their actions were honest, moral, and consistent. Unlike your average gods of the ancient world, who gloried in crushing their enemies beneath their feet, the Roman deities would bless war only when it was clearly defensive and unavoidable. For that reason, Roman law made it *illegal* to wage war except when provoked by a hostile action toward Rome itself or one of its allies.

How did this work in practice? When an act of aggression or other provocation occurred against Rome it would be formally reported to the Senate. In the early days, the provocation would likely be something along the lines of a raid on Roman farms or an attack on Roman travelers, although it could be direct attacks on Roman territory. At that point, the fetial priests would investigate the situation. If the reports were true and it seemed that the situation had a chance of being resolved peacefully, a fetial priest would be sent to the foreign power. Wearing a long veil, the priest would stand at the border of the other state, where he would loudly proclaim the Roman grievance, demand reparations for any wrongs, and call down divine wrath on himself if his claims were unjust. He would then walk into the foreign territory and repeat the same ritual for the first person he met. He did it again at the gates of the principle city and finally in the main forum. At that point the leaders of the foreign power would have thirty days to make things right and thus avoid war. Back in Rome a war standard would fly, signifying to the citizens that they should prepare themselves. If the foreign power refused to provide restitution, the fetial priests would then make an official pronouncement, calling the gods to witness that the Romans had been wronged and that their cause was just.

The fetial priests' decision simply meant that the Romans were justified in going to war, having exhausted all other possibilities and having received the approbation of the gods. It was still up to the Senate and the people legally to declare war. If that happened, a messenger would be sent to the enemy's border with a charred spear, which he would throw into their territory to signify the beginning of the war. By this act the Romans produced an *indictio belli*, a legal declaration of war. By law, this was the only sort of war that Romans were allowed to fight.

After the war (or instead of it) a treaty would generally need to be made. Treaties in the Roman Republic had the force of law—just as in the United States. No one was permitted to break them. Once the treaty was agreed to, the fetial priests would solemnize the agreement in a public ceremony in which they would make an animal sacrifice saying, "If the Roman people break this treaty, then do you, Jupiter, so strike down the Roman people as I now strike this offering, and so much harder as you are stronger."

These are not the laws and customs of a conquering empire. Rather, they constitute a system that was designed to make it *difficult* to wage war. With their inherent distrust of concentrated power and solid isolationist views, the Romans wanted to avoid war whenever possible. Such an attitude was (and is) remarkably rare. The great Athenian leader Solon, much like European colonial powers of the nineteenth century, openly advocated military conquests in pursuit of national glory. Aristotle believed that the military subjugation of barbarians (i.e., non-Greeks) was a natural by-product of Greek superiority. In the vast majority of human civilizations that have ever existed, war is something that is to be avoided only when the prospect of defeat is certain. Otherwise, it is a means to greatness. But that is not at all the way the Romans saw things. As Roman senator and jurist Cicero wrote,

> There are two ways of settling a dispute: first, by discussion; second, by physical force; and since the former is characteristic of man, and the latter of the brute, we must resort to force only in case we may not avail ourselves of discussion. The only excuse, therefore, for going to war is that we may live in peace unharmed; and when the victory is won, we should spare those who have not been bloodthirsty and barbarous in their warfare.

Romans (like Americans) lived in a dangerous world. Despite their efforts, therefore, they frequently found themselves at war. And (again, like Americans) they were good at it. This led to a thorny problem: What to do with conquered foes? When a war was concluded, the natural Roman desire was to close up the doors on the Temple of Janus and get on with life. They did not want to be involved in governing foreign peoples with strange languages and customs. Yet, on the other hand, they did not want their defeated enemies to be in a position to cause further trouble in the future. And so, as they did so many things, the Romans dealt with the problem in an ad hoc, commonsense fashion, slowly forming customary policies over the course of many years. Their solution was to transform their enemies into new friends. As Cicero wrote, "Not only must we show consideration for those whom we have conquered by force of arms but we must also ensure protection to those who lay down their arms and throw themselves upon the mercy of our generals." From the perspective of empire building, the Roman desire to turn conquered foes into trusted allies seems counterproductive. It seemed that way to the Romans too. After all, they were trying to avoid an empire. What they wanted was a lasting peace that would afford them an opportunity to be left alone. By allowing defeated states to retain their independence as allies, the Romans sought to build a network of friends rather than an empire of the conquered. They wanted the security that a far-flung empire could afford to a capital city, but without the need to actually have the empire and all the headaches that come with it.

Enough abstract discussion. What did all this mean in practice? The overthrow of the Etruscan kings in Rome did not go over well among the Etruscans themselves. It was only a matter of time before Etruscan forces would return. In order to defend themselves, the Romans organized an alliance with the other nearby towns. Rome was the major city in a small area of west-central Italy known as Latium, because it was inhabited by Latin-speaking people. Having at least that in common, the various towns made deals with Rome to support it in war and to recognize the rights of Roman citizens if Rome would do the same for them. These treaties bound the Latins to Rome for defensive purposes, yet they still retained their local independence. Overall the system worked well enough. The alliance repelled the Aequi and Volsci—hill people from the south and east who were bent on conquering Latium.

As time went on and new attacks occurred, additional towns and territories came into the Roman alliance. In 396 BC the Romans conquered the Etruscan city of Veii, about twelve miles to the north of Rome. Not trusting the Etruscans with an alliance, though, the Romans took direct control of Veii, granting citizenship to its people and incorporating it within the Roman government. Yet that was the exception. In all other cases the Romans were content with treaties of alliance and friendship. It did not escape the notice of the other Latin towns that when it came to the alliance structure, all roads really did lead to Rome. Some Latins began to resent a system that theoretically was a collection of equals, but in reality was handing Rome an increasing amount of power. Yet, although taken together the armies of the other Latin towns were much larger than that of Rome, the Romans were able to hold the alliance together because they worked directly with locals, genuinely respected their independence, and proved trustworthy when it came to meeting their obligations.

This was the birth of the Empire of Trust. Rome had insufficient military forces to conquer and hold the region, but its established track record of fair dealing and its organizational abilities gave it the authority to lead. It also didn't hurt that Rome had the single largest military force, giving it the power to punish individual states that did not maintain their treaty obligations. Even in those cases, however, the Romans were eminently predictable, using force only to right a wrong done to them and their other allies. In short, they could be trusted to use power in a particular sort of way.

The ultimate purpose of the early Roman system of alliances was to keep foreigners out of Latium. As a result, it did not look much beyond the borders of that small region. The basic idea remained isolationist. The borders of Roman interest had expanded, it is true—but only insofar as it allowed the Romans to keep the outside world at bay. They had no interest in projecting power beyond their local sphere of influence. Indeed, although they were only a few miles from the sea, they had no navy at all. Like the Americans of the nineteenth century, the Romans had little interest in people across the waves.

All of that was about to change. Far away to the north, beyond Rome's horizons or interests, was Gaul (modern France). This heavily wooded land was home to fierce primitive tribes who regularly raided the cities of the Mediterranean and northern Italy. As far as barbarians go, these were the real deal. The raiding parties were made up of thousands of men, often drunk, seldom dressed, and always looking for a good time. They would sweep down on cities raping, pillaging, and killing. They were particularly fond of collecting severed heads and did not shrink from various forms of human sacrifice. Modern archaeologists have found evidence of the carnage—whole layers of nothing but ashes, weapons, and skeletons.

The members of the Latin alliance, including the Romans, heard the reports of these atrocities in the north. One could hardly avoid them. Indeed, so many Gauls had come into northern Italy and ultimately settled there that the Romans started calling the area Cisalpine Gaul—Gaul on this side of the Alps. Nevertheless, while disturbing, the Latins could comfort themselves in the knowledge that the Etruscans were between them and the Gauls. That is until most of Etruria fell, leaving no buffer at all between Latium and the murderous hordes. Bullies themselves, the Gauls knew that the best way to knock out a gang is to defeat the leader. They planned to do just that in the land of the Latins.

In 390 BC about thirty thousand Gauls invaded Latium and made a direct line for Rome. In a panic, each of the Latin towns closed its gates, refusing to honor the alliance. Rome was left alone. At this time Rome had two legions. Both were mustered for battle, but it was a pitiful force compared to the Gauls, who outnumbered them two to one. In order to save the city, the legions marched north and met the Gauls about ten miles upriver. It was a massacre. Three days later the triumphant Gauls arrived at Rome, which was nearly defenseless. They knew what to do. The city was brutally sacked, plundered, and burned. Only the citadel on the Capitoline held out, and only because there was not much interest among the Gauls in capturing it. Finally, when the Gauls were finished, the senators in the citadel paid them a large sum of money to leave. The Gauls took the money and went home, leaving behind the smoking ruins of Rome.

The Gallic Sack in 390 BC was a turning point for the Romans. It could hardly fail to be. They learned a hard lesson for an isolationist people— just because you ignore the outside world does not mean that the outside world will ignore you. This is a lesson that Americans learned just as painfully at Pearl Harbor and on 9/11. Both peoples believed so strongly that they were safe from the outside world that they had no compunction about disregarding it. It was only when the outside world rained fire down on their homes that they learned of their mistake.

The Roman response to the horrors of the Gallic Sack could be summed up in two words—two words that would echo across America in the wake of its own tragedies: *Never Again.* They were determined to rebuild and reform so as to make another such attack impossible. In both the Roman and American instances the overriding motivation was securing the homeland. That alone mattered.

At once, the Romans chose a dictator, Camillus, who ordered the construction of a five-and-a-half-mile stone wall around the city (the still partially extant Servian Wall). The Roman military was reformed to make it more powerful and effective. It was needed. Without Roman leadership the Latin towns had fallen into anarchy, preying upon each other. Etruscans who had managed to weather the Gallic storm also took advantage of Rome's weakness by moving again into Latium. In short, things were a mess, so the first order of business for Rome was to restore order. It took almost forty years to do it. Although the Latin towns had broken their oaths, they were usually allowed to reenter the alliance with the same rights and status they'd had before the Gallic invasion. Rome could easily enough have conquered and controlled the towns, yet they treated each one with leniency and even kindness, hoping to build an alliance that would stand firm.

They succeeded. When the Gauls again attacked Latium they were met by a powerful allied Latin force that turned them away. The new Latin League had become a significant power in Italy. Surprisingly, though, this did not please the Latin towns, many of whom questioned the need for the alliance with the recent decline in external threats. Although the Romans insisted that all members were equal, it was clear that Rome had become the administrative capital of the League, and that rankled. In 340 BC the Latin towns demanded independence. The Romans refused. To allow such a thing, the Romans insisted, would leave them again vulnerable to outside attack. The alliance, the Romans maintained, was indivisible. The Latins disagreed, forcing the Romans to wage war to put down the rebellion.

The Latin Revolt of 340 BC in some ways resembles the United States' own Civil War. In both cases a group of independent political entities had bound themselves together under the loose control of a central government. In both cases some of the states later decided to withdraw from the union, forcing the government to wage war to bring them back in. Although initially voluntary, the government maintained that the union was henceforth indivisible. The argument in 340 BC, like that of 1861, was ultimately decided by war.

The Roman defeat of the rebels might well have led to the establishment of a regular Empire of Conquest. Yet even now the Romans were determined to avoid it. As the great Roman historian Tenny Frank wrote, the Romans were led by "far-sighted [*sic*] statesmen who for the first time in history showed how a republican city-state might build a world-empire, and who thus shaped a policy that endured for centuries.... The idea dominating Greek states that conquerors had a perpetual right to a parasitical life at the expense of the conquered, an idea which precluded a healthy and permanent growth of the state, was rejected entirely at Rome." Instead, the Romans brought the Latin states back into a more tightly bound confederation, one in which the question of indivisible union was at last settled. As occurred in the aftermath of the American Civil War, each of the Latin states was separately accepted back into the union.

The Romans crafted a science of union or alliance that would be crucial during their subsequent expansion. Each state was an ally (*socius*) bound to Rome by a permanent treaty (*foedera*—where we get our own word *federal*). The ally was required to supply annual military support and could not remain neutral in wars affecting members of the union. The closest Latin towns would receive Roman citizenship, with full voting rights and the right to run for Roman offices. Although they maintained local state governments, the big decisions for the region were made in Rome. Others, particularly non-Latin allies, were given citizenship without voting rights. They, too, supported the common military and allowed Rome to deal with matters of warfare and foreign affairs, but they retained more local autonomy. The lowest rung were "equal allies" who were not citizens, but could do business with Romans, although not with others without Rome's approval. These various levels of association allowed the Romans to build a strong union and to bring others gradually into it. Rome could reward good behavior with closer ties and more rights, and since the emphasis was always on equality, no one felt that they were under the subjugation of a conquering power.

This method of expansion was important for the Romans as well because it preserved for them the idea that they were simply organizing a union or alliance system for the benefit of themselves and their friends. In this way they created an empire made up of allies bound to them by a common trust in Rome's responsible, predictable, and measured use of authority. This infant Empire of Trust allowed both the Romans and their allies to maintain ideas that were extremely important to them. For the allies, it was important to believe that they were, after all, equal partners with Rome. For the Romans, it was important to believe that, appearances notwithstanding, they had no empire. That national desire to avoid empire is what is so remarkable about Rome—and what would ultimately lead to the expansion of their Empire of Trust.

The relative safety and security that the Romans had built in central Italy did not go unnoticed by their neighbors. Even Italians and Greeks in southern Italy began asking to join. Capua, for example, became a member of the alliance largely to avoid the attacks of the Samnites, another one of those warlike hill people. Centuries earlier, southern Italy had been settled by Greeks who had built beautiful cities along its coasts. Not surprisingly, many of those Greeks looked on the Roman confederation with derision, some even fearing that it might turn into a threat against their freedoms. In the Greek city of Neapolis (modern Naples), a contentious debate over joining the Roman confederation ended in 327 BC when some of the leaders invited a Samnite garrison into the city. The pro-Roman Neapolitan leaders fled to Rome, asking them to send troops to oust the garrison. The Romans agreed and the following year captured Neapolis, making it a new ally.

This same pattern continued during the next several decades as the Romans found themselves in a series of wars, all stemming from the expansion of the alliance. The building of an Empire of Trust is ironic on many levels. In this case, the Romans were motivated by a desire to bring more allies into their confederation so as to increase their own security from outside aggressors and to bring peace to the lands of the allies. Yet, every new ally expanded Rome's frontier a bit further. And over every new horizon was a new potential enemy that, when finally defeated, the Romans would naturally seek to turn into a friend. In other words, to build peace and security at home the Romans had to involve themselves farther and farther away from home and, by the same token, take part in more and more wars.

Similar dynamics are evident enough in modern American expansion.

Like the Romans, most Americans seek security and peace—not an empire. Yet, when attacked, the United States must respond, and when it is victorious it must decide what to do with its conquered foe. Americans settled on much the same solution as did the Romans: Dangerous enemies must be defeated and transformed into friends. Nazi Germany was transformed into a NATO ally: West Germany. Imperial Japan was turned into a prosperous, pro-Western democracy. Afghanistan and Iraq were conquered and accepted as new allies. In each case, American leaders were faced with the same calculus presented to the Romans many centuries before—either annex the conquered foe or transform it into an ally. The former is the strategy of an Empire of Conquest, the latter of an Empire of Trust. Even if a new friend should turn against you, as Germany did after World War I, simply conquer it again—and keep conquering it until it finally gives up and stays your friend. It may seem a bit perverse, but for an isolationist people uneasy with the whole concept of empire, it is the only option available.

During the late fourth century BC the Romans were primarily fighting against the Samnites, Etruscans, and Gauls, all of whom saw the growing Roman confederation as a threat to their power. And, of course, it was. Cities that were attacked by these powers would regularly appeal to Rome for aid. The Romans would then judge the situation and, if they thought the matter just, accept the threatened city as an ally. War would ensue. In some cases, allied cities would rebel, switching sides to the other powers. In each case the Romans would ultimately defeat the rebels, punish those guilty of the rebellion, and accept the city back as a friend. As Frank noted, "There must have been respect bred of the knowledge that the Romans were able to keep a pledge, to restrain grasping hands, and to bestow favors, as well as to strike and punish."

Although the Romans had done their best to avoid the implications of their growing power, by 300 BC it was plain even to them that they had become the leader of much of Italy. The frequent wars that they had to fight on behalf of their allies must have led many Romans to the conclusion that the only way to bring lasting peace would be to push the horizons of the confederation all the way to the sea. In other words, only by unifying all of Italy could the Romans and their allies truly be safe and secure. There seems to have been a general acceptance of this idea, because the Romans showed every willingness to accept more and more allies. And with warlike people like the Samnites or Lucanians nearby there was no shortage of towns and cities who needed help. It was almost a Roman form of Manifest Destiny, a growing feeling that their mission was to unify, secure, and pacify the peninsula.

Pick up any history of the Roman Republic and there is one phrase that you will find over and over again: "They appealed to Rome for aid." Those six words explain the central dynamic by which the Romans expanded. A people somewhere would get into trouble. They would appeal to Rome for aid. The Romans would agree, gaining a new ally, but also a new war in the bargain. In this way the confederation expanded, making it even more attractive to other states in danger of attack and even more troublesome to those powers seeking conquests. Yet this was still an Italian affair. The Romans were fighting local tribes and armies, not the great powers of the eastern Mediterranean. Events in Italy did not go completely unnoticed by the Greek East, particularly as the Roman confederation began gobbling up Greek towns in southern Italy—places like Rhegium, Locri, and Croton.

In 285 BC the small Greek coastal town of Thurii appealed to Rome for aid against the Lucanians. Rome responded, ejected the Lucanians, and made an alliance with the people of Thurii. A few years later the Lucanians again attacked Thurii, forcing the Romans to return. In order to deter future attacks and provide some stability for the region, the Romans provided a garrison for the city. It was what we would today call a "trigger presence"—a small contingent unable to defend itself against a powerful foe, but whose elimination would trigger war with the home country. This was standard operating procedure for the Romans. But in this case it had dramatic repercussions. Nearby on the Italian boot heel was Tarentum, a large Greek city of wealth and sophistication. The Tarentines were plenty tired of watching Roman barbarians take control of Greek cities in Italy. They believed that Greeks, the inventors of democracy as well as much of Western philosophy and science, should never under any circumstances be subject to a collection of Italian farmers.

It is important to remember that in the 280s BC the great powers in the Western world were all Greek. Only a few generations earlier Alexander the Great had led his armies out of Greece, conquering the Persian Empire, Egypt, and Mesopotamia before pressing on all the way to India. In a few years of conquests, Alexander had built an empire that was truly enormous. Of course, as so often happens with Empires of Conquest, it did not last much longer than the conqueror. With only an infant son to succeed him, Alexander's empire was quickly divided up among his top three generals and their families. Nevertheless, although the Greek empire may have been divided, Greek culture was not. Across the eastern Mediterranean, Greek was the culture and language of the elite. After all, the Greeks were the new masters. Regular wars in the East led to the creation of Greek professional armies, highly trained and easily able to deal with local militias.

Italy, in the poorer and less populated western Mediterranean, was untouched by all this empire building. But the Greeks in the West were nonetheless proud of the achievements of their brothers in the East. By the same token, Greeks in the East kept their eye on the West, for they believed that the natural state of all Greeks, no matter their location, was freedom. The Tarantine Greeks agreed, of course. And they decided to do something about the growing power of Rome. Tarantine envoys were sent to the Greek king of Epirus, Pyrrhus, asking for help. Pyrrhus commanded a highly trained professional army of some twenty-five thousand men and twenty elephants that he was willing to use in order to defend Greek freedom wherever it was threatened (provided the Greeks in question could pay). After hearing of Rome's encroachment into Greek territories in southern Italy, Pyrrhus agreed to come and fight for Tarentum if Rome should declare war against it. That was all the Tarentines needed.

Tarentine forces were sent immediately to Thurii, where they ejected the Roman garrison and sacked the city. Despite the clear provocation, the Romans nevertheless tried to avoid a war. Indeed, their laws required it.

A Roman ambassador, Postumius, was sent with a delegation to Tarentum to offer lenient terms of reconciliation. The hope was that the Tarentines could be convinced to join other cities in the south as allies of Rome. But the Tarentines, who knew full well that they could call on Pyrrhus, had a very different idea.

The Roman delegation was brought into the great theater of Tarentum, where they addressed the leaders and people, assuring them of Rome's desire to forge a lasting friendship with them. The audience had not come to make friends, but to contemptuously smirk at the barbarians. They listened closely for mistakes in Postumius' Greek, chortling whenever they caught one. Shouts began to come from the assembled people, demanding that the barbarians be expelled lest their bad grammar and base manners pollute the city any further. Dionysius of Halicarnassus, himself a Greek, provides the rest of the story:

> As the Romans were departing [the theater], one of the Tarentines standing beside the exit was a man named Philonides, a frivolous fellow who, because of the drunken condition in which he spent his whole life, was called "Wine Jug." This man, being still full of yesterday's wine, as soon as the ambassadors drew near pulled up his garment and, assuming a posture most shameful to behold, bespattered the sacred robe of the [Roman] ambassador with the filth that is indecent even to be uttered. When laughter burst out from the whole theater and the most insolent people clapped their hands, Postumius, looking at Philonides, said: "We shall accept this omen, you frivolous fellow, in the sense that you Tarentines give us what we do not ask for." Then he turned to the crowd and showed his defiled robe; but when he found that the laughter became even greater and heard the cries of some who were exulting over and praising the insult, he said: "Laugh while you may, Tarentines! Laugh! For long will be the time that you will weep hereafter."

Rome declared war.

Pyrrhus and his mighty army landed in Italy in 280 BC. The Romans looked on with grave concern. For more than a century the Romans had followed a policy aimed at securing their horizon, which they had come to believe meant securing Italy. Their inherent isolationism led them to seek security through alliances, organizing a system that they hoped would bring peace to the peninsula. But by its very nature the alliance system that they built, which was, after all, centered on Rome, appeared from the outside to be a growing empire. It was only natural, then, that it would attract some notice from beyond Italy. In short, although the Romans sought to secure their horizon, the attempt was now bringing even greater threats from beyond that horizon.

Still, the unique nature of Rome's developing Empire of Trust gave them an important advantage against Pyrrhus. The Greek king naturally assumed that Rome had built an empire the old-fashioned way—by conquering, bullying, and subjugating. He cast himself, therefore, as a liberator, first of the Greeks and then any others whom Rome had oppressed. After a little demonstration of his power, Pyrrhus felt certain that this barbarian empire would disintegrate into dust and blow away.

The Romans activated their alliances, marshaled their troops, and met Pyrrhus on the field of battle near Heraclea. Pyrrhus won, although he lost four thousand men in the engagement. This is the famous "Pyrrhic victory," for, unlike the Romans, Pyrrhus could not raise more troops locally. His losses were permanent. Nevertheless, he expected that his victory would lead to rebellions among the Italian towns and cities under the Roman yoke. Soon, he reasoned, envoys from the towns would arrive to congratulate him on his win and seek to join his armies in their war against Rome. That is, after all, what would happen under any Empire of Conquest. But, to his surprise, no one came. Rome's grip on the cities, he thought, must be stronger than expected. Undoubtedly, the conquered peoples feared reprisals from Rome after Pyrrhus returned to Greece. The answer, then, was to destroy Rome itself. He would begin the campaign, gathering support from the liberated along the way.

Pyrrhus started marching directly toward Rome, while at the same time sending word to all of the towns and cities that they should throw off their shackles and join him in his war of liberation. Again, there was silence. Pyrrhus failed to understand that the towns and cities did not want liberation because, quite simply, they were already free. Big cities like Capua and Neapolis slammed their doors shut to Pyrrhus, refusing to have anything to do with him. Over many decades Rome had shown itself to be a responsible leader, a first among equals that used its position for the benefit and security of all. They trusted Rome to support them provided they were faithful to the alliance. By the same token, they also trusted Rome to punish them should they now prove unfaithful. Despite brave words and a great show, Pyrrhus failed to shake apart the Roman system. The alliance held firm.

Although Pyrrhus remained undefeated, he now realized that beating Rome would require more than a few spectacular battles. This was all a bit more than he had bargained for when he took this job. Besides, there were Greek cities in Sicily that needed his help against Carthage. Time, he reasoned, to negotiate a victory. Pyrrhus sent a proposal for peace to the senators in Rome. As was the custom in the wealthy East, the proposal was accompanied by plenty of rich presents for the senators. That was a mistake. The Romans, steeped in their own culture of moral virtue, considered the gifts to be bribes and refused to accept them. The proposal, though, was another matter. Clearly, Pyrrhus was looking for a face-saving way to leave Italy. He offered to end his war with Rome if the Romans would do the same with Tarentum and if they would promise to stay out of southern Italy from now on.

To many of the senators assembled that day Pyrrhus' proposal seemed like a very good deal. Pyrrhus was dangerous—there was no doubt about that. The Romans had met their treaty obligations to their allies in the war. Although they would have to pull out of some treaties with towns like Thurii, it was a small price to pay to remove a large and powerful Greek army from Italy. Although it would have been preferable to extend the security of the confederation across the peninsula, if it was going to bring foreign armies to Italian shores it was defeating the whole purpose. News began to spread in Rome that peace was at hand, that a solution to end the war had been found. It was at this point that the aged, ill, and blind statesman Appius Claudius demanded to be led to the Senate.

There, dressed once again in his old toga, he berated the senators for their cowardice and demanded that they remain true Romans. If they were not faithful to their allies now, then they would never again be trusted. All would truly be lost. The senators were convinced. They rejected Pyrrhus' offer.

After a brief side trip to Sicily, Pyrrhus returned to Italy. This time the Romans and their allies were ready for him. In 275 BC the Roman confederation defeated Pyrrhus and sent him packing back to Greece. Bereft of their champion, the Tarentines quickly made peace with Rome. As usual, the Romans were generous to the vanquished, seeking above all to turn them into allies. The Tarentines were not alone. The defeat of Pyrrhus made it crystal clear to everyone in Italy that Rome really could provide peace and security, even against powerful foreign invaders. Within a short time virtually all of the peninsula came within the confederation. For all intents and purposes, Italy had become Roman. Like the Americans in their desire to expand from sea to shining sea, the Romans had realized their dream of organizing Italy under their leadership. They could at last rest easy in the sure knowledge of peace and security at home. Their isolationism was satisfied, for they had continued to neutralize and then befriend all of their enemies up to the water's edge. They had secured their horizon. Beyond that, they had no interest.

Yet beyond the waves that lapped onto the shores of Italy were great powers that had an interest in Rome. That is hardly surprising. Rome had become the ruler of Italy, was able to put large armies into the field, and had even managed to defeat the famed Pyrrhus. That qualified them as a power to be reckoned with. Much like the United States after its own continental expansion, Rome began to attract serious attention abroad. It was now widely recognized as a member of the "powers," something that the Romans, like the Americans, had not wanted. Only two years after the victory over Pyrrhus, the Roman Senate received ambassadors from Ptolemy Philadelphus, the Greek king of Egypt. It caused quite a stir in Rome to have such richly dressed visitors from the exotic and sophisticated East. The Egyptians asked the Romans to send a goodwill embassy to the court of Ptolemy in Alexandria, which they did. In Egypt, the three Roman ambassadors were treated with every courtesy and showered in unaccustomed luxury. When they departed, they were each given an abundance of rich gifts, according to the Eastern custom. The ambassadors knew enough not to protest, lest they offend their hosts. Nevertheless, when they returned to Rome their first stop was the public treasury, where they handed over every gift that they had received. Romans do not take bribes.

Although it is true that Romans and Americans reluctantly began to step onto their own worlds' stage after the consolidation of their home territories, the means by which they did so were very different. From the beginning, the Romans worked through alliances of equals—even when members were anything but equal. They formed a united Italy in an attempt to bring peace and security to the region while keeping it separate from the wider world. Americans had the same idea, but they created the continental United States through purchase, conquest, and settlement—not alliance systems. The difference comes from the facts on the ground before the expansion. The Romans were dealing with well-established states with governments and militaries of their own. The Americans, on the other hand, were dealing largely with tribal groups without cities or comparable military technologies. When it was their turn to face the wider world of powerful civilizations, the Americans would do so in much the same fashion as the Romans, building power through alliances. By the same token, when the Romans later moved into the tribal areas of western Europe, they did so in much the same manner as the Americans during their westward expansion.

No two empires have parallel histories. Certainly Rome and the United States do not. But both had qualities that would lead them to create powerful and extensive empires. Isolationism, born out of an agrarian frontier society, ultimately brought both states step-by-step into an unwanted world of empire building. In the next chapter, we will see how.

Chapter 5

Becoming a Superpower

It was a quiet, foggy night on the North African coast. Dark waves rolled up onto the shore and flowed back into the whispering Mediterranean Sea. It seemed a night like any other. But it was not. For on this night in 202 BC and on this lonely stretch of beach, Rome was coming to Africa. Slicing through the fog, the first ship prows appeared, followed by dozens and then hundreds more. As the vessels were pulled onto the shore, quietly, cautiously, they spilled out their contents—thousands of armed troops. Fanning out, the well-trained soldiers quickly secured the area, made a defensible camp, and prepared for war. Splashing ashore, too, came their leader, the famed Roman general Publius Scipio. With quiet confidence he issued orders to his men, a collection of Romans and their allies. At great peril they had sailed from Sicily across the sea to the shores of Africa. They had come to put an end to a long war.

More than two thousand years later, in the dark early morning hours of June 6, 1944, another massive seaborne invasion was about to begin. Vessels poured across the English Channel, unloading their soldiers onto the beaches of Normandy. D-day had begun. The collection of allied troops was led by the famed American general Dwight D. Eisenhower. At great peril, the American and allied soldiers pushed onto the beaches, fighting to secure a foothold. Thousands would die. But the invasion, so far from home, was crucial. For they, too, had come to put an end to a long war.

The Roman invasion of Africa and the Allied invasion of Normandy have a number of other interesting parallels. Both were expected for some time, although shrouded in great secrecy. Both were the result of a good deal of political and strategic wrangling in which very different approaches to the war were proposed and debated. But most importantly for our purposes, both operations would profoundly shape the future direction of the states that launched them. For both Rome and the United States, these invasions signaled the beginning of a major overseas involvement. In this way, the Empires of Trust were becoming superpowers.

Of course, launching an invasion into a faraway country is standard procedure for an Empire of Conquest. But how did an Empire of Trust find itself in that circumstance? As most people today know, the United States and its allies invaded France not as an act of conquest, but as a means to defeat the Axis powers in Europe. They were successful. France was liberated and returned to its people. Yet for all that, the United States would continue to keep significant numbers of troops in Europe even after war's end. They remain there still. Americans and Europeans would strongly deny that the more than a hundred thousand American troops stationed in Europe today constitute an occupation force or that European countries are part of an American Empire. They would be right, of course—provided we are talking about a standard Empire of Conquest. But we are not. The Romans and their allies would also have strongly denied that they were building an empire in Africa or anywhere else. But, little by little, they were. And the first steps toward those far-flung international Empires of Trust were taken during those two massive seaborne invasions.

How did the Romans, isolationists who secured their Italian horizon while studiously avoiding any connections to overseas powers, end up overseas? One might just as well ask how Americans, whose country was born out of a desire to escape European problems, found themselves fighting their way into Europe. In both cases the answer is the same: They were there to defend themselves and their allies. That's what Empires of Trust do. That is, after all, why they are trusted.

In the last chapter we left the Romans happy enough, having defeated Pyrrhus and subsequently expanding their confederation to include all of Italy. At long last their horizon was the sea, and they felt reasonably secure in that. Indeed, although Rome's armies were large and powerful, it had a navy so small that it was hardly worth the name. In fact, it probably did not exist at all. In other words, the Romans had achieved much the same level of security as the United States after it covered the continent from the Atlantic to the Pacific. And, like the United States, Rome had no desire to project its power beyond those shores. The United States, too, had a tiny navy.

In the days of the Romans, it was the Greek-dominated eastern Mediterranean that was the "Old World." By contrast, the western Mediterranean was sparsely populated, with only a smattering of Greek cities, smallish kingdoms, and primitive tribal groups living along its coastline. By 275 BC two major powers had arisen out of this jumble. Rome, we know about. The other was the Carthaginian Empire. Carthage was a large city on the coast of North Africa, on the site of what is today the city of Tunis. Like Rome, it had been settled in the eighth century BC, although it did not arise from indigenous tribes. Instead, it was a colony of Phoenicians, the well-traveled merchants of the ancient Near East. Eventually becoming independent, the Carthaginians proceeded to build an empire across North Africa. They expanded through conquest primarily, although they were not opposed to making treaties with kingdoms that had something to offer. The overriding motive for Carthaginian expansion was the acquisition of wealth. They wanted rich lands, raw materials, good ports, and large cities. By the fourth century BC Carthaginian forces had pretty good control of the western Mediterranean, including the Pillars of Hercules (the modern Straits of Gibraltar), which they kept closed lest anyone try to move in on their lucrative trade with tin merchants from Britain or gold and ivory sellers from sub-Saharan Africa.

From a modern (and, not coincidentally, Roman) perspective, the Carthaginian culture was rather unattractive. They were wealthy—at least by western Mediterranean standards. They used that wealth to pay other people to do the menial jobs that their citizens disdained. This increasingly included military service, which the Carthaginians preferred to outsource to mercenary armies led by Carthaginian generals. Those generals were powerful men, celebrated for their victories and crucified for their failures. The Carthaginian government was complex, and our understanding of it is sketchy. We do know, however, that it was ultimately controlled by a small oligarchic council. The Carthaginian religion was brutal. Unlike the Roman gods, Carthaginian deities did not go in much for quiet moral virtue. They liked things a bit noisier. Religious rituals in Carthage usually involved various forms of self-mutilation and human sacrifice. In times of emergency, the gods developed an appetite for plump babies, who were thrown onto open flames by the cartload. Unattractive, yes, but it was stable. As Cicero later remarked, "Carthage would not have held an empire for six hundred years had it not been governed with wisdom and statecraft."

Of course Rome and Carthage knew about each other, but neither one wanted any trouble. For the Romans, Italy was all that really mattered. They had little interest in Carthaginian doings across the water. That was fine by the Carthaginians, who wanted a free hand to expand their empire in the western Mediterranean. Rome and Carthage made several treaties in the fourth century that defined their respective "spheres of influence." From the perspective of empire building, these treaties were decidedly in Carthage's favor. While Carthaginians promised to stay out of Italy, the Romans promised to stay in it, putting the sea and everything beyond it off limits to them. But that, of course, is what the Romans wanted and so the Carthaginians were glad to oblige.

By the third century BC Carthage was busy trying to eliminate its last serious rival in the west—Sicily. The large island, resting as it does in the middle of the western Mediterranean and between Italy and North Africa, had always been a thorn in Carthage's side. Settled by Greeks many centuries earlier, it was largely controlled by Syracuse—a beautiful city that would later give birth to Archimedes. All in all it was a lovely place that Carthage desperately wanted to conquer. The Carthaginians began waging war in western Sicily, slowly pushing their conquests eastward. Pyrrhus, after crushing Roman forces at Heraclea, had landed in Sicily, where he did his best to save the Greeks. Although he was able to push back the Carthaginian advance, when he returned to Italy Carthage simply made up the lost ground. Not surprisingly, the Carthaginians were keen on seeing Pyrrhus stay in Italy, so they happily provided money and support to Rome while it fought against the Greek leader.

After Pyrrhus returned to the East in 275 BC, Carthaginian forces began a major offensive to finish off Greek resistance in Sicily. Syracuse was barely hanging on to its last territories in the eastern part of the island. At first, the Romans do not seem to have given these events much thought. After all, what was it to them if Carthage wanted to conquer Sicily? But their new Greek allies in southern Italy gave it plenty of thought, and they increasingly worried that when the Carthaginians were finished with the Greeks of Sicily, they would make a move on the Greeks of southern Italy. That was a concern, of course, but the Romans felt it was manageable. The solution was to make it crystal clear to the warring parties in Sicily that hostilities were not to cross over into the Roman confederation in Italy.

Easier said than done. As any map will show, Sicily and Italy are not very far apart. On a clear day you can stand on one side of the Strait of Messina and see easily to the other side. Ferrying troops across the strait is not difficult—today car ferries make the trip in just twenty minutes. The Romans were worried about invaders doing the same thing (although not in cars, of course). Years earlier they had sent a garrison force to Rhegium, the Greek city on the Italian side of the strait (modern Reggio di Calabria). That had not gone well. The Roman contingent, led by a ruthless general named Decius and made up primarily of Italians from Campania, had looted Rhegium, treating it like conquered property. The Romans were horrified when they heard of this breach of trust. They dispatched new forces to Rhegium to destroy the Roman garrison and bring Decius and his lieutenants back to Rome to stand trial. After their convictions, the leaders were flogged and beheaded in the Forum. The people of Rhegium were glad to see justice done, but the Roman crimes there would remain a favorite taunt of Greeks for centuries. Whenever the Romans insisted that they used their power only for peace and security and always in a responsible fashion, their critics would waste no time bringing up the bloody events at Rhegium.

Garrisoning Rhegium allowed the Romans to better monitor the chaos in Sicily. And it was becoming dangerously chaotic. Perched on the other side of the strait was the port city of Messana (modern Messina), which constituted a perfect spigot for the Sicilian war to spill over into Italy. At that time it was under the control of a ragtag band of Italian mercenaries who had garrisoned it for King Hiero of Syracuse, but eventually decided to just take it for themselves. These men were a bad lot, having mistreated the people of Messana and generally made a mess of things. Hiero was determined to reclaim the city and it looked like he had the forces to do it. To save their skins, the leaders in Messana decided to look for some outside help. After all, they were sitting on a strategic port that one of the other powers must surely want. The problem was that they could not make up their minds about whom to ask for help—the Carthaginians or the Romans. So they asked both. Or rather, various leaders made their own separate appeals to both powers to garrison and protect Messana from Syracuse.

Since the Carthaginians were already in Sicily, they quickly accepted the offer and sent a small contingent of troops to Messana. In Rome the Senate heard Messana's request for aid and alliance, but they were torn about how to respond. On the one hand, these "leaders" were little more than thugs who had brutally preyed upon the people of their city. Accepting them as allies could be seen as a tacit endorsement of their methods—something that the senators were sensitive to, given recent events at Rhegium. On the other hand, if the Romans allowed the Carthaginians to control Messana it would give them the perfect launching point for an invasion of Italy. Given Carthage's aggressive expansionism, that was not something to be taken lightly. Bringing Messana into the confederation would have the effect of placing the straits under Roman control, making a Carthaginian invasion that much more difficult. Although Messana was in Sicily and thereby outside of Italy, it was only barely so.

And the fact that it was controlled by Italians could be used as a justification for its inclusion in the Roman alliance.

And so the debate in the Senate raged on. In the end, they found themselves deadlocked, unable to establish a consensus for any course of action. Without much guidance, then, the popular assemblies took up the question. After another long debate they agreed to respond to Messana's request for aid. The consul, Appius Claudius Caudex, was sent to Messana with two legions. In short order he expelled the Carthaginian garrison, restored the Rome-friendly leaders, and stationed a Roman contingent of troops there for the defense of the city. The general assumption in Rome was that Syracuse and Carthage were too busy trying to destroy each other to worry much about little Messana. From the Roman perspective, though, Messana was an important cork in a bottle, which they hoped would keep the warfare in Sicily from pouring out into the peaceful plains of Italy.

But the Romans misjudged the situation. When they sent friendly notices to the Greeks of Syracuse and the Carthaginian commanders telling them to keep their war away from Messana, the response was declarations of war from both foreign powers. King Hiero resented barbarous Romans crossing over the straits to garrison a Sicilian city that by rights belonged to him. The Carthaginians, for their part, considered the Roman ejection of their garrison in the city to be a flagrant act of war. They claimed that the Romans were in violation of their treaty obligations, which excluded Romans from Sicily, a Carthaginian "sphere of influence." On the last point, though, the Romans were insistent that no such treaty existed. And they would know.

The Romans were surprised by the hostile response. In their view they had projected their power only slightly beyond their "borders" in order to keep a dangerously unstable situation from crossing into their own lands. Of course, they, too, were a bit uneasy about the whole thing. But that was because it seemed to compromise their principles and violate their isolationist tendencies, not because they believed it was unjustified or illegal. In this way the Roman decision was similar to the United States' entry into the Spanish-American War, when American power was itself projected a short way across the sea in order to put an end to dangerous instability. As we saw earlier, though, that war was the occasion for much soul-searching in the United States as Americans wondered whether they were losing their moral compass and becoming an imperial power. Like the Americans, the Romans would find themselves pulled into a much larger engagement than they had originally bargained for.

It is along the narrow straits of Messana that we can once again see an important dynamic that impelled Roman expansion—a dynamic plainly visible in the expansion of American power as well. Rome's desire for security at home repeatedly led it to secure its horizon through the acquisition of allies. The homeland became more secure, that is true, but this policy required Romans to project their power farther and farther away from that home. That is the problem with horizons, there is always another one just over this one. In each case, the Romans could take solace in the fact that they were simply meeting treaty obligations, or being faithful friends, or even righting terrible wrongs. But it also meant that Roman power was further extended to new areas, where new horizons and new enemies waited. The Romans, therefore, expanded in a constant search for an ideal peace and prosperity that is simply not of this world. A naturally optimistic and self-confident people, it was just not in their nature to give up.

Two foreign states declaring war against them, the Romans had no choice but to respond in kind. With control of the straits, the Roman legions began to march into Sicily. In short order the Romans defeated Hiero of Syracuse. The vanquished king immediately became Rome's close ally, supporting its continuing war against Carthage in Sicily. But Carthage was not so easy to beat. The Carthaginians were furious that their opportunity to capture Sicily had been short-circuited by the Romans. They funneled enormous resources into the war, passionately determined to push the invading Romans off the island once and for all. This, of course, led the Romans to respond in kind by pumping more and more of their own resources into the war. It would be a long and a bloody one.

There is no need to bother here with the details of the twenty-three-year-long conflict that historians call the First Punic War. What is important is that when it was over Rome had defeated the Carthaginians and ejected them from Sicily. How did they do it? There are two factors that principally explain Rome's success. First, the Romans fought with citizen armies built on the foundation of loyal alliances and trust in Rome. That trust was the lifeblood of their empire. It insured that the Romans could continue to recruit committed troops from Italy who were themselves personally invested in victory. The Carthaginians, on the other hand, used their great wealth to purchase mercenary armies. By their nature, mercenaries are never as reliable or committed as citizen soldiers. They serve for pay, not love or honor. When push comes to shove, as it always does in war, that distinction becomes crucial.

The second factor in Rome's victory is bound up in the character of the Romans—a character forged in the frontier days of the Roman family farm. The Romans had what the American military today calls a "hoo-ah" spirit—a confident belief that "technology, and Americans, can fix anything." When the war first broke out in Sicily, Carthage ruled the waves. Remember, the Romans had no navy to speak of. Their legions were trained to fight on the good hard earth, not on the choppy seas. Very early in the war, though, the Romans discovered that they could not take and hold an island without first obtaining naval superiority. How to get it? How could a state with no experience on the water hope to challenge the greatest naval power in the western Mediterranean?

For the Romans, with their ancient equivalent of "hoo-ah," there was never any doubt that they *could* do it. The first job was to learn how to make a war vessel. Simple enough. They proceeded to capture a Carthaginian warship, carefully dismantled it, labeled all of the parts, and then made lots and lots of them. When the parts were put together the Romans had a fleet. Mission accomplished. While they were building the fleet they also started training their new marines. In the ancient world this meant teaching the recruits how to man the oars. On the sun-drenched beaches of Italy rows of Roman men would sit on makeshift benches and pretend to pull imaginary oars to the beat of drums and the calls of their commanders. When ancient oarsmen engaged another vessel they transformed into soldiers, for they kept their weapons just under their benches. So the Romans practiced that too. Pretending that they had grappled an enemy boat, they reached for their swords and rushed off to dispatch the imaginary enemy. In this way, thousands of Roman marines were ready to take the war to the Carthaginians on the sea.

Although the Romans could build ships and train marines, there was one significant advantage that the Carthaginians still had on the water— they were much better sailors. With great maritime skills honed over centuries, the Carthaginian commanders could outmaneuver the amateur Romans and ram them on the broadside. Carthaginian warships had a nasty ramming prow designed to pierce the hull of the opposing ship below the waterline. Once that was done, the Carthaginian rowers would simply put the boat into reverse, disengage, and watch as their enemies went to the bottom of the sea. The Romans understood their limitations, so they set about finding a technological solution. They developed a new device, the *corvus* or "crow's beak." This invention was mounted on the main deck of the new Roman vessels. It consisted of a wide gangway plank that was hinged to the deck and kept in an upright position during normal operations. On its end was a long spike. The genius of the *corvus* was that its inventors recognized that Roman vessels were going to get rammed. But when that happened, the *corvus* would swing down onto the Carthaginian vessel and trap it before it could get away. Then the Roman marines would grab their weapons and storm over the *corvus* onto the Carthaginian boat, killing or capturing all aboard. It worked like a charm.

The First Punic War was all about Sicily. When it was over, Rome found itself with a new island but not exactly sure what to do with it. The initial plan was simply to treat the area as they had any other in Italy. That would mean that each of the Sicilian cities would become a Roman ally, keeping its own local government, but contributing troops to the military forces of the confederation. But that system was not well suited for Sicily. The main city, Syracuse, had already been declared free by the Romans when King Hiero joined their side during the war. Several other cities had received similar concessions. As for the rest of the island, the Sicilian Greeks were simply not used to military obligations. They liked the Hellenistic practice of paying a tribute to the ruling state for their protection. In the past the Sicilians had paid tributes and taxes to Syracuse and then to Carthage. Now they wanted to pay that money to the new master, Rome. That was not what the Romans had in mind, but over time they modified their approach to take into account local customs. That meant, however, that Rome would need to permanently station their own troops in Sicily in order to provide for defense and maintain order. But how was that going to work within the Roman constitutional framework? Remember, only consuls had the legal authority to use force in foreign territories. The Romans could not permanently station one of their two consuls each year in Sicily.

In the end, the Romans simply modified their constitutional system in a commonsense way. In Rome, two praetors had always been elected annually who had authority to use force for public order and administration, yet only within Rome itself. To deal with Sicily, the Romans simply began to elect an additional praetor who would have the same authority on that island. The legal area of responsibility for a praetor was called his *provincia*, so the Romans naturally referred to Sicily in that manner. But the term, in English "province," would later gain a wider meaning as a territory directly controlled by an empire through its officials. The Roman praetors in Sicily quickly took on the role of governors. They commanded all military forces and acted as a supreme court for civil and criminal cases involving the locals. (Roman citizens could still appeal to the courts in Rome.) This was far greater power than the praetors in Rome had. Nevertheless, local city and town governments in Sicily still remained in place. Provided that the Sicilians kept the peace and paid their taxes, the Romans took no interest in their local affairs. With Rome firmly in control of the island, its inhabitants knew peace for the first time in living memory. And Rome, although it had not wanted it, found that it had acquired its first province.

With regard to its expanding power, Rome in 235 BC was not unlike the United States in AD 1900. It was secure and prosperous and had begun to cautiously project power beyond its own borders. As a result of the Spanish-American War, the United States found itself with effective possession of Guam, Puerto Rico, Cuba, and the Philippines. It subsequently annexed Hawaii. All of these territorial acquisitions would require additional American troop involvement and, ultimately, the further extension of American power beyond U.S. borders. No longer focused only on their own insular world, American leaders were increasingly engaged in international matters, at least in the New World and Asia. Like the Romans, Americans still tried to remain aloof from the problems of the ancient, wealthy, and very powerful Old World. President Theodore Roosevelt, expanding on the Monroe Doctrine, embraced his "big stick" policy of using force if necessary to keep European powers out of the Western Hemisphere. Yet he never imagined that the United States would use that force in Europe itself. Isolationism remained at the heart of American foreign policy. There was no mistaking the fact, though, that the United States had become a world power.

Although we can see similarities between the methods, motivations, and dynamics behind Roman and American expansion, that does not mean that their histories are parallel. Although the United States waged war beyond its borders in the late nineteenth and early twentieth centuries, none of its enemies had the ability to seriously threaten the United States itself. American isolationism, therefore, was able to flourish in a world without jets and rockets, a time when the United States truly was isolated from the great powers. Rome did not have that luxury. Its first war across the sea was against the powerful Carthaginian Empire. Rome's victory in 241 BC had denied Sicily to Carthage, but that was all. Carthage still controlled North Africa and began moving into southern Spain. More importantly, it was still an extraordinarily wealthy state with a large and effective military and a grudge against Rome. The Romans could not afford a "big stick" policy. They crafted instead a plan to achieve what they had wanted in the first place: secure horizons and peace.

The treaty that ended the war between Rome and Carthage was an agreement between equals. Given that the war was fought in someone else's country, that is not too surprising. Above all, the Romans wanted to lay out a legal basis for avoiding similar conflicts in the future. The treaty of 241 made clear that Rome and Carthage would henceforth respect and refrain from attacking the allies or friends of the other. Given the apparent balance of power between the two, there was every reason for both of them to adhere to this provision closely. Excluded from Sicily, the Carthaginians made do with Spain, where they founded cities like New Carthage (modern Cartagena). In those days Spain's hinterland was thickly wooded and its mountains were jammed full of precious metals. The Carthaginians found it all quite to their liking.

As the years went by, more and more Romans began to look with some apprehension at Carthaginian expansion in Spain. New acquisitions brought additional wealth and also more lands that were closer and closer to Italy. Rome had expanded, too, acquiring control over Corsica and Sardinia and organizing both of them into provinces. It was all getting a little too close for comfort. To avoid conflicts, the Roman Senate sent ambassadors to the Carthaginian general and governor in Spain—a man named Hasdrubal. The ambassadors pointed out the necessity of avoiding any possibility of misunderstandings between the two powers. Hasdrubal's expansion in Spain was of little concern to Rome, but they feared that if it continued eastward it might cross into areas provocatively close to Italy. They suggested, therefore, that they sign a treaty that would guarantee that the Carthaginians would never advance in arms beyond the Ebro River. Rome did not control the lands beyond that boundary, but it seemed a good place to put a buffer zone between Carthaginian expansion in Spain and Roman territories in Italy. Hasdrubal agreed and the treaty was ratified by the Senate in 226 BC.

So far so good. These treaties between Rome and Carthage served their purpose, keeping the peace for fifteen years. In the ancient world (and even in our own) that was no small thing. But despite their best efforts, it would all soon unravel. In 221 BC Hasdrubal died and was succeeded by Hannibal. You have probably heard of him: the elephants and the Alps and all of that. We are not there yet, but it is the same person. Hannibal was a young man, only twenty-six years old when he took command in Spain. A natural leader and a brilliant general, Hannibal was eager to build up Carthaginian might so that it would never again be humiliated by Rome. To begin with, he continued Hasdrubal's policies of expansion and consolidation in Spain. Within two years most of the Iberian peninsula south of the Ebro was under Hannibal's control.

Most, but not all. There was one important holdout. Nestled on the Mediterranean coast the citizens of the prosperous city of Saguntum (modern Sagunto) had shut their massive gates and manned their formidable walls, refusing to be incorporated into the Carthaginian Empire. For the time being Hannibal had other matters to attend to, but there was no doubt that he would have to turn his attention to Saguntum—and soon, for Saguntum's defiance might lead other conquered areas to revolt. Recognizing their danger, the citizens of Saguntum sent ambassadors to Rome, where they asked for and received a formal alliance with the Romans. Saguntum was pretty far afield for the Roman confederation, but the senators genuinely felt sorry for the Saguntines, who had showed such courage and strength against great odds. They also recognized that by protecting Saguntum's independence, Rome would keep Hannibal's project in Spain—whatever it was—incomplete.

Or so they thought. The decisions of the Roman Senate and the people of Saguntum were predicated on the bedrock principles of the Empire of Trust. These included a certainty that Rome did not begin wars, but it would never fail to defend itself or its allies if attacked. Although the Romans did not send a single soldier to Saguntum, they did send a scroll of confirmation that the city was a Roman ally and thereby under Roman protection. That should be enough. The faith put into a Roman guarantee of protection was, after all, the glue that held together the entire Roman confederation.

Hannibal did not see things that way. In the first place, he was outraged that the Roman Senate would attempt to meddle in faraway Spain. Allying with Saguntum was a clear provocation, and the Roman proclamation almost an assertion of the right to command Hannibal. He took orders from Carthage alone. In the second place, Hannibal judged that the Romans had overreached. At that moment both Roman consuls were busy with problems in the Adriatic Sea. It would be some time before they could turn their attention to the distant shores of Spain. By then, Hannibal expected that he would have rich Saguntum firmly in hand

and the Romans would have no choice but to accept it. Surely they would not go to war with the Carthagian Empire over a small Spanish city so far from Italy.

Taking Saguntum was not so easy. Hannibal's siege of the city stretched on for month after difficult month. The men, women, and children inside the walls remained defiant, putting their hopes in their Roman allies. Each day they watched the sea, always expecting a Roman squadron to come sailing over the horizon laden with troops. And then, one day the Romans did come. But their invasion consisted of only one vessel. And it did not carry soldiers, just a few diplomats. The Senate had sent ambassadors to meet with Hannibal and to insist that he leave Saguntum in peace. Hannibal listened and refused. Saguntum, he said, was a threat to his Spanish holdings and he would deal with that threat. Besides, Saguntum was well south of the Ebro River. The treaty that Hasdrubal had made with Rome obliged Carthage not to cross that border and Hannibal had kept that promise. As for Saguntum, the Romans had only themselves to blame if they insisted on making far-flung alliances with Hannibal's enemies. That was their concern, not his. He would defend against threats to Carthaginian territories in Spain no matter their origin. Let the Romans see to their own domains.

Surprised by Hannibal's response, the ambassadors went back to their boats, waved good-bye to the frightened Saguntines, and sailed to Carthage itself. There, they demanded that Hannibal be ordered to cease his attack against a Roman ally. The ruling council of Carthage was unimpressed. Like their general, they insisted that Saguntum was a threat to Carthaginian control of Spain. The Saguntines were known to be stirring up rebellion against Carthage, they claimed, so Hannibal was clearly within his rights to put a stop to it. Surely, the Romans were not saying that they valued their ill-considered alliance with these Spanish troublemakers more than their ancient friendship with Carthage!

The ambassadors left Carthage and returned to Rome with grim news. Unless the Romans sent troops immediately to relieve Saguntum, it would fall. The Saguntines were engaged in a heroic defense of their city, but their provisions were running low and parts of their defensive works were in ruins. Nevertheless, each and every man, woman, and child there continued to work hard and endure great deprivations because they trusted the Romans to come to their aid. Hannibal did not share that trust. In fact, he was proceeding on the assumption that Rome would not commit itself to a war so far from home for the sake of this one city.

The principles of trust behind Rome's success worked because they were eminently simple. Roman allies contributed to the confederation in the sure knowledge that they would be defended by it. It had taken more than a century for the Romans to build that level of trust among their allies. The situation in Saguntum threatened all that they had done. The Roman people found themselves wrestling with a new shade of gray that could seriously jeopardize their own self-image as well as their reputation among others. In order to meet their treaty obligations to Saguntum, the Romans were forced to act almost like an Empire of Conquest—issuing demands to foreign powers and waging foreign wars if those demands were not met. This was not the Roman way. It was contrary to the isolationism that continued to pervade the Roman spirit and which had built the confederation. The Carthaginians had stayed far away from Rome's territories. Why should the Romans march forth to attack them in their own?

But, as with all shades of gray, there are always other considerations. If the Romans failed to relieve Saguntum it would not go unnoticed by the allies. If the Carthaginians should later decide to threaten the confederation closer to home, perhaps even in Italy or Sicily, would the allies stand firm with Rome? Or would they instead make what deal they could rather than stake their lives and property on Roman promises? Trust in Rome is all that held the confederation together. If Rome betrayed that trust, could the confederation survive? And if the confederation collapsed, the security that Romans craved would naturally collapse with it. Trustworthiness and honesty were core principles of Roman culture. To turn away from them would bring shame—and probably divine retribution too. The Romans did, after all, call on the gods to punish them if they were ever untrue to their treaty commitments.

Given these vexing questions, it is perhaps not too surprising that matters stalled in Rome. It is difficult for historians to discover precisely what was going on at this time because the sources themselves are contradictory. Some claim that the Senate debated all sides of the issue but the members were torn as to what was right and just. Others insist that the Senate did not debate at all. Who is right? The problem is that for centuries after these events the Romans continued to debate among themselves as to whether or not they had done the right thing. It was a touchy subject, which naturally led to different interpretations of the events. For us, however, the important thing is that the Romans cared about the question at all. Empires of Conquest do not fret for centuries over the moral or legal justifications of their conquests. They celebrate them as victories. For Romans, though, the very act of conquest was a necessary evil, the result of a failure to find a peaceful solution to a problem. Every conquest, every victory, brought the Romans face-to-face with the fruits of empire. And each time they sought to deny that empire—turning conquered foes into allies, thereby maintaining the illusion that they were just one power among many. But it was, after all, an illusion.

The parallel with the American self-image is striking. Americans, too, believe that they are simply one power among many in the world. They are strong, yes. But Americans insist that they are coequal with their allies. American military interventions in foreign countries are invariably referred to as coalition actions, even if the other members of the coalition contribute only a few soldiers. Troop levels, like those of the "Coalition of the Willing" that invaded Iraq, may be more than 90 percent American, but they preserve the principle that the United States is acting as one ally among many. In American politics "unilateralism" or "going it alone" is still considered to be a bad thing. The U.S. military is larger than the militaries of all other NATO allies combined. American military bases are planted in many NATO countries, while no allied bases are in the United States at all. Yet, Americans will still insist that NATO is an alliance of equals, not the structure of an empire. That, too, is an illusion. But it is a necessary one for an Empire of Trust.

Back in Saguntum things had become desperate. The hardy Saguntines, so confident at the beginning of the siege, were weakening.

Food was scarce, disease was spreading, and a feeling of dread was descending on every family. Hannibal had already conquered a portion of the city and he was poised to take the rest. He informed the citizens that if they surrendered immediately he was willing to let them leave with their clothes and their lives. Nothing else. The Romans, he assured them, were not coming. They had bet on the wrong horse, and they should accept their losses and save themselves. Hannibal especially wanted the riches of the Saguntines, which were said to be extensive. When the people of Saguntum heard this bitter news they returned to their homes and gathered up their gold and silver. They then brought their treasures to a common pile within sight of the Carthaginians, who looked on with glee. Finally, the Saguntines built a large fire and burned it all. They would not give one penny to the Carthaginians. Solemnly, the beleaguered citizens returned to their homes and killed themselves. Saguntum was no more.

When news of these horrifying events reached Rome it rocked the city. Stories of Saguntine fathers gently kissing their wives and children and then setting their own homes on fire filled the streets. It was heart-wrenching. The Romans' anger at Hannibal was matched only by their anger at themselves, for it had been their inaction that had allowed this to happen. The people of Saguntum had died waiting for the Romans to keep their promises. They had failed their allies. That fact alone dramatically changed the mood in Rome. Livy tells us that "such was the distress of the Senate at the cruel fate of their allies, such was their feeling of shame at not having sent help to them ... that they were in no mood for deliberating, shaken as they were by so many conflicting emotions." Everyone agreed that Hannibal must be held accountable for this act. The Romans must make clear to the Carthaginians and to the world that they would ever stand with their friends—even if they had failed to act quickly enough to save these poor people. The priests began the rituals, the armies began to muster. Rome was preparing for war.

It has not been in the American, any more than in the Roman, character to let down allies. Yet it has happened. In 1974 the United States withdrew from South Vietnam, leaving it to fight its Communist enemy alone. The following year Saigon fell and an American ally was no more.

In Cambodia, Pol Pot and the Khmer Rouge took advantage of the American withdraw to kill 1.5 million people. As with the Romans, the decision to abandon an ally was a difficult one, which would lead to long controversy afterward. It is the controversy that is important here. Both cultures, the Roman and the American, abhor cowards, liars, and quitters. And yet, their actions seemed to fit just that pattern. The result was centuries of tortured and conflicting explanations for a dark chapter in their histories.

In 1974 Americans had been fighting a long war and they were tired of it. In 219 BC the Romans were only just getting started. Impelled by their outrage and shame, the Senate made plans to send out the two consuls with a large number of troops. The first would go to Spain to punish Hannibal, while the second would head to Africa to defeat Carthage itself. Nevertheless, Roman law required that Carthage be given a chance to settle the matter peacefully. A delegation of distinguished senators, led by Quintus Fabius, went quickly to Carthage and addressed the ruling council there. They brought with them a simple question: Had Hannibal destroyed Saguntum on his own initiative as a private citizen, or had he done so as a Carthaginian general under orders from the council? The Carthaginian leaders responded with a long and legalistic analysis of their treaties with Rome. One can imagine the Roman senators quietly fuming as they listened to the Carthaginians expound endlessly on a simple and straightforward question. The Carthaginians' main argument was that they had perfectly observed their treaties with Rome. They had promised not to attack Roman allies and they had not done so, for Saguntum was not a Roman ally when they made the treaty in 241 BC. They then made it clear that they considered the Roman envoys' demeanor to be overbearing and hostile and implied that the Romans were simply looking for an excuse to declare war.

As for the Romans, they listened quietly but did not respond to the Carthaginian assertions. There was no need. Only by claiming that Hannibal acted without state sanction and only by handing him over to Rome for punishment could the council have avoided war. Plainly the council had no interest in doing either. When the Carthaginians finally stopped talking, one of the Roman senators walked forward to the assembly, gathering up the folds of his toga as he went. When he stopped to address them, it looked as if he was carrying something in those folds—and indeed he was. With a calm and steady voice he said, "Here we bring you both war and peace. Take whichever you wish." A shout rose up in the council. These oligarchs of Carthage were not used to having ultimatums flung at them. They angrily told the Romans to leave whichever they wished. And so the Roman senator let drop the folds of his toga saying, "Then I leave you war." The Carthaginians accepted the gift.

Although the Roman ambassadors were not much interested in debating with the Carthaginians, generations of Romans would later debate the question. Again, it tells us much about the Roman character that long after winning the war, the Romans continued to question whether it was truly just. Was Hannibal within his rights to attack Saguntum? The Carthaginians did have a point about the city not being a Roman ally in 241 BC when the treaty was made. And the 226 BC treaty with Hasdrubal at least implied that the Carthaginians could act without Roman interference south of the Ebro River. Was it the Romans who had violated Carthaginian rights when they made an alliance with Saguntum and then declared war when that illegal alliance was not honored? Or did the 241 BC treaty include both present and future allies and thereby allow Saguntum to come under Roman protection? These muddled questions regarding the justness of Rome's war would exercise Roman minds just as much as similar questions regarding some of America's recent wars are troubling ours. Modern opponents of the war in Iraq, for example, have claimed that it was unjust because Iraq attacked neither the United States nor its allies. Supporters, on the other hand, cite a doctrine of preemption in which one is justified in attacking an enemy if it appears that he is attempting to acquire sufficient force to attack you. Behind both arguments, though, lies a common belief that the United States is not an Empire of Conquest. Like the isolationist Romans, it is crucially important for Americans to believe that all of their wars are defensive in nature.

It is also important that trust, the lifeblood of the alliance, be maintained. How often are American foreign policy decisions made on the basis of "having our word count for something" or "maintaining America's credibility in the world"? These are not idle words. There are many countries today that rely completely on the United States for their defense because they trust that Americans will honor their alliances. Consider, for example, Britain, France, Italy, or almost any other country in western Europe. All of them have smaller effective military forces (i.e., actual fighting soldiers as opposed to public service workers) than at any time in their modern history. Why? Is it because Europeans have recently become nicer and would therefore never consider attacking one another? No. It is because each country knows well that the United States will not allow a major war in Europe and would move quickly to defend anyone who was attacked. If any of these countries did not believe that, if any one of them believed that the Americans might not defend them or might turn a blind eye to an attack against their neighbor, they would rearm. And when one power rearms, its neighbors must also rearm. Then comes the shooting. This has happened occasionally in the last century—the occasions were called World War I and World War II.

The point is that doubt among allies regarding the trustworthiness of the Empire of Trust is toxic. Americans cannot allow it and neither could the Romans. Hannibal understood that very well. As a result of the failure to defend Saguntum, Rome's word already meant nothing in Spain—something that Roman envoys learned when they arrived to seek allies in the war against Hannibal. Wherever the Romans went they heard the same answer from Spanish tribal leaders:

> Are you not ashamed, Romans, to ask us to form a friendship with you rather than the Carthaginians, seeing how those who have done so before have suffered more by you, their allies, cruelly deserting them than through any injury inflicted by the Carthaginians? I advise you to look for allies where the fall of Saguntum has never been heard of; the nations of Spain see in the ruins of Saguntum a sad and emphatic warning against putting any trust in alliances with Rome.

Hannibal's plan was to bring those same sentiments to Italy. Unlike Pyrrhus, Hannibal understood that it was trust that held Rome's empire together. Saguntum had shaken that trust. Hannibal meant to break it utterly.

The Romans believed that the war (which historians call the Second Punic War) would be fought in Spain. But Hannibal surprised them. With astonishing speed he moved his armies and elephants overland and across the Alps into Italy, arriving almost a year before anyone believed possible. Northern Italy went into a panic. The Romans moved quickly, but the quality of their troops and leaders was simply not up to Hannibal's standard. At Lake Trasimene, Hannibal wiped out nearly two Roman legions. While defeating the Romans at home, Hannibal also sent out envoys to the Italian allies, reminding them of Saguntum and pointing to his own military victories over the Romans. He hoped to demonstrate vividly that the Romans were both unfaithful and incompetent. The allies should abandon them and join Hannibal before it was too late.

But Rome was not yet beaten. The consuls still commanded many troops and so the allies held firm. That is until 216 BC. It was in that year that Rome suffered one of its greatest military defeats ever. At the Battle of Cannae, Hannibal destroyed the bulk of Rome's military forces in Italy. Altogether twenty-five thousand allied troops were killed and more than ten thousand captured. Worse than that, the victory at Cannae gave Hannibal free reign to march across Italy at will. The Romans no longer had the forces to stop him. He took advantage of the situation, destroying crops and spreading carnage in the lands of all those that remained loyal to Rome. The alliance was no longer able to defend its members.

And so it crumbled. Towns in Samnium, Apulia, Lucania, and Bruttium were the first to break with Rome and go over to Hannibal. These areas had been the last to join the confederation, so their defection was not too surprising. But the betrayal of Capua, the second largest city in Italy, was a bitter pill for the Romans to swallow. Along with it went most of Campania. Rome's experiment in empire might well have ended right there. Unable to rely on the Romans, the allies had begun to make their own deals with Hannibal. Unlike Pyrrhus, who could not stay in Italy indefinitely, Hannibal was there for the long haul. After six years in Italy he showed no signs of leaving.

But Roman forces in Spain had won a few victories. Cutting Hannibal off from his Spanish supply base forced him to rely on his Italian supporters, which necessarily constrained his actions in Italy. For that reason Rome's oldest and closest allies in Latium, Etruria, and Umbria remained loyal. Nevertheless, the Romans were just hanging on. One more major defeat in Italy would break what was left of the alliance. Rome's strategy, which was articulated by the venerable leader Fabius Maximus Cunctator ("the Delayer"), was to play for time. As a general, Hannibal was just too good. The answer, then, was to keep Roman forces just beyond his reach, limiting his movements and waiting for him to make a mistake. After all, Hannibal couldn't remain in Italy forever. Could he?

It seemed that he could. By 211 BC Hannibal was the de facto ruler of much of Italy and the Roman offensive in Spain was stalled after the death of its generals. Still the Romans clung to the strategy of delay. Without a Roman leader of Hannibal's caliber, they had little choice. That changed with the election of young Publius Scipio, who was given command of Roman forces in Spain. In his mid-twenties, Scipio was part of a new generation of Romans raised in a wealthier, more powerful, and more cosmopolitan Rome. Scipio had Greek teachers—something unheard of before his time. He was a well-educated and cultured man of the world. He was a Roman, of course, with a strong sense of duty, common sense, and moral virtue. But he was a Roman of a new age, one who questioned the traditional isolationism of the past. Like his countrymen, he believed that Romans should mind their own business, seeking peace by securing their horizons. But Scipio and his generation saw those horizons stretching well beyond the fields of Italy and Sicily. They firmly believed that ignoring the world across the sea was no longer an option.

Aside from being a charismatic man, Scipio was also a very good general. Within three years after arriving in Spain he had defeated the Carthaginians and captured the entire southern peninsula, including the rich silver mines. In a city starved for victories, news of Scipio's success was welcomed with loud cheers in the streets of Rome. When Scipio returned to the city in triumph he used his popularity and political capital to argue for a new strategy in the war against Hannibal. Carthage was able to wage indefinite war in Italy because it cost little to do so. It was time, Scipio argued, to bring the war to Carthage. A large-scale Roman invasion of Africa would force the Carthaginian council to recall Hannibal in order to defend the homeland. Italy would be free and the Romans could deal Carthage so great a blow that it would never again threaten them.

The Senate majority, led by Fabius Maximus and other elder statesmen, strongly opposed Scipio's plan. Fabius cast Scipio as a brash glory hunter who was simply trying to build his political résumé with high-profile initiatives that were dangerous to Rome. If Scipio were really interested in defeating Hannibal, Fabius asked, why not do so in Italy where Rome is strongest, rather than in Africa where Hannibal is strongest? Scipio responded that waging war at home meant that the damage was felt there. Had Italy not been damaged enough by all of Fabius' delays? Let Carthage now feel the pain of this war. It was time, Scipio insisted, to bring fire and sword to Africa.

The angry speeches that rang through the Senate house reflected a much deeper division among Romans about their own future. For Fabius and his generation, Rome was an Italian power and that was all. Italy and its defense was what mattered. These Romans had little use for the intrigues, disputes, or troubles of the outside world. Let the ancient kingdoms and empires wage wars against each other. Rome had Italy and that was enough. Like most Romans of his generation, Fabius admired Greek culture for the beauty of its art and literature, but he wanted nothing to do with its immoral ways or intellectual obfuscations. The Greeks, most Romans believed, were brilliant but weak, for they had become drunk on their own wealth and affluence. Sending Roman troops overseas to attack a foreign power like Carthage would necessarily involve Rome in foreign cultures. For Fabius and the majority of the Senate, Rome must defend itself at home while avoiding foreign entanglements.

Scipio and his supporters saw things differently. The idea that Rome would be safe once it no longer had enemies in Italy, they believed, was naive. While the Roman Senate had dithered, Saguntum fell and Hannibal invaded Italy. Since then many of the allies had abandoned Rome. Was Rome now safe? The senators needed to recognize that as Rome became more powerful it would naturally attract the interest of more powerful enemies. Just as Rome had neutralized its enemies in Italy, it needed to do the same wherever they appeared overseas. Like any other Roman, Scipio was not interested in expanding Roman power simply for its own sake. But he was determined to respond to threats when they arose. Whether the senators liked it or not, for its own safety Rome must become a Mediterranean power. And was that so bad? Surely the sophisticated and ancient cultures of the world had something they could teach Romans, if the Romans would only listen.

And so the debate went on. Scipio cast Fabius as an ossified relic of a failed strategy, while Fabius described Scipio as a Greek-loving hedonist whose recklessness would doom them all. Livy tells us that Scipio was "taunted for his style of dress as being un-Roman and even unsoldierly. It was asserted that he walked about the gymnasium in a Greek robe and Greek slippers and spent his time amongst rhetoricians and athletes, and that his military staff were ... living a life of similar self-indulgence and effeminacy."

Scipio was opposed by the Senate, but he had the support of the people. After his election as consul, the Senate grudgingly approved Scipio's plan, but in such a way as to ensure its failure. Arguing that it was foolhardy to send Roman troops overseas while the enemy remained undefeated in Italy, the senators assigned to Scipio only those legions already based in Sicily. Nevertheless, Scipio was so popular that he attracted his own soldiers who volunteered to serve under him as he marched south and then prepared for the sea crossing. And so it was that the Romans stormed the beaches of Africa in 202 BC, ushering in a new era in the history of their empire. As Scipio predicted, the Carthaginians recalled Hannibal, who was forced to leave Italy after seventeen years of victories. Later that year Hannibal and his armies met Scipio at the Battle of Zama. Scipio won. Carthage sued for peace. The war, at last, was over.

The Romans had now twice been forced to wage exhausting wars against Carthage. They were determined that Carthage would never again be a threat. As with all of their defeated foes, the Romans' plan was to turn Carthage into a dependent friend. The Carthaginian Empire was reduced to the city of Carthage and the nearby region. Carthaginians were henceforth forbidden to wage war outside of Africa. Even within Africa they could declare war only with the approval of the Roman people. The Carthaginian army and navy were reduced to tiny forces and the Carthaginian people were required to pay a large war indemnity in annual installments for the next fifty years. Rome kept its Spanish conquests of the war. Rich in natural resources and sparsely populated, the area held much promise for the Romans. Like the American version, Roman isolationism did not extend toward undeveloped tribal areas, which they saw as an opportunity for colonization and exploitation. Well-civilized Africa, though, was another matter. Although they could have kept it easily enough, the Romans wanted nothing to do with the various kingdoms of the North African coast. Instead, they parceled out the former Carthaginian territories to the rulers who had helped them in the war. They then withdrew from the continent altogether. Despite the Roman evacuation of Africa, their treaties with Carthage and the other kingdoms meant that they would remain heavily engaged in the region. There was really no other choice.

The end of the Second Punic War in 202 BC brought the Roman Republic to a position in their world similar to that of the United States at the end of the Second World War in 1945. Like the Romans, Americans were strongly isolationist when the war began. Groups like the America First Committee insisted that the United States not involve itself in foreign entanglements. Even when Adolf Hitler conquered most of continental Europe and declared war on Britain, the majority of American citizens and the American Congress were strongly opposed to entering the war. They clung to the traditional belief, articulated by the Monroe Doctrine, that if the United States secured its American horizon it could avoid the dangers of the rest of the world. Like the Romans, the Americans learned differently.

The Japanese bombing of Pearl Harbor in 1941 was as great a shock to Americans as the fall of Saguntum had been to Romans more than two millennia earlier. The situations were by no means identical. Hawaii was an American territory, while Saguntum was a Roman ally. Yet both were under the protection of the Empire of Trust and both were well outside the traditional boundaries of that empire. That is why Hannibal doubted that Rome would either relieve Saguntum or go to war as a result of its conquest. That is also why the Japanese high command believed that the isolationist sentiments saturating American public opinion in 1941 would lead the United States to accept the loss of its faraway Pacific holdings rather than wage war on the other side of the planet. But both attackers misjudged the situation. They mistakenly equated isolationism with timidity. The same elements in the Roman and American characters that led them to favor coalitions of allies rather than conquering empires also infused in them a determination to steadfastly defend themselves and their allies when they were attacked.

Admiral Yamamoto knew this. Having studied at Harvard, the Japanese leader understood the American character very well. In 1940 the Japanese government asked him whether he could successfully attack Pearl Harbor. Yes, Yamamoto responded, he could do that. American military power was sufficiently weak that it would be a relatively simple thing to remove it from the Pacific. That was the answer that the high command wanted to hear. But Yamamoto continued speaking. After the attack, he said, Japan would have free run of the Pacific for six months and perhaps as much as a year. "But then what?" he asked. Yamamoto knew that the United States would not accept the defeat. The Americans would be back and they would be very, very strong.

Before World War II it was a compliment to call an American an isolationist. Afterward it was an insult. Although they dithered, argued, and delayed before Pearl Harbor, Americans were determined to bring the war to the enemy after Hawaii was attacked. More importantly, victory in the war fundamentally changed the United States. Having learned that instability overseas can bring insecurity at home, Americans would not again ignore the outside world. When World War I ended the United States had refused to join the League of Nations. When World War II ended the United States not only joined the United Nations, it hosted it.

When World War I ended every soldier overseas returned home. When World War II ended thousands of American troops stayed. Having twice fought a bloody war in Europe, Americans would not allow it to happen again. West Germany and Japan, like Carthage in 202 BC, were stripped of their empires, reduced to token military forces, and turned into friends of the United States.

The United States that emerged from World War II remained isolationist in sentiment, yet became interventionist in practice. Average Americans still focused on their own country, noticing the outside world only when dramatic events occurred. Yet the American military remained a powerful force, responsible for defending not only the United States but its new allies in Europe and Asia. Rome had much the same experience. After 202 BC the Roman military was extraordinarily powerful. Through their alliances the Romans controlled most of the western Mediterranean. The great powers of the East could not help but look on Rome with interest and fear. In their attempts to forge security in a dangerous world, both the United States and the Romans had extended their power far beyond their homelands, involving themselves in the affairs of increasingly distant peoples. Without seeking it—indeed, while actively attempting to avoid it—both republics had become superpowers.

Chapter 6

The Empire and Its Aging Cultural Parents

In 200 BC Rome, either directly or indirectly, controlled the entire western Mediterranean. It had become a superpower. But it was not the only one. Far older, far wealthier, and just as powerful, the empires of the East slowly began to spare a moment to notice the barbarian upstarts in the backwater West. For them, Rome was an oddity, but not much else. Rich, Greek-speaking elites might have made a casual remark about Rome during their gala parties and lavish banquets. But it was an unpleasant subject and therefore best passed over quickly. As near as they could tell, Rome appeared to consist of a collection of primitive westerners who had managed to cobble together something that resembled a civilization. But, as one of the dinner guests would surely note, in no way could the Romans be called civilized. There was no denying that Rome was beginning to rival the military power of the ancient Eastern empires. Still, the people and rulers of the East considered the Romans boorish nouveaux riches to be kept at arm's length, if not farther.

That was fine with the Romans. They had long ago recognized that they were not as refined or educated as the citizens of the Old World in the Greek East. Indeed, they reveled in it. While Romans admired, even idolized, the high culture of the Greeks, in their daily life they preferred their own simple Latin ways. Although the city of Rome was growing all the time, in 200 BC it remained mostly a collection of wood and mud huts. Its simple temples were adorned with crude terra-cotta decorations that even the tiniest Greek city would have disposed of as eyesores.

Like the United States, Rome was a young country when it became a superpower. Both were less than three hundred years old. Born on the frontier, both countries suddenly found themselves forced to deal directly with the elder cultures of their world. In the case of Rome that meant the Greek East, from which so much of Roman cultural identity flowed. In the case of the United States, that meant Europe, which was itself the great font of American culture. In both cases, the relationship would be rocky from the start. The new Empire of Trust (both the Roman and the American version) was the cultural child of the Old World. As such, it was both attracted to and repelled by its elders. Attracted, because of the beauty, elegance, and brilliance of the ancient culture, as well as a desire, like that of any child, to be well regarded by its parent. Repelled, because the intricacies of the high culture seemed not only at variance with the simplicity of the new empire's character, but an open gateway to immorality and decadence. In the same way, the elder cultures (both the Greeks and the Europeans) found themselves equally attracted and repelled by the new empire. Attracted, because of the empire's strength and wealth, which could serve and protect them. Repelled, because that very strength and wealth served as a constant reminder of their own impotence and decline.

Much has been written about the causes and manifestations of anti-Americanism in Europe today. For most Americans it poses a vexing and frustrating problem. Americans, after all, love Europe. They revel in its history, its culture, its landscape. By the millions, they flock to Europe every year to experience its rich past and vibrant present. Europe, for many Americans, is like a beautiful museum, holding the treasures of the Western past. In two world wars—both started by Europeans—the United States sent millions of troops and lost thousands of lives in order to establish a peaceful and liberated Europe. Throughout the twentieth century Americans have given billions of dollars to European countries to help them rebuild and spent billions more providing for their military defense. Yet, despite all of this, gratitude seems to be an alien concept in modern western Europe. Against European protests that rang across the region, the United States deployed troops and missiles that ultimately won the Cold War, thus freeing Europe from the threat of the Soviet Union. Why, then, Americans ask themselves, is anti-Americanism still so prevalent there?

As we shall see in this chapter, the Romans faced the very same sort of reactions from their own elder culture, the Greeks. Like Americans, ancient Romans poured out their money, time, and blood in order to secure peace and liberty for the Greeks. Yet, more often than not, they were repaid with insults, accusations, and derision. Can any lessons be drawn with regard to the same dynamics at work in our own world?

Let's set the scene of the eastern Mediterranean world in antiquity. There is a reason that the East had more people, money, and cities than the West—it was older, much older. Human civilization, after all, began in the East, principally in Mesopotamia (modern Iraq). The Greeks were relative latecomers, settling in what is today Greece around 1600 BC. What made them important, though, is their development of a new and uniquely Western culture, quite different from those of earlier civilizations like Mesopotamia, Persia, or Egypt. Unlike those peoples, the Greeks were not unified into powerful empires with god kings. Rather, they were heavily divided into separate city-states, each one fiercely independent. Not surprisingly, the Greek cities frequently clustered together into various leagues, making war against each other. The Trojan War—that was one.

By 800 BC Greek civilization had developed the concept of the polis— an important milestone in Western political thought. The polis was the city-state, but not the walls or the buildings. It was the body of citizens, all freeborn males, committed to each other and their common defense. The Greek military was made up solely of these free citizens, each bringing his own weapons and serving without pay. Although the Greek cities had various forms of government, all put great emphasis on the individual citizen, who should have rights, responsibilities, and a voice commensurate with his contribution to the welfare of the polis. It was in these amazing cities that art, architecture, literature, and philosophy flourished.

Men like Plato fashioned a Western approach to philosophy, Aristotle gave birth to a Western style of science, and Cleisthenes introduced Western concepts of democracy. The Greeks tilled the land, but they also plied the waterways, doing business in faraway ports and founding new Greek cities in Asia Minor (modern Turkey) and southern Italy. Each city was independent, each Greek inside committed to preserving his individual liberty at all costs. Yet these scattered people naturally saw each other as members of the same Greek culture, which they were. For ancient Greeks, true civilization existed only in a polis. Non–polis dwellers were by definition barbarians.

Disjointed and scattered, the Greeks were the small fry of the ancient world. To their east was the massive empire of Persia, which stretched all the way from India across the Middle East and Asia Minor. It was in Asia Minor that the Persians first came into contact with Greek cities, who steadfastly refused to be incorporated into an eastern Empire of Conquest. The Persians were not accustomed to refusals. Between 490 and 479 BC the Greeks on both side of the Aegean Sea fought for their lives against the Persian Empire. It was their finest hour. Banding together to defend their civilization, the Greeks at home were ultimately successful, defeating the Persians and sending them back to Asia Minor. That victory meant the survival of Greek culture. It is difficult to imagine what our world would look like today if the war had gone the other way.

Over the course of the next several decades the Greeks saw a magnificent flowering of their culture and an increase in their wealth. But the Persian threat had not disappeared. It loomed to the east, always threatening Greek liberty. To defend against it, the Greeks developed various alliances, the largest being the Delian League, headed up by Athens. In time, the Delian League, which was supposed to be an arrangement of equals, turned into an Athenian empire that brooked no rebellion. Greek cities not in the Delian League joined up with the Spartans' own Peloponnesian League for defense. Given the frequency with which Greeks generally waged war on each other, it was a bad idea to have so many of the cities organized into just two unfriendly leagues. The inevitable happened in 431 BC when the two leagues went to war. The destruction was severe, straining the fabric of Greek society and leaving it beaten and battered. When the war finally ended in 404 BC, a weak and exhausted Greece was all that was left.

To the north of Greece was Macedonia, a rugged country inhabited by rugged people who were distantly related to the Greeks. They spoke Greek and did their best to mimic Greek culture. The Greeks in the south considered the Macedonians to be poor cousins, hill people with violent natures, poor education, and bad hygiene. But they were better than barbarians. Busy with their own wars, the Macedonians did not often bother the Greeks. That changed with the reign of King Philip II of Macedon, who was able to defeat his rivals and claim control over all of Macedonia. For the first time in memory, the region was at peace. Philip decided to do the same thing for Greece. Leading his armies south, he managed to conquer all of the Greek cities by 338 BC. As a Macedonian, Philip naturally admired Greek culture. Yet he believed that the incessant warfare between the Greeks was fundamentally harming that culture. By conquering the peninsula Philip forced a peace on the Greek cities but, in the process, deprived them of their liberty. There was, he believed, no other way.

In 336 BC Philip was assassinated by a noble, unhappy with his rewards. The throne passed to his son, Alexander the Great. Alexander's plan was to pick up where his father had left off. Like his father, Alexander was deeply committed to the ideals of Greek civilization—minus the part about democracy and the liberty of each polis. He decided to use the unified Greek forces now under his command to deal once and for all with the continuing threat of the Persians. With approximately thirty thousand men and five thousand horses he marched into Asia Minor, defeated the Persians, and liberated the Greek cities there. This was an amazing reversal of fortunes for Greek civilization, which was now for the first time on the offense. But Alexander was not finished. Not content simply to push the Persians past the Greek horizon, he meant to utterly destroy their empire. He pressed on into Syria, which fell to his armies in 333 BC, then quickly into Egypt, which also surrendered. With all of the eastern Mediterranean under his control, Alexander plunged deep into Mesopotamia, where he conquered Babylon before moving into the heart of Persia (modern Iran). No one could stop him. The Greek military innovation known as the phalanx, consisting of rows of well-disciplined foot soldiers, defeated all that stood in its way. After demolishing the Persian Empire, Alexander continued eastward to India. It was at this point that his soldiers balked, for they had only signed on to defeat the Persians, not the world. During his return journey Alexander died. In thirteen years he had marched twenty thousand miles, never lost a battle, and built a Greek empire that spanned the Near and Middle East. No longer a small and threatened culture, Greek was henceforth the very definition of civilization in the eastern Mediterranean world.

Alexander's heir, a posthumously born son, was in no position to assert his rights of inheritance. In short order the conqueror's generals proceeded to split up the empire among themselves, each one establishing a new dynasty. In the end, what had been one empire became three. The Seleucids received the lion's share, claiming Syria, Mesopotamia, and Persia. The Ptolemids were content to become the new rulers of Egypt, while the Antigonids were largely confined to Macedonia and parts of Asia Minor. As the years went by tensions grew between these three empires, but the basic template was established. These Eastern powers were fundamentally Greek in character—what historians call Hellenistic, or Greek-like—although the populations themselves were not ethnically Greek. The real Greeks (i.e., those in the original Greek cities) were understandably proud of these victories, but that did not stop them from continuing to find reasons to wage war against each other, which they tended to equate with liberty. Still searching for freedom, the old cities would fashion leagues in order to keep the Hellenistic kings at bay. Sometimes this worked.

This, in a nutshell, was the Old World that the Romans knew, insofar as they knew very much at all about events in the East. Culturally, the Romans owed a great deal to the Greeks. But, as we saw earlier, they also brought to the mix their own experiences forged on the periphery of the civilized world. More important in the early years of Roman development was the cultural impact of the Etruscans. There is still a lively scholarly debate over the origins of the people of Etruria, who lived just to the north of Rome. They developed their own unique and fascinating culture that appears to have been drawn from a cocktail of peoples including Iron Age tribes, Greeks, and other unknown groups. They flourished, although like the Greeks they were divided into frequently warring independent cities. Developing impressive engineering skills, the Etruscans mined the hills of Italy and engaged in active trade with other Mediterranean civilizations.

Etruscan religious practices had a strong influence on the early Romans. The Etruscans lived by omens. It was the Etruscans who introduced the Romans to anthropomorphic gods like Jupiter and Juno, who began to muscle out the humble household spirits of earlier days. Etruscan political ceremonies and rituals were adopted wholesale by the Romans, including such things as the toga, fasces, rod, and golden wreath. More than that, the whole concept of a divided government, popular assemblies, and a Senate came directly from the Etruscans. Although the Etruscan language was different, the Romans nevertheless adopted and modified the Etruscan alphabet in order to write their own Latin. With some modifications, those are the letters that you are reading right now.

Either as a league or individually, the Etruscans expanded southward in the seventh century, which is probably when they came to control the small village of Rome. But they found the Greeks who lived in southern Italy to be formidable opponents. After suffering a defeat at the hands of the Greek city of Cumae in 524 BC, the Etruscans began to withdraw back to the north of Italy. Roman independence was one part of this general disintegration of Etruscan authority. As we saw earlier, the Romans were able to defend themselves and their new Latin allies against Etruscan attempts to reimpose their authority in central Italy. The subsequent Gallic invasions then left the Etruscans so weak that they were obliged to join the expanded Roman confederation. After years of fighting the Romans, the Etruscans joined their confederation and became one of their most trusted allies.

Rome, therefore, was first and foremost a child of Etruria. Yet Rome was also situated between the Etruscan north and the Greek south of Italy, giving it an opportunity to learn from both. As the Romans began to project their authority farther away, they became better acquainted with the sophisticated cultures of the East. In the fifth century BC, for example, a traveler to Rome could find very simple temples to the Greek gods Apollo and Demeter. By the fourth century the Romans had their own copy of the *Sibylline Books*, a collection of prophecies dictated by the oracles of Apollo at Delphi. These mystic writings were commonly consulted in the Greek world, where diviners could discern the meanings of the cryptic remarks (although typically only after the event had happened). That the Romans introduced this Greek practice alongside their own homegrown auguries is suggestive. A century later, in 222 BC, we find the Roman people actually sending a votive offering to Delphi to thank Apollo for a military victory against the Gauls.

Despite these contacts, high Greek culture remained foreign to the early Romans. It was not until the late third century BC that a significant Greek influence began to be felt in the city. Recall that Scipio Africanus, the young general who led Rome to victory in the Second Punic War, was taught by Greeks and he greatly valued their culture. By 200 BC, this was becoming a standard for young Romans in affluent families. It was natural that wealthy Rome, which had come to control the western Mediterranean, would find itself increasingly exposed to the culture of the East. No longer content with just the Latin tongue, Roman elites made certain to learn Greek—even if only a few words to sprinkle into their cocktail conversations. Greek was the language of culture, after all, so using a Greek phrase or two always gave the well-heeled Roman a certain je ne sais quoi.

Within a generation of the victory over Carthage every educated Roman could speak Greek and was familiar with at least the basics of Greek history. Philhellenism became a central feature of Roman elite culture. Romans were hungry for Greek culture and they had the money to buy it. Droves of Greek tutors flocked to Rome to take advantage of the new market. Greek philosophers, who were finding times increasingly tough at home, relocated to Rome, where rich benefactors competed to become their patrons. Pockets stuffed with new cash, the Romans sought to buy an elite culture—or at least its trappings. Greek plays, music, literature, everything—it all became the rage in the Rome of the second century BC. Well-known Greek philosophers were treated like modern rock stars. In an ancient counterpart to the "British invasion," two Greek intellectuals, Carneades and Diogenes, made a tour of Rome, where they were literally mobbed by young Romans. Plutarch tells us:

> The charm of Carneades especially, which had boundless power and a fame not inferior to that power, won large and sympathetic audiences, and filled the city, like a rushing mighty wind, with the noise of his praises. Reports spread far and wide that a Greek of amazing talent, who disarmed all opposition by the magic of his eloquence, had infused a tremendous passion into the youth of the city, as a result of which they abandoned their other pleasures and pursuits and were "possessed" about philosophy.

Although not quite *The Ed Sullivan Show*, the two famous Greeks were given a rare senatorial audience. They impressed the senators, even though Roman law required them to speak though translators. Greek might be learned and fashionable, yet only Latin could be spoken in the Senate House.

At least a few similarities between Rome's approach to its elder cultures and that of the United States begin to suggest themselves. Although Americans threw off control of British kings and subsequently warred against them, nevertheless the foundation of American culture lies squarely in England. The English, like the Etruscans, acquired some of their own culture from their sophisticated neighbors in Europe. But in many ways they are quite different than other Europeans—and it is generally those aspects of English culture that Americans absorbed. England, for example, uses common law rather than the European Roman Law, and so, too, does the United States (except in Louisiana). English religious denominations, principally the Church of England (or in America, Episcopalianism), Presbyterianism, Congregationalism, and other forms of Puritanism, became the bedrock of America's religious culture. It is no coincidence that for many Americans the King James Version of the Bible is still *the* Bible. They may have rejected the English king, but Americans were sticking with his Bible.

Although Americans ejected the British from their lands, they held on to British ideas and rituals of government. In 1776 Britain was a constitutional monarchy in which a parliament, with its lower and upper houses, held virtually all of the power. Since the Glorious Revolution of 1688, monarchs in England had served under the law, not above it. It was an Englishman, John Locke, who developed the intellectual underpinnings of the British system as it emerged in the late seventeenth century and who provided the philosophical inspiration behind the American Revolution. The Declaration of Independence is in every way a Lockean document. Even today, American culture is in large part British, as any visitor to the two countries can attest.

Although at first the British were the enemies of the United States, in time they, like the ancient Etruscans, became firm and fast allies. The same cannot be said of the Europeans, who more closely resemble the ancient Greeks in this context. American culture adopted much from Europe, but it was generally brought by immigrants and was modified by the "melting pot," already largely filled with a stew of British origin. European religion, particularly Catholicism, was an early import. Yet an appreciation of the high culture of Europe—such as the literary, artistic, dramatic, or even culinary expertise of Europeans—was some way off. Most average Americans in the early nineteenth century knew full well that Paris was a beautiful and cultured city. They were just unclear on what it looked like or what made it so cultured.

We will explore more similarities between American and Roman attitudes toward their elder cultures a bit later. For now, though, let's look through the other side of the lens, at the Old World perceptions of the growing Empire of Trust. Indifference would best sum up the ancient Greek attitude toward Rome during its first three centuries as an independent state. In general the Greeks took little notice of events in the West. Why should they? There was not much there to command their attention. A handful of Greek scholars mentioned the Romans, but only as one among many barbarians and only by virtue of their proximity to western Greeks. In the fourth century BC the Romans were forging a powerful confederation of allies in Italy, but the Greek world, including many of those Greeks in Italy, took little notice. Remember the boisterous scene when the Roman senatorial delegation addressed the Greeks of Tarentum? Although Postumius came to discuss grave matters of war and peace, the assembled people had come to make fun of his bad Greek and laugh at his rude and rustic manner. For the Greek citizens of wealthy and sophisticated Tarentum, the Romans were buffoons, nothing more. When they became troublesome, the Tarentines simply called in a professional Greek army, led by the famed general Pyrrhus.

In the end, though, the Romans defeated Pyrrhus and brought all of the Greek cities and towns in Italy into their confederation. Yet even that did not elicit much of a response from the Greeks of the East. It was bad luck for the Greeks in Italy, to be sure. But, after all, one must expect that sort of thing if one is going to live in the wild and woolly West. Rome's wars in the third century BC held about as much interest for contemporary Greeks as modern African struggles do for Americans today. They happen, and one might even hear something about them. But they do not impact American lives very much. Timaeus of Tauromenium, a Greek scholar writing in the third century, mentioned Rome and Carthage only in his *History of Sicily* (an island filled with Greeks, and therefore worthy of a history). Around 230 BC the Greek mathematician Eratosthenes referred to Romans as barbarians, but admitted that they might be "refined barbarians." This remained the Greek perception when Rome became a superpower in 200 BC. As Erich Gruen has noted, "the Hellenic perception of Rome remained nebulous and blurred ... scholars and intellectuals had accumulated fragmentary items of interest, foundation legends, alien customs, geographic data, a few historical particulars, some ill-digested research into Roman institutions ... [yet] no distinct Hellenic image of Rome had taken shape."

That all changed in the next few years. It was not the Roman victory over Carthage that grabbed Greek attention, but the subsequent Roman intervention into Greece itself. Like the United States, Rome wanted to avoid intervening in the Old World, but found itself step-by-step drawn into its perilous and tangled web. As usual, things were complicated in Greece at the end of the third century. King Philip of Macedonia was waging on-again, off-again wars against various Greek cities or leagues. He had some minor dealings with the Romans—none to his liking, since the Romans naturally idealized the famous Greek cities and their culture. In 202 BC Philip made a deal with one of the other Hellenistic kings, Antiochus of Syria, who ruled the massive Seleucid Empire just to the east. As it happened, a succession struggle in Egypt had left the Greek dynasty there, the Ptolemids, in disarray. That opened all sorts of possibilities for an enterprising tyrant. Philip and Antiochus agreed to start carving up what they could from the Ptolemaic pie. For Philip this meant attacking various independent Greeks, such as the Aetolians (a league of cities in west-central Greece), the kingdom of Pergamum (a small Greek state on the Asian side of the Aegean coast), and the island of Rhodes. What had once been a balance of power between three Hellenistic dynasties looked like it would become an alliance of only two.

In desperation, the independent Greek cities under attack by Philip sent ambassadors to Rome to beg for aid. Suddenly Greece had discovered Rome. The Greeks made the trip to the Roman Senate because they simply had no other good options. They knew that Rome was powerful and that without a powerful friend they would soon be gobbled up into Philip's expanding Empire of Conquest. When speaking to the senators, the ambassadors naturally played on the ideal image of the Greek, who should always be free of tyranny. They knew that this worked with the Romans, who themselves hated tyranny in all of its forms. Just as Americans instinctively believe that European states should be independent and free, so the Romans also believed as they gazed across the sea at the marble-columned cities of Greece. The Greek appeals for aid also tell us something about the growing reputation of the Romans. The Greeks sent ambassadors to Rome for two simple reasons: The Romans were strong and they were known to use power in a trustworthy manner. They knew that Rome, despite its power, was not building an Empire of Conquest— in other words, that the Roman people were nothing at all like the Macedonians.

An appeal for aid—once again this was the crucial dynamic that led the Romans to their empire. It was not that they sought expansion. Rather, it came groveling to their door, begging to be let in. In this case, the request posed a unique problem for the Senate. There was no doubt in the senators' minds that helping the Greeks in their struggle against Philip was good and just. But was it legal? We will return to this question later. Ultimately, though, the Senate agreed to support the beleaguered Greeks and found the legal basis to do so. There were two reasons for this decision. First, the senators understood that Rome's new stature was attracting the attention of great powers in the East. If Antiochus and Philip were successful, their combined strength would constitute a powerful threat to Roman control of the West. That could not be a good thing. Second, the senators, most of whom were well-educated in Greek culture, really wanted to help. They saw the situation in Greece as a clear case of tyranny versus freedom, and they honestly wanted to help preserve Greek freedom.

Once again Rome's military forces were mobilized in what historians refer to as the Second Macedonian War (200–196 BC). Greek cities that had asked for Roman aid, like Athens and the cities of Aetolia, were very pleased to have the legions landing on their shores. Yet other Greeks looked on the Romans' arrival with dread. Although they did not relish conquest by Philip of Macedonia, they worried about the invasion of these Italian barbarians. Weren't the Romans the ones responsible for taking over Greek cities in southern Italy and Sicily? What if the Romans did defeat Philip? What then? Were the Greeks simply trading one tyrant for another?

The ambassadors of Philip, who hoped to rally the Greek cities against the Romans, were quick to exploit this fear. It is the first time that we can hear a genuine anti-Roman diatribe delivered by ancient Greeks. Like anti-American arguments made today, the speaker purposefully ignores the good that Rome had done, dwelling instead on specific incidents in Roman history in which the Romans had failed to meet their own standards of behavior. With a Roman ambassador in attendance, the envoy of Philip approached the assembled Greek delegates, saying:

> In the First Punic War they [the Romans] went to Sicily, ostensibly to help Messana; in the Second, to deliver Syracuse from Carthaginian tyranny and restore her freedom. Now Messana and Syracuse and in fact the whole of Sicily are tributary to them. They have reduced the island to a province in which they exercise absolute power over life and death. You [Greeks] imagine, I suppose, that the Sicilian Greeks enjoy the same rights as you, and that as you hold your council at Naupactus under your own laws, presided over by magistrates of your own choice, and with full power of forming alliances or declaring war as you please, so it is with the councils which meet in the cities of Sicily, in Syracuse or Messana or Lilybaeum. No. A Roman governor manages those meetings. It is at his summons that they must assemble. They see him issuing his edicts from his lofty tribunal like a despot, and surrounded by his lictors. Their backs are threatened with the rod, their necks with the axe, and every year they have a different master [Roman governor] allotted to them. Nor should they be surprised at this, given the situation in Greek cities of Italy such as Rhegium, Tarentum, and Capua, lying prostrate beneath the same tyranny.... If men of an alien race, separated from you as much by language, customs, and laws as by intervening sea and land, obtain a foothold here, it is folly and madness to hope that anything in Greece will remain as it is now.

Imperialists! If such a word had been coined, the ambassador would have flung it at the Romans. Of course, he had to play a bit loose with the truth. Although Rome had made Sicily a province under the control of a governor, that was at the request of the Greeks of the island, who did not want to be bothered with their own military defense. The attacks on the people of Rhegium by Roman soldiers were deeply embarrassing to the Romans. Those who were responsible were quickly and severely punished. Yet, just as with Abu Ghraib or Hiroshima today, Rhegium would become a favorite taunt of those who opposed the growing preeminence of the Empire of Trust.

When the Greek ambassador from Philip finished his speech, the Roman ambassador rose and gave a point-by-point rebuttal, which again reveals much about the core beliefs of the Empire of Trust. Above all he stressed that throughout their history the Romans had always and only waged war to defend themselves or their allies. The Italian Greek cities of Tarentum and Capua had declared themselves to be the enemies of Rome. Yet even after the Romans had defeated them, they were still given a lenient peace that allowed the inhabitants to enjoy lives of peace and prosperity. The Roman ambassador also pointed to Carthage, which had attempted not only to destroy Rome but to conquer all of Italy. After twice defeating the Carthaginians in long and costly wars, the Romans still allowed them to live in freedom, removing every Roman soldier from the shores of Africa. In short, the Roman ambassador responded to the imperialist taunt by underscoring the extreme caution and great patience that his people had used when wielding power. Rome was an Empire of Trust, not an Empire of Conquest.

When the speeches were finished and the armies marched, some Greek cities declared for Philip, others for Rome. But most debated and played local politics with the question until it was clear which of the two sides was going to win. In 199 BC Roman forces in Greece were commanded by the well-respected general Flamininus. He defeated Philip in battle after battle, pushing the king step-by-step northward and back into Macedonia. That was enough for the wavering Greeks. They began to sign up with the winning side, supporting the Romans in mopping-up operations. It helped that Flamininus was a well-educated Roman who spoke excellent Greek and who clearly had a deep respect for the Greeks and their culture. Although the Greeks were weak and clearly no longer the masters of their own destiny, Flamininus flattered them, recalling their past achievements and extolling their leaders as if Greece were still at the pinnacle of its power.

By 197 BC Flamininus had effectively managed to undo the conquests of Alexander the Great's father more than a century earlier. Greece was free of Macedonian control. Many of the liberated Greeks urged the Roman leader to continue his war into Macedonia, crushing Philip in his home. That is, after all, what any great empire would have done. Yet Flamininus refused. That was not why the Romans had come to Greece. His legal charge was to eject Philip from Greece and this he had done. Flamininus replied to the Greek allies that "the Romans have never after a war destroyed their adversaries, as was proved by their conduct towards Hannibal and the Carthaginians, at whose hands they had suffered grievous injuries, but afterwards, when it was in their power to do whatever they wished, they took no extreme measures." Flamininus had never, he said, "entertained the idea that Rome should wage war on Philip without any hope of reconciliation."

Once again we can see here the consequences of a military conquest for an Empire of Trust. Although ancient Rome and modern America routinely defeated their enemies, both abhorred the idea of conquest. Instead, both turned conquered enemies into friends. They did so for the simple reason that they did not want foreign territories. They wanted allies. In war after war—including the current war in Iraq—the United States first defeated its opponent and then turned it into an ally. After the Cold War the United States began bringing eastern European countries into NATO. There continues to be discussion of Russia itself joining the alliance. Today, many of the strongest and most faithful allies of the United States, countries like England, Germany, Italy, Austria, Turkey, and Japan, were at one time America's enemies. Philip of Macedon, defeated by Rome after more than two years of difficult fighting, was allowed to keep his kingdom and become a Roman ally. He gladly accepted.

Having expelled Philip from Greece, the Romans were left to deal with the fiercely proud and independent Greek city-states. Without the Macedonian threat, the Roman presence in the Greek homeland became odious for those who lived there. Yet those who took the time to notice also worried about what would happen if the Romans simply withdrew their forces. Philip seemed to be pacified—at least for the moment. But there remained the problem of Antiochus, whose massive empire lay just to the east in Asia Minor and who would very much like to claim what Philip could not. If the Romans returned home, who would protect the Greek cities from him? Just as importantly, who would protect them from each other?

For the proud and sophisticated Greeks, the idea that they needed protection from barbarians was naturally insulting. In a few places it led to the same sort of resentment that can be seen in European anti-Americanism today. As writers like Jean-François Revel have chronicled, European thought and politics has become increasingly permeated with anti-Americanism. Things were not that bad in Greece in 197 BC. Not yet. Too many Greeks were still genuinely grateful for Rome's defeat of Philip. But anti-Romanism was stirring in a few areas.

Take, for example, the situation in the renowned Greek city of Thebes, situated in Boeotia, just to the northwest of Athens. The Thebans were divided in their allegiances during the war, with most of the people opting to support Philip. When the Roman legions entered and garrisoned the region, they captured and imprisoned the Boeotian forces that had fought against them. In wealthy Thebes, where anti-Romanism was spreading, the leaders petitioned Flamininus to release the captured Boeotian troops. As a gesture of goodwill, Flamininus agreed. But it generated neither goodwill nor gratitude. Instead, the Thebans sent a formal declaration of thanks *to Philip*! They then proceeded to elect as their new leader Brachylles, a man fresh from a Roman prison, having served as the leader of Boeotian forces that sided with Philip. Pro-Roman Boeotians could not get elected to any office. This double slap in the face of the Romans was followed up by a string of nighttime murders of Roman soldiers, who were stationed in Boeotia for its defense. When Flamininus protested these actions, the Boeotian leaders responded that there was nothing that they could do, since their government had not sanctioned the killings. It was only when the exasperated Roman general prepared to attack that the Boeotians agreed to arrest and hand over those guilty for the murders. But they were not happy about it.

Anti-Roman sentiments like this could be found elsewhere in Greece, particularly in those areas that had fought on the Macedonian side and were now garrisoned by Roman troops. When Greeks got together in the forums to discuss current events they naturally wondered what Rome was going to do with all those regions. Given that they had fought against Rome, most agreed that the Romans were justified in holding on to them. Some suggested that the Romans would establish military bases at strategic locations in Greece, while removing their troops from the more famous and high-profile cities like Thessalonica and Corinth. With each new dispatch from Rome to Flamininus the rumors became more heated and more bizarre.

But the suspense was almost at an end. In the spring of 196 BC all of the Greeks were invited to the Isthmian Games, an event that always drew vast crowds. It was known that Flamininus himself would be there and that he would have something important to say. The games were opened with great fanfare to a packed stadium. Then to the surprise of the people a single herald walked out into the middle of the arena, accompanied only by a lone trumpeter. A loud blast brought the thousands of people in the stands to a complete silence. This was it—the announcement they had been waiting for. No one wanted to miss a word.

The herald took one step forward, opened a scroll, and read the following in a loud voice:

THE SENATE OF ROME AND TITUS QUINCTIUS [Flamininus], THEIR GENERAL, HAVING CONQUERED KING PHILIP AND THE MACEDONIANS DO NOW DECREE AND ORDAIN THAT THESE [Greek] STATES SHALL BE FREE, SHALL BE RELEASED FROM THE PAYMENT OF TRIBUTE, AND SHALL LIVE UNDER THEIR OWN LAWS.

The herald then proceeded to list every Greek city-state not already free—including all of those that had fought against Rome. Having finished his announcement, the herald pocketed his scroll and with the trumpeter walked out of the silent arena. For a moment nothing happened at all. Stunned, the Greeks began to turn to each other, not certain if what they had heard was a bad joke or just a horrible mistake. Then, like a thunderclap, a great roar of surprise exploded from the crowd. According to Plutarch, the noise was so great that crows flying overhead were knocked unconscious and fell out of the sky. Suddenly no one cared at all about the games. They demanded that the herald return and read his scroll again. Surely he could not have said what they thought he had said! After a few minutes, the herald reappeared and reread the scroll. It was true. It was really true. Rome was freeing the Greeks.

The games were then held, although no one paid much attention to them. As soon as the prizes were handed out and the games formally concluded, the crowds rushed out of the stands, mobbing Flamininus' box. They showered him with accolades, tossing garlands and ribbons at him, and pressing in so tightly that for a moment he began to fear for his life. The Greeks were grateful—grateful that the Romans had come so far to free them and had asked nothing at all in return. This was something unheard of in human history. It seemed impossible to believe. Yet, for the Romans as an Empire of Trust, it was the natural choice. As the news spread across Greece, Roman officials and soldiers were stopped in the streets and warmly thanked. According to Livy, Greeks everywhere were saying:

> There is but one nation which at its own cost, through its own exertions, and at its own risk has gone to war on behalf of the liberty of others. It renders this service not to those across its frontiers, or to the peoples of neighboring states, or to those who dwell on the same mainland, but it actually crosses the seas in order that nowhere in the wide world may injustice and tyranny exist, but that right and equity and law may be everywhere supreme.

No doubt the Roman people felt great pride and satisfaction at having freed the Greek people, just as Americans felt at the end of World War

I. It was then, in 1918, that the European allies celebrated the Americans for their decisive role in the defeat of the Central Powers. Parisians poured out into the streets to welcome President Woodrow Wilson, greeting him with a parade and an electric banner proclaiming VIVE WILSON! They, too, were genuinely grateful to the Americans for having crossed the sea to end a war that they had not started and secured a freedom that they did not imperil. The United States did not send troops across the Atlantic in 1917 to conquer territory. Instead, American forces came "to make the world safe for democracy." Wilson insisted that the United States would not conclude a peace with despots or tyrants, but would relentlessly wage war against them until all Europeans lived in freedom. The overriding message that Wilson brought with him to Europe was one of "national self-determination" in which every nation was to be free, none fettered by the bonds of empire. Like the Romans, Americans felt a natural pride at bringing freedom to the Old World, where their own ideas of liberty had been born.

When the Great War was over, the United States brought every single American soldier home from Europe. The Romans did the same thing in Greece. Both actions were risky, for by their involvement in the war both empires had staked their own reputation on the continued peace and liberty of the elder cultures. In the case of the United States, this led to various attempts to help European powers get back on their feet financially. Yet, by the 1930s, when totalitarian governments began to spread across Europe, Americans simply shook their heads and turned away.

That did not happen in Rome. In the great proclamation of Flamininus the Roman state had not only freed the Greek states, but by implication had guaranteed their continued freedom. Strictly speaking, the Greeks were not allies, because they owed Rome nothing. But Rome owed the Greeks a great deal, for the Romans had taken on the job of artificially creating and defending a world of Greek liberty that had long ago passed away. They did this, quite simply, because they could. Greek independence was worth protecting because it was genuinely cherished by the Romans. Yet, although it may have given Romans a warm feeling, committing themselves to being the sole defender of Greek liberty was still a daunting task. Greek cities in Asia Minor, many of whom were supporters of Rome in the war, naturally assumed that their independence was also guaranteed. All of a sudden those eastern Greeks felt quite self-assured when dealing with King Antiochus of Syria. After all, didn't they have the people and Senate of Rome behind them as well?

If Antiochus had been the only threat to Greek liberty, that would have been enough. But the gravest danger was—and had always been— from the Greeks themselves. For ancient Greeks, freedom meant not only individual liberty, but also the freedom to attack one's neighbor. How, for example, could the Romans say that Corinth was truly free if it was forbidden to attack Sparta? Yet, by the same token, how could Sparta be considered free if it was conquered by Corinth? These were the arguments that would now make their way to the Roman Senate, for obviously no one could attack anyone without making certain that it would not bring a Roman legion down upon their heads.

Without a single soldier stationed in Greece, the Romans maintained the peace there. It was not easy. In time, as so often happens with humans, gratitude turned into resentment and then hatred. The Greeks were free because the Romans made them so. There was no other reason. The Greeks were like aged, weakened parents under the protection of their brash, powerful children. This humiliating state of affairs was made all that much worse by the fact that the Romans were, after all, barbarians.

As for the Romans, they could not understand this resentment. Greeks loved freedom. The Romans, out of their own generosity, had given them that freedom. Why not take advantage of it? Go philosophize, create some art, engage in debauchery—all of those things that Greeks were famous for. The Romans made a point of reminding the Greeks that despite all the heroic battles of their past, only a few of them, during the Persian War, were fought for the sake of freedom. All the rest were just attempts to kill or enslave their fellow Greeks. Now the Romans had handed, without cost, them the freedom that they claimed to crave. In only a few years, Rome had done more for the Greeks than their own generals had done in many centuries. Why, then, were the Greeks so resentful?

133

King Antiochus of the Seleucid Empire, himself a Greek, was also upset with the Romans. He sent several ambassadors to the Senate to protest the Roman policy toward Greek cities. With Philip defeated and Egypt still in disarray, Antiochus led the only remaining superpower in the East, controlling almost everything from Persia to Syria, south to Egypt and west into Asia Minor. He wanted no trouble from the Romans, whom he was willing to accept as an equal in the West. But he refused to accept Rome's blanket guarantee of Greek freedom. By right and tradition Antiochus' lands included Thrace and all of Asia Minor. Those areas, of course, were thick with Greek cities, which demanded to be free as a result of the Roman decree. Antiochus protested that he would never think to interfere in Italy. Why, then, should the Romans interfere in his empire?

For years this remained simply a battle of words. It was the Greeks themselves who turned it into a real war. The continued rise of anti-Romanism in Greece led the Aetolian League of Greek cities to start seeing the Romans as the real enemy. In 192 BC, they proclaimed their eternal liberty and, in good Greek fashion, began attacking their Greek neighbors to prove it. Naturally, their neighbors appealed to Rome to defend their liberty. It was an exasperated Senate that sent troops to Greece to separate the combatants and restore order. But at that point the Aetolians appealed to Antiochus to liberate the Greeks from Roman oppression. Believing that the Romans would not invest too much time or energy into the matter, Antiochus sent a small force to help the Aetolians. He was wrong. Within a year the Romans had defeated the Aetolians and sent Antiochus' forces back to Asia.

For the Roman Senate this was the last straw. Not only had Antiochus refused to free the Greek cities of Asia Minor, but he had now demonstrated that he was willing even to invade Greece itself. Clearly, the Greeks would never be free while Antiochus remained in the region. The Senate sent him a tersely worded ultimatum. He was to immediately free all Greek cities in Asia Minor and withdraw completely from the region or face the consequences. Antiochus refused, of course; Rome declared war.

Asia Minor was a place of enormous wealth. It was home to massive Greek cities such as Ephesus, Smyrna, Halicarnassus, and Antioch. It would be tempting, therefore, to imagine that the Romans were simply seizing on any pretext to take this rich prize for themselves. Yet that would be wrong. This was the Romans' first entry into Asia, a land that was for them both famous and exotic. Nevertheless, just as with their invasions of Africa and Greece, the Romans came in force—but they did not come to stay. They conquered; but they did not claim.

Scipio Africanus, the hero of the war against Hannibal, was given command of the Roman invasion forces along with his brother, Lucius. The moment of truth came in 189 BC when the Romans decisively defeated Antiochus' main army, forcing the king to retreat back to Syria. With the evacuation of Antiochus, all of the cities and kingdoms of Asia Minor sent representatives to the Scipios to make terms with the new conquering masters. The Senate in Rome sent a ten-man delegation to investigate claims and make recommendations regarding the final settlement of Asia Minor. In the end, the Romans rewarded their friends, like the kingdoms of Rhodes and Pergamum, but otherwise simply pronounced all of the cities of Asia Minor to be free and independent. The following year, the Roman troops withdrew completely. Despite their amazing victories that would have netted any other state in history an impressive Empire of Conquest, by the end of 188 BC there was not a single Roman soldier east of the Adriatic Sea. This was something new—something that the Old World found difficult to understand.

The Romans hoped that the removal of Antiochus would pave the way for a new golden age in the Greek world. They were to be disappointed. As the Roman historian H. H. Scullard noted, Rome "left the Hellenistic world free to abuse its liberty, and only when this occurred was she again unwillingly forced to intervene. But her patience was not inexhaustible."

It is safe to say, then, that by 188 BC the Greek world knew all about the Romans. Although powerful kingdoms still existed in the eastern Mediterranean and Middle East, with the decline of the Seleucids there was no longer any power to rival that of Rome. Amazingly, through a constant quest for peace and security and with a strong and abiding aversion to foreign conquests, the Romans had become the lone superpower in their world. There was no longer any question that Rome would have to be noticed.

Since the fall of the Soviet Union in 1991, Americans have found themselves in a situation that bears some similarity to that of the Romans in 188 BC. During the Cold War, the United States opposed the extension of Soviet power abroad, because it was a threat to the American homeland and American allies. Moreover, the growth of communism necessarily meant a commensurate loss of freedom in the world, a commodity that Americans value highly. Like Rome, the United States committed itself to difficult wars far from home in order to defeat powers that, if left unchecked, would destroy freedom in the Old World and threaten it in the New World. Of course, neither Philip nor Antiochus had nuclear weapons. But the nuclear dynamic only forced the Cold War struggle to be fought through proxies—a complication with which the Romans had no need to contend.

With the defeat of Antiochus by the Romans and the Soviet Union by the Americans, both Empires of Trust were free of serious threats to their existence. Although today there remain many potential threats to U.S. security—one thinks readily of North Korea, Iran, China, and groups like al-Qaeda—none have the capability to conquer or destroy the United States. Even Russia, the heir to the Soviet Union, no longer has the military capacity to seriously threaten the United States.

The fall of the Soviet Union freed eastern Europeans from cruel dictatorships and western Europeans from a dangerous enemy. After the fall, most Americans reasonably expected Europeans to be grateful for bringing freedom and security to the continent. Eastern Europeans, who for so long looked to the United States as a beacon of hope, were indeed grateful. Pro-American feelings remain quite high in countries that were formerly behind the Iron Curtain. They remain eager to join NATO and eager to see American military installations in their countries.

The same cannot be said for western European countries. That well of gratitude seems to have run dry long ago. Public opinion polls chronicle the rise of anti-Americanism in western Europe beginning in the late 1960s—not coincidentally when a similar strain of thought was making its way through the United States as well. By 1983, when President Ronald Reagan was deploying additional weapons and troops into Europe to defend it against the Soviet Union, anti-Americanism had risen to even higher levels. A Gallup poll in that year revealed that most western Europeans believed that the American military was making the world more dangerous, actually increasing the chance of war. These sentiments were expressed in large anti-American demonstrations across Europe. The subsequent fall of the Soviet Union did little to change European minds. Indeed, since 1991 anti-Americanism in continental western Europe has not only grown, but has become a standard of discourse. Politicians in France, Germany, and Italy insult their opponents by suggesting that they admire or support the United States. For example, in the 2007 presidential election in France, Ségolène Royal castigated her opponent, Nicolas Sarkozy, for imitating President George W. Bush. Sarkozy quickly defended himself, calling Royal's accusation "extreme." In books, newspapers, and conversation anti-Americanism has become the coin of the realm. Americans are derided as overbearing, swaggering imperialists who debase everything that they touch. They spread like a virus across the world, leaving McDonald's, Disney, and Coca-Cola in their wake.

This characterization is disturbing to most Americans (except, of course, to those who agree with it), but it may help to know that the ancient Greeks felt very much the same way about the Romans after their liberation from the threat of the Seleucid Empire. Freed by the Romans from any serious external dangers, the Greeks wrapped themselves in their own cultural superiority, sniffing at their boorish, overbearing protectors. Like anti-Americanism in modern Europe, anti-Romanism in ancient Greece became a necessity of politics and a commonplace in popular opinion. The Greek politician Callicrates explained this fact to an astounded Roman Senate in the 170s BC. He told them that all democratic Greek states had a powerful anti-Roman party and a weak pro-Roman party. The anti-Romans were much more popular among the people, "the result being that the partisans of Rome were constantly exposed to the contempt and slander of the mob, while it was the reverse with their opponents." He told the senators that anti-Romanism had become the ticket to power in Greece, that "even now there are people who have no other claim to distinction, have received the highest honors in their states simply for the reason that they are known to oppose your policies."

All of this occurred in a Greek world that was inherently artificial. The Greeks were free, prosperous, and protected from the outside—something that is almost never true for any civilization. But it is true today in western Europe, and it has been for many years. Numerous commentators have observed that western Europeans live in a postmodern world in which all is peaceful and ideas no longer have any real meaning. Niall Ferguson has noted that in Europe, "otherwise intelligent people choose apartments on the basis of feng shui. They delude themselves into thinking that attendance at a concert will reduce poverty in Africa. They are simultaneously against poverty and against global warming, when it is precisely the reduction of poverty in Asia that is increasing emissions of carbon dioxide."

Fixated on their own gratification, Europeans have not bothered much to procreate. Birthrates have plummeted to unprecedented lows, leading observers like Ferguson and Mark Steyn to conclude that Europe is slowly committing suicide. Although the fertility rate in the United States is sufficient to replace the current generation (more than two children per woman), it is below that rate in every western European country today. In some countries, like Italy and Spain, the next generation will be one-half the size of the current one. In other words, Europeans are disappearing. The same sort of problem afflicted the ancient Greeks under Roman protection. Polybius lamented that:

> In our own time the whole of Greece has been subject to a low birth-rate and a general decrease of the population, owing to which cities have become deserted and the land has ceased to yield fruit, although there have neither been continuous wars nor epidemics.... For as men had fallen into such a state of pretentiousness, avarice, and indolence

that they did not wish to marry, or if they married to rear the children born to them, or at most only one or two of them, so as to keep themselves in affluence and bring their children up to waste their substance ... so by small degrees cities became resourceless and feeble.

Under the protection of a devoted child, both Greece and Europe entered their old age, becoming decrepit, angry, barren, and confused.

The 180s BC were difficult for the Romans, because they not only had to contend with growing anti-Romanism in Greece but, as the guarantors of Greek freedom, were forced to referee nasty quarrels among the Greeks themselves. The latter only compounded the former. When the Achaean League attacked and conquered Sparta in 184 BC, the Romans sent envoys to Greece to demand that Sparta be restored. The Greek response, delivered by Lycortas (the father of the historian Polybius), was the standard complaint of Roman arrogance. Lycortas reminded the Romans that it was they who had declared the Greeks free. Why now were they issuing demands? The old black marks on the history of Roman trustworthiness were, as usual, trotted out for another airing. Lycortas asked:

> Why should I not ask what you Romans did when you took Capua, since you demand from us an account for what we Achaeans did to the Spartans, after we had conquered them in war? Some of them were killed. Suppose they were killed by us, what then? Did not you, Senators, behead the Campanians? We destroyed the walls; you deprived the Campanians not only of their walls but of their city and their fields!

This, of course, is much the same response that is returned to Americans when they lecture others in the world about keeping the peace. Invariably, they will remind Americans of their own history with regard to African slavery or the treatment of American Indians or Hiroshima and Nagasaki. In other words, they use those cases in which it appears the empire did not use power in a trustworthy fashion in order to chide the

Empire of Trust. They know it is a sore spot, and they use it for precisely that reason.

But the response is also demonstrative of the extraordinary trust that the Greeks continued to put in the Romans' use of power. It was certainly a trust that they seldom mentioned, but it pervaded all of their actions, indeed it formed the foundation of their open anti-Romanism. They realized that the Romans put a high premium on Greek freedom and would tolerate a lot of verbal abuse to preserve it. They had no fear that the Romans would take offense and launch a devastating attack on their lands. It was simply not within the character of the Romans to do so. Of course, it was in the character of most states—indeed most Greek states— to act in precisely that fashion. As a strategy of diplomacy, the Greeks relied on the fact that, as Philopoemen of the Achaean League said, the Romans "set a very high value on fidelity to oaths, treaties, and contracts with allies." He urged his fellow Greeks to take advantage of this by rigorously criticizing and complaining about Roman involvement in Greece as a means of securing for Greeks maximum freedom of action.

This strategy, though, guaranteed that the Romans would find themselves more and more involved in Greece, which in turn only stoked the fires of anti-Romanism. In Europe today one will not go broke writing a book that excoriates the United States as an imperialist state bent on world domination and environmental destruction. Just so in ancient Greece, where anti-Roman tracts were gobbled up by a ready market. Metrodorus of Scepsis made a career of writing harsh attacks on the Romans, calling them insulting names, accusing them of heinous crimes, and wishing every misfortune down on their heads. Although he lived in a world under Roman protection, Metrodorus was free to criticize and even lie about the Romans with no repercussions whatsoever. Similarly, the Greek author Timagenes wrote tract after tract against Rome. He was fond of saying that "the only reason he was grieved when fires occurred in Rome was his knowledge that better buildings would arise than those which had gone down in the flames."

There is a school of thought in Europe today that holds that the United States is, in fact, not powerful at all. Instead, it is a rather oafish and cor-

pulent state that just happened to be around when the Soviet Union collapsed. America then convinced itself that it was the cause of the
collapse—that it had won the Cold War. Whatever Americans have,
then, they have by chance. The reasoning not only has the benefit of de-
riding Americans, but likewise flatters Europeans who, it is said, can
unite and build a great and powerful state. Emmanuel Todd is perhaps
the most prominent recent proponent of this view. He explains that:

> Two real empires stood face to face and one of them, the Soviet Union,
> fell apart. The other one, the American empire, was also engaged in a
> process of decomposition; however the abrupt fall of communism cre-
> ated the illusion that the United States had risen to a level of absolute
> power. After first the Soviet and then the Russian collapse, America
> thought it could extend its hegemony over the whole planet at the very
> moment when its control over its own traditional sphere was weaken-
> ing.... America has resorted to making a show of empire by choosing
> to pursue military and diplomatic actions among a series of puny pow-
> ers dubbed for dramatic effect "the axis of evil." ... The ostentatious
> militarism of the United States, which supposedly intends to prove the
> technomilitary incapacity of everyone else in the world, has ended up
> worrying the three big real powers—Europe, Japan, and Russia—and
> is pushing them closer together. Herein lies the great counterproduc-
> tive ricochet of America's game.

Noting that "Europe is industrially more powerful that the United
States," Todd urges his fellow Europeans to "emancipate" themselves
from the Americans by building a powerful "nuclear strike force." "This
is a taboo subject, but the mutual fear that still exists between the United
States and Russia leaves Europe plenty of time to build up this potential
if it wants to." Although not directly advocating a nuclear buildup, the
French newspaper *Le Monde* urged its readers in 2004, "We must stop
talking about America as a hyperpower. America's power is only an echo
of Europe's impotence."

The ancient Greeks hit upon this same argument several millennia earlier. Dionysius of Halicarnassus noted that in his day it was common among Greeks to assert that the Romans were a low form of barbarian who had simply stumbled into their empire through dumb luck. They "arrived at world domination not through reverence for the gods and justice and every other virtue, but through some chance and the injustice of Fortune, which inconsiderately showers her greatest favors upon the most undeserving." Dionysius also tells us that there was a great market for fraudulent and slanderous histories of the Romans among "kings who detested Rome's supremacy." Although Dionysius condemns these as lies, he nevertheless goes on to argue that the real secret of Rome's success was the fact that the Romans were actually Greeks who simply forgot their civilization in the wilds of Italy.

It was also common for Greeks to discount Roman military strength, saying that although the Romans never lost a war, they frequently lost battles, while Alexander the Great had never lost either. The Roman historian Livy dismissed this criticism, saying that Alexander was only one man and a young one at that. The Romans had been winning wars for centuries. Many were the Roman consuls who had died undefeated. Also, Alexander was a king who could do as he wished, while Roman commanders were strictly limited in their power and had to succeed while still preserving the republican state.

The point that needs to be underscored here is that all of this anti-Romanism grew up in a world in which Rome held all the cards. The Romans not only had supreme military power, but they guaranteed Greek freedom against all threats (even Greek threats) free of charge. If they had wished, the Romans could have crushed Greece, killed all of their critics, and set up a province in which only the most complimentary sentiments could be expressed toward the Senate and People of Rome. But then they would not have been an Empire of Trust, which is what made Rome Roman. The Greeks, of course, knew this. Indeed, they depended on it. Anti-Roman parties in Greece could flourish because they trusted that the Romans would use their power responsibly according to their treaty commitments. In other words, they trusted that the Romans would protect the Greeks' right to defame the Romans. Every anti-Roman speech or tract was an open declaration of that trust.

The same dynamic is at work in modern Europe—indeed around the world. Anti-Americanism spreads. Books are written, speeches are made, whole political parties are based on it. But all of them are grounded on a firm trust that the United States will use its power in a responsible and predictable fashion. Anti-American politicians in France, Italy, Germany, Spain, or elsewhere in Europe base their rhetoric on that trust. If they truly believed, as 53 percent of Europeans say they believe, that the United States is one of the biggest threats to world peace today, then why taunt it openly? If President Hugo Chávez of Venezuela truly believes that the United States is demonic, why then does he shower it with insults and expect it to respond with angelic tolerance? As a purely military matter, the United States has the capacity to destroy Venezuela or Spain or any other home of anti-Americanism with ease. Yet it does not do so, nor would it ever come into the collective heads of Americans to do such a thing. And that is what Mr. Chávez and his ilk rely upon. They trust so completely in the United States' responsible use of power that they literally stake their lives on it. It is worth remembering that Mr. Chávez's most incendiary anti-Americanisms have been delivered at the United Nations in New York, on American soil.

Criticizing the invincible is fun. We all do it. Americans regularly criticize their government, but they know that it is in no danger of collapse. If it were, if the survival of the republic were really at stake, then the criticisms would stop—or else. The Sedition Act of 1798 and President Abraham Lincoln's suspension of habeas corpus in 1861 make that point clearly enough. In both cases the threatened U.S. government took steps to halt criticism of itself or its officials. By the same token, Europeans and others around the world enjoy criticizing the United States while still consuming the fruits of its protection and the peace that it has brought. When called on the telephone in 2005, western Europeans told pollsters that they were much more favorable toward Communist China than to the United States. Yet this sort of criticism is only enjoyable in so far as it does not actually harm the United States or its ability to keep the peace. After all, is there another country that could be trusted with the power that the United States now wields across the globe? Would European countries be safer if American troops left the continent and were replaced by German, French, or even the much-admired Chinese armies? Or perhaps the European Union military, which many anti-Americanists in Europe now dream could do the job?

These sorts of questions have not had to be seriously addressed in our time, but they were in ancient Greece. By the late 170s BC the famed power of Macedonia had again grown to impressive levels. Indeed, Philip had managed to assemble an army that rivaled the one that Alexander the Great had led out of Greece to conquer the world. By this time everyone knew that when a Macedonian army marched it always headed first to conquer the Greeks. Anti-Roman sentiment in Greece, therefore, increasingly began to hold up King Philip as a would-be savior against the barbaric Romans. Of course, those Greek critics knew full well that Philip, for all of his power, was no match for Rome, should the Romans decide to prosecute an all-out war. It was precisely that knowledge which made it safe to support him. Anti-Roman elites could commend Philip as a great ruler, safe in the knowledge that they would never have to be ruled by him. Philip knew this too, so he avoided any trouble with the Romans. But then he died. And his brother and successor, Perseus, had a very different perspective on things.

In 171 BC Perseus moved his armies south in order to conquer Greece. Rome declared war. Like his brother, Perseus knew that he could not win a military war against Rome. But he had a relatively new strategy to deploy against the Romans, one that would be used again and again by subsequent enemies. It is a strategy that has been discovered in the modern world, too, and is regularly used against the military might of the United States. It is one that is not often used in human history, for it only works well against an Empire of Trust. Perseus knew that he could not win a prolonged war against the might of Rome. But he could win some battles. His plan was to draw out the war, making it costly to the Roman people. At the same time, he would do his best to leave the impression that the Romans were not wanted in Greece and were therefore fighting for nothing. His hope was that the Romans, who still remained isolationist and strongly averse to the concept of empire, would soon give up and go home, leaving Greece to him. In other words, Perseus planned to use his armies to win a political victory in Rome rather than a military victory in Greece. The result, however, would be the same. This is, of course, the same strategy that has been used against the United States since the Vietnam War, when it became clear to America's enemies that the empire could more easily be defeated on the battlefield of American public opinion and politics than it could in the trenches.

Perseus was a good general and he therefore scored some impressive victories against the initial Roman forces that landed in Greece. Nevertheless, most Greeks still assumed that Rome would win, so it was safe enough to cheer on the underdog, who at least was giving those swaggering Romans a lesson in humility. Polybius insists that his fellow Greeks did not seriously want Perseus to drive the Romans out of Greece. He writes:

> For if anyone had commanded [the Greeks'] attention, and asked them frankly if they really would wish to see the supreme and absolute power fall into the hands of a single man and to experience the rule of an absolutely irresponsible monarch, I imagine they would very soon have come to their senses and, changing their tune, have had a complete change of heart. And if one had reminded them briefly of all the hardships that the Macedonians had inflicted on Greece, and of all the benefits that Roman rule had brought, I imagine the reaction would have been sudden and complete. But now, when they gave in to their initial unthinking impulse, the delight of the people at the news [of Rome's defeat] was conspicuous. Simply because of the strangeness of the event, they cheered the appearance of someone who was actually a capable adversary for Rome. I have been led to speak of this matter at such length lest anyone, in ignorance of what is inherent in human nature, may unjustly reproach the Greeks with ingratitude for being in this state of mind at the time.

Polybius, who was in Greece at the time, can be trusted on this point, at least insofar as it describes most Greeks. The enthusiasm for Perseus, particularly among Greek elites, began to take on a momentum of its own. This caused untold problems for the Roman commanders in the invasion forces, for they not only had to deal with the Macedonian enemy, but also those opinion makers and leaders in the Greek cities who were supposed to be Roman supporters.

Perseus continued to do his best to make the war costly and troublesome to the Romans. He frequently asked for meetings to discuss peace, hoping that the Romans would abandon the Greeks in disgust. The Roman people were displeased with the situation in Greece—that is true. But they would not accept defeat. The Roman commander, Paullus, was able to turn the tide of the war, finally defeating Perseus and his Greek allies in 168 BC. After a long and bloody struggle to defend Greek freedom—a struggle that the Greeks themselves largely sat out—one might assume that Roman admiration for the Greeks would have waned. Yet even now, after so many Roman deaths and so many Greek insults, the Romans remained determined to provide liberty and security for the Greeks. The Senate decreed that all Greek cities—even those who had helped Perseus—were to remain free and independent and ordered the complete withdrawal of Roman forces from Greece. Even Macedonia was declared free and independent, although it was split into four separate republics so that it could no longer threaten the Greeks.

And so it was that the Greeks were once again set free, thanks to the people of Rome. They hated it—or at least they hated the idea of it. They accepted the freedom and the protection, of course. In the aftermath of the war, Roman officials put pro-Roman leaders into power in many Greek cities. But they had a hard time of it, for they were dismissed as Roman lackeys. Polybius tells us that when these leaders would go to the public baths the superintendents had to replace all of the water that they used, since the common people considered it to be polluted. "Even the children in the streets on their way back from school dared to call [the leaders] traitors to their faces. So deep was the prevailing aversion and hatred of them."

Over the next two decades anti-Romanism in the Greek world grew to extraordinary levels. In 162 BC a Roman ambassador to Greek Syria was assassinated, leading to a short-lived scandal. Countless Roman travelers and merchants in Greece were rewarded for their country's protection and support with insults and ridicule. Like modern Americans, most Romans seemed to have taken all of this in stride. They preferred to focus on their long friendships with the Greeks and imagined that, in their heart of hearts, the Greeks remained appreciative of all that Rome had done and continued to do for them. And, of course, many Greeks did. Nevertheless, there were some anti-Greek feelings in Rome that were slowly coming to the surface. In the 190s BC the sitcom writer Plautus (well, his plays were like modern sitcoms) was able to make use of well-known Roman stereotypes of Greeks in his comedies. Characters that led lives of hedonism and debauchery were regularly described by Plautus as "Greek-like." The Greeks that appeared in his plays were always "philosophizing" when not living lives of moral decay.

In order for Plautus' Greeks to be funny, the stereotype of Greek behavior had to be firmly set in the Roman mind. Remarkably, it is a stereotype that almost exactly mirrors the one Americans have of western Europeans. The Spanish, Italians, Belgians, and most of all French, are regularly lampooned in America as effete, immoral, and overly intellectual. Take for example a piece written by Rob Long, himself a sitcom writer, that appeared in *National Review* after the election of French president Nicolas Sarkozy in May 2007. In it, President Bush calls Sarkozy to congratulate him on his victory:

"Allo? Who is thees, please?"

"Sarko? Sarko, it's George Bush."

"Oh, oui. Yes. Allo, Mister *le Président*."

"Back at ya, Mr. President. Congrats, Sarko. Fabulous, fabulous victory. Really."

"Yes, well. It had the elements of the essential human crisis. Ultimately, it became a battle between a nihilist and an absurd clown."

"Um. Right."

"With me being the absurd clown, *bien sûr.*"

"Gotcha. Anyways. Just wanted to reach out and say 'hey' and tell you how happy I am that France and America are getting back to being friends."

"You know, Mister *le Président*, we are not so different. I often think of the loneliness of the open spaces that your country has—I think primarily of the magnificent sadness of *Aree-zona* or *Wee-ohming* and I would say that France, too, has her magnificent and wonderful sadness."

"Right. Right. Think that myself sometimes. But if we could maybe have some kind of new thinking on Iraq, that would—"

"As I was saying to my lover last night, as I was leaving her to return to my wife, I said to her that the stupidity and meaninglessness of philosophy can be mirrored in the *terroir* of a place, and that for man to find purpose in life, he must also grasp the concept of non-purpose, correct?"

"Hmmm? Oh, sure, yeah. Yeah. But if we could get back to Iraq—"

"My lover laughed sadly. She is depressed. She has just recently lost election to the presidency of France."

"Wait. What?"

"My lover. She is the other candidate."

"Wait. Your girlfriend was the gal who ran against you?"

"But of course."

This nicely encapsulates all of the elder culture stereotypes—as well as the stereotype of the terse, commonsense American. The new president of France cares only for obscure philosophy and illicit sexual liaisons. While the president of the United States wants to talk policy, his counterpart in Europe is more concerned with the intellectual terroir of Wyoming.

This sort of good-natured ribbing can give way to genuine hostility—and it did in the ancient world. We see this for the first time in Rome with the famous senator Cato the Elder. Cato lived through the wars in Greece in the first half of the second century BC and he did not like what he saw. He was convinced that the flood of Greeks pouring into Rome to teach the young leaders of tomorrow were, in point of fact, killing the Republic. Hard-nosed, homespun Roman values were being exchanged, he argued, for weak-kneed, eggheaded sophistry. Although Roman elites flocked to Greek doctors, who were acclaimed for their superior medical knowledge, Cato would have nothing to do with them. He reminded his countrymen that when the greatest of all Greek doctors, Hippocrates, had been offered a large fee to examine the king of Persia, he replied that he would never put his skill at the service of barbarians who were enemies of Greece. Cato was sure that Hippocrates' principle was at work among the Greek doctors in Rome, who he believed were poisoning Romans rather than curing them. To combat this, Cato even wrote his own book of home remedies, which differed markedly from Greek prescriptions. Plutarch, himself a Greek, noted with some satisfaction that "such presumption on [Cato's] part seems not to have gone unpunished, for he lost his wife and son."

When Cato visited the magnificent city of Athens and addressed the Assembly there, he scandalized the Athenians by refusing to speak Greek. Like all elite Romans, Cato could speak the language well enough, although he pretended that he could not. Instead, he addressed the Assembly through an interpreter, speaking Latin himself. He later joked that what he said in a few simple Latin words took the interpreter whole paragraphs to say in Greek. For Cato, Greek was a language of style, not substance. "The words of the Greeks are born on their lips," he said, "but those of the Romans in their hearts." Cato would have been very much at home in modern America, where postmodern French thinkers like Jacques Derrida and Michel Foucault are regularly criticized as the pinnacle of European intellectual vacuity. In characteristic fashion, Cato complained that the Greek spirit questioned everything and settled nothing.

We may assume that some Romans agreed with Cato, but most remained firmly in love with Greek culture, if not always with the Greeks themselves. The Romans of Cato's day did not come so much to hate the

Greeks, but simply to become exasperated with them. The same could not be said of the Greeks, most of whom truly loathed the Romans. Indeed, the Achaean League of Greek cities had become a hotbed of anti-Romanism. In 150 BC it was led by Diaeus, an anti-Roman extremist. He promptly issued demands, some of which the Romans granted in an attempt to win him over. This, however, only emboldened him more, leading him to conclude that Rome was a paper tiger. The idea spread across Greece. In 149 BC a Macedonian named Andriscus attempted to reunite the region and declare himself its king. The Roman consul, Metellus, and his two legions persuaded him otherwise. But Rome's patience with Macedonia was at an end. The Macedonians had demonstrated time and time again that they could not remain both free and peaceful. The Senate declared Macedonia to be a Roman province and sent a magistrate to take charge. No longer free, Macedonia would henceforward be at peace.

The Roman annexation of Macedonia had the predictable result down in Greece. Anti-Roman speeches and rallies echoed across the land. They were the loudest in the cities of the Achaean League. The Romans were widely condemned for their unprovoked conquest of the freedom-loving people of Macedonia. Not all of the Greek cities of the Achaean League, though, were so pleased with this inflammatory rhetoric. Sparta, a long-time supporter of Rome, tried to resign from the League. In retaliation, the other member cities attacked. Naturally, the Spartans sent to Rome for aid. In 147 BC the Romans sent a senator, L. Aurelius Orestes, to address the Assembly of the Achaean League regarding the matter. On behalf of the Senate and People of Rome he ordered the Achaeans to leave Sparta alone, allowing it to retain its freedom and independence. He also warned them against any further attacks on their Greek neighbors, suggesting that if they did not cease these provocations the Romans would disband the League. The Assembly erupted in shouts of outrage. A torrent of insults were heaped upon Orestes, castigating him for the arrogance of the Romans. Orestes returned to Rome and reported the situation to the Senate, which had become depressingly used to this sort of treatment from the Greeks. They sent another embassy, this one led by Sextus

Julius Caesar, in an attempt to cool heads. Caesar apologized to the Achaeans for the earlier threat to disband the League, but he reminded them that they should treat their Roman friends with more respect. The Assembly accepted the apology in stony silence.

Diaeus, the leader of the Achaean League, took the conciliatory Roman embassy as evidence of Rome's unwillingness to fight yet another war in Greece. In a direct challenge to Roman protection of Sparta, Diaeus led the League in an all-out attack on the city. The Roman commander, Metellus, led his legions south from Macedonia in an attempt to contain the war, but he had too few soldiers to stop it. And Diaeus was right—Rome did not want to fight another war in Greece. In an attempt to find a peaceful solution the Romans responded to the provocation by sending a high-level delegation of senators to meet with the Achaean Assembly in the great city of Corinth. But Diaeus had no intention of meeting with them. Instead, he led the people of the city in a mass anti-Roman demonstration, which violently turned on the visiting senators, overwhelming their bodyguards. In a desperate attempt to save themselves, the toga-clad senators ran through the streets of Corinth. Waiting for them, the locals opened their second-story windows and joyfully emptied their chamberpots on Rome's most revered men. The senators barely escaped with their lives.

The laughter and exultation among the Greeks had scarcely died down before the Romans took action. On a clear summer morning in 146 BC a squadron of warships arrived off the Greek coast. The Romans were finished talking. Their commander, Mummius, led four Roman legions against the armies of the Achaean League. After defeating them he went on to capture Corinth. The Greeks were used to seeing Roman soldiers marching into their cities. Yet this time, the Romans had not come as liberators. The citizens of Corinth had flagrantly and gleefully violated the sanctity of Rome's ambassadors. More than a provocation, this was an act of war. And it was only the latest in decades of anti-Roman activities supported or engaged in by these people. Ungrateful, sneering, and treacherous, the Greeks could no longer be trusted. The Romans had come to the reluctant conclusion that they simply could not afford to pay the extraordinary cost of a Greek liberty that the Greeks themselves valued so little.

When the dust had settled and the fighting stopped, Mummius announced that the citizens of Corinth should assemble to hear the decree of the Senate. No doubt many of them expected the Romans to read yet another scroll that confirmed Greek liberty and announced the complete withdrawal of Roman forces. Although this had been startling enough to cause birds to fall from the skies in 196 BC, fifty years later it would hardly have disturbed a housefly. The Greeks had not only come to expect it, they believed that it was their due. As free people they were entitled to have the Romans clean up their messes and leave quietly, bowing and groveling before the cultural magnificence of the Greek people.

Mummius read the decree of the Roman Senate. The people of the city of Corinth were ordered to evacuate. After its precious art objects were relocated to Rome, Corinth was to be leveled. It would literally be taken off the map. The assembled Greeks were thunderstruck. This was not at all what they had come to expect. This was not how Romans had responded in the past. It had taken half a century, but the Greeks had finally exhausted the patience of the Roman people. The Corinthians evacuated and their city was destroyed. Afterward, all of Greece was reorganized into various administrative regions supported by Roman military installations in order to keep the peace. Theoretically, the Greeks remained free. However, the close proximity of Roman forces told a different story. They would never again be allowed to wage war against each other or against the Roman people. Corinth had served its purpose. The Greeks were at last convinced that the Romans were not to be trifled with.

The peace that now descended upon Greece would last for the next four hundred years—an unprecedented achievement. Yet that does not mean that Greeks and Romans suddenly began to love and respect one another. The Greeks stopped provoking the Romans, that is true. But they still considered them to be barbarians. The poster child for Roman oafishness among Greeks became Mummius, who had overseen the destruction of Corinth. A swarm of stories spread in the Greek world that were meant to show the bumbling boorishness of this conqueror. It was said that he ordered priceless art objects packed up hodgepodge for transport to Rome, telling the movers that they would have to replace anything that they broke. Others contended that Mummius could not even tell a statue of Zeus from one of Poseidon. Still others recounted how he rounded up artwork that he did not fancy and sold it at public auction. However, when one particular piece started fetching large bids, Mummius pulled it from the block, saying that it must be good after all. All of these stories were meant to characterize Mummius, and thereby the Romans, as the ancient equivalent of cowboy capitalists—people who understood culture only in terms of monetary value. The fact that these stories were untrue, that Mummius not only appreciated Greek culture but generously restored ruined Greek temples, was irrelevant. The construction of the stereotype was complete and he was the natural one to bear it.

The luster of the Greeks had faded among the Romans. After the incident at Corinth it was no longer just Cato who distrusted and derided Greeks as immoral, tricky, and weak. Although Rome's elites still embraced Greek culture, extolled Greek customs, and complained about Roman baseness, the majority of Roman citizens did not feel that way at all. Being called a Greek-lover became a death sentence for a Roman politician, since it implied that he was a haughty dandy, not a man of the people. The Roman consul Marius, a "new man" who came from common parentage, made a virtue of the fact that he had no education at all in Greek learning. "Nor have I studied Greek literature," he boasted. "I had no interest in a branch of learning which did nothing to improve the characters of its professors." Cicero, another new man, remembered that his grandfather used to say that "the better one learns Greek the more a scoundrel one becomes." Although Cicero himself was thoroughly educated in Greek learning, on the political campaign stump he pretended not to remember the names of Greek artists and liberally dished out contempt for Roman elites who affected Greek manners. Even among Rome's patrician class it was a good idea to hide one's familiarity with Greek ways. Two rival Roman orators in the late second century BC,

L. Crassus and M. Antonius, chafed under the label Greek-lovers. Crassus claimed to hate Greek learning, while Antonius claimed to be completely unfamiliar with it.

The similarities between the relationship of the Greeks and Romans in the second century BC and that of the Americans and western Europeans in the twentieth and twenty-first centuries are apparent. Of course, American-European relations have not yet sunk to the chamberpot-dumping, Corinth-destroying level. But there is no doubt that anti-Americanism is a powerful force in Europe, while anti-Europeanism is growing in the United States. Nevertheless, while the dynamics at work are similar, the facts on the ground are different. Rome twice invaded Greece in order to crush its dictators and conquerors and twice withdrew its troops, guaranteeing the freedom of the Greek city-states. The United States did that only once—in World War I. The second time—after World War II—the Americans decided to stay. They did so not only to protect western Europeans from a powerful outside empire, the Soviet Union, but also to keep the peace among the European states, which would receive an American guarantee of freedom in the NATO alliance. A good thing, too, for the Romans were ultimately forced to return to Greece, push out Antiochus, and conquer most of the Seleucid Empire, all at the cost of much Roman blood.

Both elder cultures were given the protection of the Empire of Trust and, while enjoying those benefits, began to hate the empire itself. Of course, not all western Europeans hate America, just as not all Greeks hated the Romans. But a great many did and do—and for much the same reasons. It is a hatred brewed from a mixture of potent ingredients, including strong feelings of cultural superiority, relative military weakness, and dependence on the "barbarians" for security. Unable and unwilling to reject the Empire of Trust, the elder cultures content themselves with chiding it for its "arrogance" (i.e., the empire does not do what it is told) and urging it to act multilaterally (i.e., the empire should do what it is told). We have already seen this in the ancient world and it is only too easy to demonstrate it in our own time. Simply peruse the numerous books and essays written by Europeans and elite Americans urging the

United States to stop acting alone and start acting in concert with world opinion. Anatol Lieven's *America Right or Wrong: An Anatomy of American Nationalism* (2004) and Will Hutton's *Declaration of Interdependence: Why America Should Join the World* (2004) are just two examples.

It is worth noting that the anti-Roman Greeks in Greece were not the only Greeks in the ancient world. Greek people in the cities and kingdoms of Asia Minor and Rhodes, whom the Romans later liberated from the Seleucid Empire, remained pro-Roman for a very long time. In that respect, they resembled modern eastern Europeans, who still remain deeply grateful for the role the United States played in their liberation from the Soviet Union. Compare, for example, the attitudes expressed in the Romanian Parliament in May 2007 when the lawmakers there voted 257–1 to allow up to three thousand American troops to be permanently stationed in their country. Prime Minister Călin Popescu-Tăriceanu praised the vote, saying that for decades Romanians had "only one hope: that the American troops would come and free us from communism. [Today,] Romania is no longer a victim looking for a savior, but a partner of the United States." If ancient history is any guide, countries like Romania, Poland, Hungary, and Bulgaria will remain strong allies of the United States for many years to come.

The case of Britain is also different. Given its close association with the founding of the United States, it has more in common with the Etruscan relationship to Rome. Although Britain is a member of the European Union, the relationship between the two is by any reckoning a strained one. Conversely, the "special relationship" between Britain and the United States is quite solid. The common bonds of history, language, and culture are so strong that Americans and Brits cannot avoid seeing a reflection of themselves when they look at each other from across the "pond." This is not to say that anti-Americanism does not exist in England. It does—but at nowhere near the levels that it is found on the Continent. Indeed, it is not much more prevalent in Britain than it is among America's own elites. Except for a brief moment in 2003 as the Iraq War was heating up, British public opinion has been steadfastly and overwhelmingly pro-American. It is not just England, but much of the old

British Empire that continues to come more and more into the American orbit. Like the peoples of ancient Italy, the countries of the so-called "Anglosphere," including Australia, Canada, and New Zealand, find that they have much more in common with each other than with the rest of the world. Naturally, this draws them together. When Prime Minister Tony Blair of Britain addressed a joint session of the Australian Parliament on March 27, 2006, he did not decry American arrogance or imperialism. Quite the opposite, to an approving audience he proclaimed: "The danger with America today is not that they are too much involved. The danger is that they decide to pull up the drawbridge and disengage. We need them involved. We want them engaged." It is much more difficult to imagine such a speech being made by a leader in Brussels, Rome, or Madrid.

Taken as a whole, American relations with continental western Europe seem to have much in common with relations between Romans and Greeks in the 170s BC. This fits well with the level of Roman power in the world at that point when compared to the similar level of American power today. But can the example of ancient Greece give us some clues about the future of Europe? For example, should we expect to see in thirty or forty years American troops marching into a European capital, removing the art, and toppling the buildings? Probably not. History is a wonderful teacher, but a poor fortune-teller. We can use it to help us understand our world, but we should not expect history to repeat itself in a way that can be divined beforehand. Although relations between the United States and western Europe may continue to decline, that does not mean that we will witness another Corinth. The Romans only took that action after the Greeks themselves banded together in the Achaean League and attacked their neighbors. As the guarantors of Greek liberty, the Romans could not allow a Greek military power to conquer other Greeks.

But is such a thing possible in Europe? Could Europeans join together to build a powerful military machine? That is clearly the hope that many Europeans today have for the EU. Americans are frequently reminded that the combined GDP of the EU countries exceeds that of the United

States. Similarly, the EU boasts that its members have a combined military force of some two million soldiers. American active duty personnel only numbers about 1.5 million. It is not surprising, then, that some European leaders have begun to talk about creating a single EU military in order to "balance American hegemony." Prime Minister (now President) Zapatero of Spain has said that "Europe must believe that it can be in twenty years the most important world power." If that happened, if an EU military force began threatening pro-American governments that refused to join the league, then, yes, the United States would necessarily have to become involved—just as the Romans did in Greece. In truth, though, the United States would almost certainly take some form of economic, diplomatic, or even military action long before an effective EU military force appeared.

But all of that is extremely unlikely. President Zapatero's dreams to the contrary, it is difficult to imagine a scenario in which Europeans would be able to combine into one, effective military force. Like the ancient Greeks, western Europeans have never combined their strength unless under the heel of conquering dictators. Public opinion polls in Europe continue to show low levels of identification with the EU. Predictions of a new European superpower, therefore, are neither convincing nor borne out by the facts. It is worth pointing out that only 3 to 5 percent of those touted two million European troops are actually trained and ready for military deployment. The rest are in service positions, office jobs, or used for public works around their countries. Perhaps the clearest example of this is the extraordinary difficulty that EU countries had in deploying just forty thousand battle-ready troops to Kosovo, which is in Europe itself. And once they arrived they were largely ineffectual. The war stopped only when American power was deployed to the region. More recently the EU has begun the creation of "battle groups," military forces available for rapid deployment. On January 1, 2007, the battle groups were declared to have reached "full operational capability." They consist of two deployable units of fifteen hundred soldiers each. By contrast, the United States has approximately a hundred thousand soldiers deployed in Europe alone.

Europeans today have strong economies but weak militaries. Economies are, in any case, beside the point. It is a fallacy to believe that powerful militaries are only sustainable by powerful economies. That has never been true. The Soviet Union, with an economy smaller than that of the state of California, managed to develop and deploy a military larger and more lethal than that of the United States. China currently has the largest army in the world, with a GDP one-sixth the size of the United States. Ancient Rome had its largest military force in the third century AD—when its economy was in shambles. Besides, the combined GDP of all EU countries is only slightly larger than the United States' single figure. In short, it seems very unlikely that anti-Americanism in Europe will ever translate into anything more than graffiti and rude waiters. And Americans are used to that.

As for the people of the United States, like the Romans more than two thousand years ago they still love European culture but are starting to find European attitudes a bit tiresome. In 2003 the French refusal to support the U.S. invasion of Iraq and President Jacques Chirac's comments criticizing those European countries that did engendered plenty of bad feelings among Americans. Suddenly the cafeterias on Capitol Hill were offering "freedom fries" and the term *cheese-eating surrender monkeys* for a time came into common parlance (although originally coined on *The Simpsons* years earlier). The late-night comedians in the United States started churning out jokes about the French that a Roman in 100 BC would have understood perfectly if said about the Greeks. Dennis Miller, for example, remarked that "the only way the French are going in is if we tell them we found truffles in Iraq." Jay Leno later quipped that "American tourists in Paris are reported to being yelled at, spit upon, and attacked by the French. Thank God things are getting back to normal."

Just as in ancient Rome, these popular sentiments are naturally reflected in American politics. In the 2004 presidential election John Kerry ran as a candidate who would restore credibility to the United States in the eyes of the European allies. To many Americans, though, that sounded like taking orders from the French. It did not help matters that Kerry and his wife spoke French and were clearly people of elite tastes. When Kerry was shown in opinion polls to be the overwhelming favorite of western Europeans the damage was done. In other words, Kerry's familiarity with and appreciation for European culture actually worked against him. As Cicero could have told him, it is best to hide such things while on the campaign stump.

Events in the ancient world make depressingly clear that anti-Americanism in Europe, while frustrating, is to be expected. There is no reason to believe that it will subside anytime soon. Indeed, anti-Romanism never did decline among the Greeks until they themselves became Roman citizens several centuries later. That is not in the cards for Europeans—at least not in the near term. But it might be of some comfort to Americans to know that for a thousand years after the Roman Empire fell in the Latin-speaking world, after Rome had been sacked by German barbarians and its people scattered, the Greeks in the East still proudly and defiantly called themselves "Romans."

Chapter 7

How an Empire of Trust Grows . . .
and Grows

In Egypt, at the eastern edge of the Nile Delta, stood the prosperous and well-fortified city of Pelusium. In 168 BC it was a city in trouble. Although a part of the Ptolemaic Empire, Pelusium was slated to become the first conquest of King Antiochus IV, the ruler of the Seleucid Empire of Syria. Antiochus had marched his great armies into the area and established a military camp. The weak king Ptolemy in Alexandria was powerless to defend Pelusium or stop the invasion. But he did have some good friends. Ptolemy had previously sent word to the Senate in Rome, appealing for aid against Antiochus. Responding favorably, the Senate had dispatched a small Roman force to Egypt under the command of Caius Popilius Laenas. Popilius carried with him a copy of the *senatus consultum*—the decree of the Senate. When he and his men arrived on the muddy banks near Pelusium it was obvious to everyone that the city could not hold out against Antiochus. But Popilius took no military action. None was needed. Instead, bringing some of his friends and staff, he walked calmly into the Seleucid camp, making his way directly toward the tent of the king. Hearing of the visitors, the king quickly came out to meet them. With a broad smile Antiochus extended his hand to Popilius in a gesture of friendship. Rather than the Roman's hand in return, Antiochus received only the *senatus consultum*. The king unrolled the decree and read it hastily. It was short and to the point. The Senate and People of Rome ordered the king to cease his war against Ptolemy, who was a Roman ally.

When Antiochus looked up from the scroll he saw the stern faces of the Romans. They were serious, that much was clear. The Roman commander tersely asked Antiochus whether or not he would obey the Senate's decree. The king needed time to think. After all, he had sufficient forces on hand to conquer Egypt with ease. There was nothing that Popilius and his few countrymen could do about that. But then what? Would the Romans declare war against him in defense of their Egyptian allies? Yes, he knew that they would. He *trusted* that they would, just as Ptolemy had trusted that they would. Perhaps, Antiochus thought, a compromise could be worked out. He responded that it was necessary for him to first confer with his councilors and nobles about this serious matter. He would summon the Romans again when he had made his decision.

What followed was an awkward moment of silence. Popilius bowed his head slightly and then from the corner of his eye caught sight of a nearby grapevine. Without a word he walked over to it and, drawing his short sword, cut off a sturdy stick. He then walked back to Antiochus and traced a circle in the dirt around the king. Tossing the stick aside, Popilius told him to take all the time he wished to make his decision. But he must do so before leaving the circle. The king was astonished. The Romans were resolute. If Antiochus was Rome's friend, he would respect Rome's allies. There was no need to confer on that point. After several minutes of anxious hesitation in which Antiochus quickly weighed his options he at last spoke. He agreed to withdraw his forces from Egypt just as the Roman Senate had decreed. Instantly, the hard demeanor of Popilius and his fellow Romans melted. Smiling warmly, they came forward to shake Antiochus' hand and embrace him as their very good friend.

This episode on the banks of the Nile provides a vivid snapshot of the power and methods of a mature Empire of Trust. Over several centuries the Romans had gained a solid reputation for the responsible use of power and a determination to protect their allies. Even at Pelusium, when the two remaining empires of the Hellenistic World were on the brink of war, the Romans were able to call the whole thing off simply by sending a scroll. But it was the contents of that scroll that mattered, for it held the determination of the Roman people to keep the peace.

That determination was backed by the extraordinary power that Rome now wielded. Some fifty years earlier a similar delegation to the city of Saguntum in Spain had been sent packing by Hannibal, who would not be ordered about by the Romans. But back then Hannibal had commanded forces that were at least equivalent to Rome's. Antiochus, who was easily as powerful as Hannibal had been in 220 BC, was no match for the Romans in 168 BC. And he knew it. He may have resented the arrogance of the circle-drawing incident, but he was in no position to object. The Romans offered him friendship or war and Antiochus knew that they would be faithful in whatever choice he made.

As we saw in the last chapter, Roman power continued to grow in the decades after this incident in Egypt. There is no getting around the fact that by 146 BC the Romans had acquired a truly impressive empire. Aside from turning Macedonia and much of Greece into provinces, they had also recently conquered their old enemy, Carthage, and turned the land around it into the Roman province of Africa. A glance at a map of the Mediterranean at about this time also shows that Rome's empire included Italy, Sicily, Corsica, Sardinia, part of southern Gaul, and most of Spain. Pretty good work for a bunch of barbarians. Even the Greeks had to admit that Rome had become a great empire. Indeed, Polybius wrote his history of Rome in Greek so that foreigners would be able to understand the new superpower. "For who is so worthless or lazy," he asked, "not to wish to know by what means and under what system of government the Romans in less than fifty-three years have succeeded in subjecting nearly the whole inhabited world to their sole rule—a thing unprecedented in history?"

But no Roman would have admitted to such a thing. Even Polybius did not mean that the Romans had actually conquered the world (they hadn't, after all), but rather that almost everyone in the known world

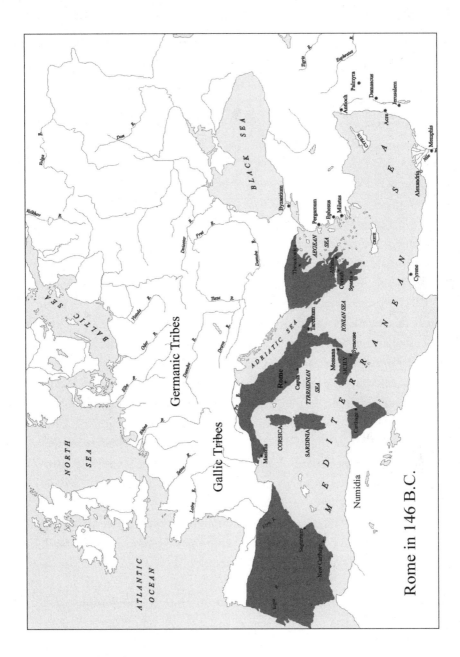

Rome in 146 B.C.

now had to obey them. And as for our map of the empire, a Roman at the time would have strongly denied its accuracy. Rome, he would have insisted, was no empire. It was a state and a people. That was all. With the exception of a few places like Veii or Capua, Italy was not under Roman rule. It was made up of free allies. The same went for most of the Greek cities. Even provinces like Sicily or Macedonia, a Roman would insist, were not part of an empire. They were merely administrative arrangements created in order to keep peace and provide order for Rome's friends. To say that Sicilians or Greeks were citizens of a Roman Empire was not only an insult to those proud and free people, but a lie. Rome was Rome, our Roman would insist. Nothing more. It had organized a powerful coaltion of allies, but it was simply a first among equals.

Technically, that Roman would be right. Yet no historian today would take him very seriously. For all practical purposes our map is correct, for the shaded areas were under the control and/or protection of the Roman confederation, which was headquartered, after all, in Rome. In all but strictly local matters, the Romans were the ones calling the shots.

Now let's try the same exercise with a modern American. Look at another map—this one of the American Empire. The map on pages 166–167 is a depiction of current American troop deployments around the world. What is most startling is the small number of countries that do *not* have American troops in them. Even if we exclude countries with fewer than ten thousand American troops, we are still including a large number of countries around the world. This sort of map makes a compelling case that the United States is not only an empire, but that it is, in fact, the largest one in history. The greatest conquerors who have ever lived only dreamed of a military presence as expansive as the United States has already achieved.

Like our Roman friend, though, most Americans would strongly deny that the United States is in any way an empire. It is the United States— that is all. Yes, it is true that hundreds of thousands of American troops are deployed around the world. But those forces do not constitute an empire. Most of them are assisting or defending our friends and allies, all of whom remain free. It would be an insult to the Germans or Italians or

Japanese to categorize them as subjects of an American Empire. They are free, proud peoples. America has no empire.

Technically, that American would also be right. But will future historians agree? Or will they gloss over the technicalities and simply speak of a growing empire of the United States—the way that we speak of Rome today? Much, of course, depends on the future of American power, something that we will discuss later. For now, though, it is worth noting that Americans today and Romans before 146 BC did not see their numerous alliances and organizations as anything other than a means toward a safe, secure, and prosperous life for themselves and their allies. The historian Erich Gruen has argued that the Romans only came to the realization that they had an empire sometime in the late second or early first century BC. And even then it came as a shock. "Overseas empire as an articulated concept," he writes, "gained formulation only after Rome had achieved it as a fact. Worldwide supremacy appears first not as a goal but as an accomplishment." When the Roman statesman Cicero later looked back on Roman history he remarked that in those early days "our government could be called more accurately a protectorate of the world rather than an empire."

In the same way, despite decades of being labeled imperialists by foreigners and years of citizenship in the world's only superpower, not many Americans have concluded that they are citizens of an empire. Americans remain firmly isolationist, even as they insist on interventionism. More than three-quarters of Americans today believe that the United States should share world leadership with others, each carrying an equal load. Since the fall of the Soviet Union, polls have consistently shown that only about one in ten Americans believe that the United States should be the single most important leader in the world. Clearly, there is a deep-seated desire among Americans to see the United States as no more than a first among equals.

But that is as much a fiction today as it was in 146 BC. When engaging in military activities it may console Americans to hear about what "we and our coalition partners" are doing, but the fact remains that it is the United States that is responsible for almost all of the doing. At the time

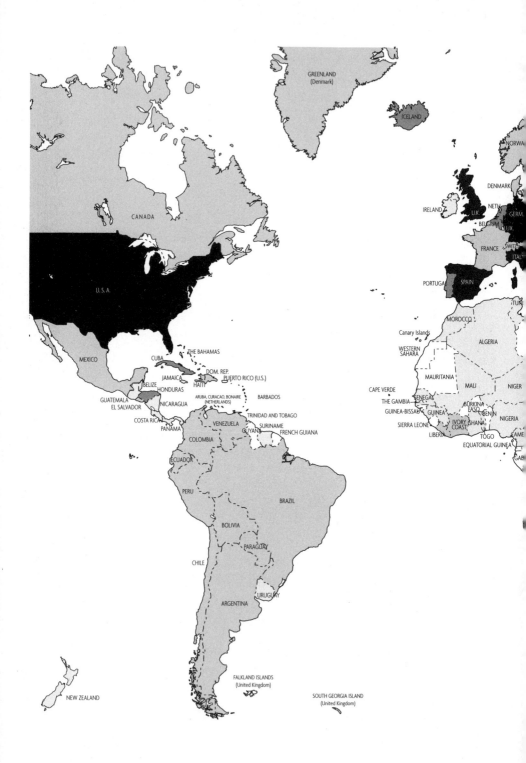

GREENLAND
(Denmark)

ICELAND

NORWAY

CANADA

DENMARK

IRELAND
U.K.
NETH.
BELGIUM
LUX.
GERM.

FRANCE
SWITZ.
ITALY

PORTUGAL
SPAIN

TURK

U. S. A.

MOROCCO

Canary Islands

WESTERN
SAHARA

ALGERIA

MEXICO

THE BAHAMAS

CUBA

DOM. REP.

JAMAICA
HAITI
PUERTO RICO (U.S.)

MAURITANIA

MALI

NIGER

BELIZE
HONDURAS
GUATEMALA
EL SALVADOR
NICARAGUA

BARBADOS

CAPE VERDE

THE GAMBIA
SENEGAL

BURKINA
FASO

BENIN
NIGERIA

GUINEA-BISSAU
GUINEA
IVORY
COAST
GHANA
TOGO

COSTA RICA
PANAMA

ARUBA, CURACAO, BONAIRE
(NETHERLANDS)
TRINIDAD AND TOBAGO

VENEZUELA
GUYANA
SURINAME
FRENCH GUIANA

SIERRA LEONE
LIBERIA

EQUATORIAL GUINEA

CAME

GAB

COLOMBIA

ECUADOR

PERU

BRAZIL

BOLIVIA

PARAGUAY

CHILE

URUGUAY

ARGENTINA

NEW ZEALAND

FALKLAND ISLANDS
(United Kingdom)

SOUTH GEORGIA ISLAND
(United Kingdom)

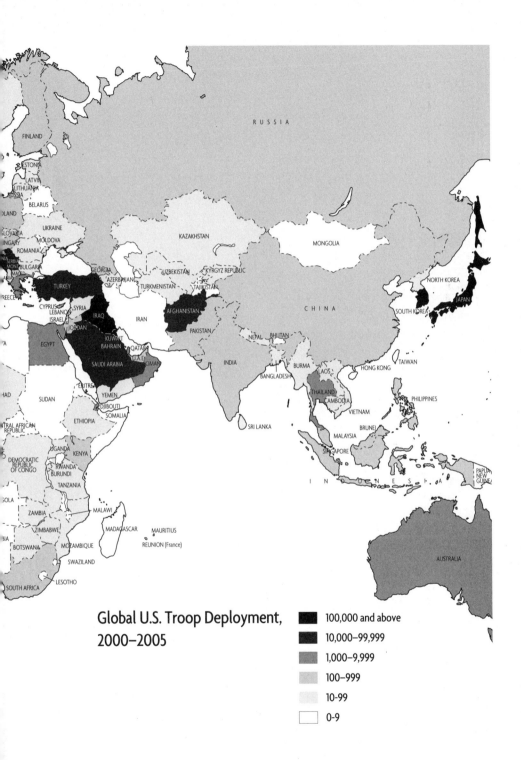

Global U.S. Troop Deployment,
2000–2005

- 100,000 and above
- 10,000–99,999
- 1,000–9,999
- 100–999
- 10–99
- 0–9

of this writing, although almost two dozen countries are members of the coalition forces in Iraq, the combined number of troops from countries other than the United States is somewhere around 14,000—half of which come from the United Kingdom. By contrast, American forces in Iraq currently number around 160,000. In other words, one member of the "Coalition of the Willing"—the United States—constitutes 90 percent of its total troop strength. Similarly mismatched ratios were seen in other "coalition efforts" such as the First Gulf War and the Korean War.

Given such ratios, it is safe to say that the United States could undertake these various military actions without any coalition help whatsoever. Well, actually, it is *not* safe to say that. In fact, it would be political suicide for an elected leader in the United States to say any such thing. It suggests that the United States should "thumb its nose at the world" or "go it alone," both of which smack of an imperial arrogance that Americans abhor. That aversion to the idea of empire, to unilateralism, to world domination, is crucial to understanding the dynamics behind both America's and Rome's rapid rise to power.

The year 146 BC is a good place to stop a moment in our trek through Roman history, since it was then that the Romans reached a supremacy in their world not unlike that achieved by Americans today. What is both startling and rare, at least from a historical perspective, is that neither state sought that supremacy. Indeed, both went out of their way to deny that it existed at all. It was this fact that led other states and peoples to trust them with an unprecedented concentration of power that would ultimately lead to an Empire of Trust. Trust was crucial. It took centuries to build up and would take centuries more to erode. In this chapter we will look more closely at the basic components of that trust and the dynamics that these two empires shared. In other words, we will strip away the chassis of events and watch the motor hum underneath.

The first of these components is a profound distrust of concentrated power. For most human cultures a concentration of power into the hands of a leader and possibly his nobility or inner circle is the norm. Kings, emperors, sultans, khans, chiefs, rajahs, pharaohs—they all work on this same basic principle. The power of the ruler is frequently defended or justified by religion or ideology, although in some cases brute force is sufficient. While many people in those cultures might wish to supplant the ruler, few have a problem with the concept itself. The Romans did. Americans do. Both of these peoples forged their states in reaction to royal authority and both were determined to build political systems that would resist tyrants and despots. They did this by dividing authority among different groups and introducing plenty of checks and balances on the exercise of power. Both were republics. Indeed, as we saw earlier, the American republic was consciously modeled on the Roman one.

This is important for two reasons. First, this distrust of concentrated power is transferred to the state's foreign relations. Just as no one person should have preeminent power in ancient Rome or modern America, so also their citizens believe that no such preeminence should exist among nations either. Like citizens, nations should be equal, each working for the benefit of the whole. That's what an alliance is all about. Second, the republican form of government precludes the capriciousness of a conqueror. This is important for the development of foreign trust. When a garden-variety emperor or king makes a treaty with an ally he may keep it—if it is in his interest to do so. That means that the trust levels between states when traditional monarchies are involved is not very high. The monarch can be trusted to keep his word as long as he wishes—and no longer. But Rome had no monarch. There was no one to decide one day over breakfast that he wanted to attack his neighbor after all. There was no spoiled brat heir to throw away his deceased father's friendships. There was only the Senate and People of Rome. And they were ruled by laws, not men. The same dynamics are at work in the United States. The president (whatever his critics may say) is no king. His power and term of office are strictly limited. Although foreign powers may not like the president or his policies, they know that he is bound by laws that not only restrict him, but insure that he will not be around for very long.

The second important component of the Empire of Trust is an isolation that breeds isolationism. Both the Americans and the Romans rejected outside powers at the beginning of their history—in the case of Rome, the Etruscan kings; in the case of America, the British kings. Their relative isolation in frontier societies shaped their culture. However, this isolation also protected them, for it meant that the great powers of their world were very far away. In their early days the Romans were able to deal with military threats from Etruscans, Latins, Campanians, and the like because they were, from a world perspective, small-fry. The same is true for the United States. There were no serious threats to its existence in its first century of history. The European powers were far away and although American Indians could be troublesome, there was no danger of them marching into Washington, D.C. This isolation, mixed with the rejection of outside control, led to a deep-seated isolationism among the people of both states.

Isolationism did not mean that the people of the two empires were not interested in learning about the outside world or even doing business with it. But they did want it to remain firmly outside. They considered the projection of power beyond their borders, no matter how often it occurred, to be an anomaly. By creating alliances, both the United States and Rome were able to build large and powerful empires while still remaining fundamentally isolationist. The sole purpose of those alliances was to provide security—first for the homeland and then, by necessity, for the allies. Security and isolationism always went hand-in-hand. It was the constant search for an unattainable total security that led both peoples into their Empires of Trust.

The Roman statesman Cicero famously remarked, "By defending our allies our people have gained the whole world." This sums up the visible dynamic that led to the rise of Roman power. Faithful, strong, and isolationist, the Romans posed a threat only to those who attacked them or their allies. For them, Cicero was stating the obvious when he wrote that "no war can be undertaken by a just and wise state, unless out of faithfulness or self-defense.... And no war can be considered just unless it is duly announced and proclaimed and preceded by a reasonable demand for restitution." Each new conquest brought new conquered people, whom the Romans then turned into allies. The alternative—annexing their conquests or ruling over them—was contrary to the isolationism of the Roman character.

It is precisely these ideas that led to some of history's most extraordinary spectacles: massive Roman invasions of Greece, Africa, and Asia Minor and then the complete withdrawal of all Roman forces from the conquered regions. If the Romans sought an empire, why repeatedly withdraw from hard-won conquests? What other empire in history has done such a thing unless forced? For the Romans, though, it was a natural choice, flowing out of their isolationism. Rather than an empire, the Romans wanted peaceful friends. And so conquered enemies were transformed into friends. Only when a region proved itself incapable of remaining peaceful did the Romans annex it as a province—as they later did in Greece, Macedonia, and Africa.

In this phase the Empire of Trust grows through a positive action of the state and people. In other words, it is being pushed. Romans and Americans made a conscious decision to fight long and difficult wars in order to build and defend alliances and defeat those who disturbed the peace. Success in these wars led to conquered states lying prostrate at the feet of the Empire of Trust. In both cases the conquered were picked up, dusted off, and accepted as friends. This had the effect of expanding the alliance, which in turn made the homeland safer. However, it also meant that Romans and Americans were responsible for helping to defend states that were farther and farther from home.

At a certain point the dynamic of the push is replaced by that of the pull. To give an example, by the early third century BC the Romans were, because of the extent of their alliances, feeling relatively secure. They controlled most of central and northern Italy and had made some friends among the Greeks to the south. In building the confederation they had acquired a reputation for faithfulness toward allies and mercy toward enemies. It was this reputation that began a pull toward empire from the outside. We saw it with the city of Thurii, which asked the Romans for an alliance because they feared the power of their neighbor, Tarentum. We saw it also with Messana, with Saguntum, with Athens, and with numerous other cases. In each instance it was a reputation for strength and trustworthiness that led foreigners to appeal to Rome for aid. The foreigners knew that the Romans could protect them from their enemies.

In return, the Romans asked that the foreigners assist with the common defense and keep the peace, thus further augmenting Roman military power. It was trust that pulled the Romans beyond Italy, ultimately across the known world, to the far reaches of their Empire of Trust.

How was this trust understood? Well, let's hear about it from those who actually had it. In 189 BC the Greeks of Rhodes sent an embassy to the Senate in Rome to speak about the situation in Asia Minor. The legions had just finished ejecting King Antiochus from the region and the Romans needed to decide what to do with their newly conquered lands—particularly those states that had sided with Antiochus. The Rhodeans made a startling suggestion—give everything away. They asked the Roman conquerors to withdraw and leave the Hellenistic cities and kingdoms of Asia Minor as independent states. The ambassador told the assembled senators:

> Wherever your arms have penetrated, there also should the laws of Rome penetrate. Let barbarians, who have the commands of their masters for their laws, keep their kings to their joy. The Greeks submit to their fate, but they have the same love of freedom that you have. At one time they too grasped at empire in their own strength, now they pray that where the seat of empire is there it may remain. It is enough for them to protect their freedom with your arms. "But," it may be argued, "some cities took sides with Antiochus." Yes, and others before that with Philip, the Tarentines sided with Pyrrhus, not to mention others. Even Carthage remains free under her own laws. See, senators, how you are bound by this precedent that you yourselves have established?

The argument here is not that the Greeks of Asia Minor deserved to be given their freedom. They did not—and no other empire would have considered such a proposal. But the ambassador appealed to the Romans' own unique standards—of mercy, fidelity, and friendship. He reminded the senators of previous enemies who deserved harsh treatment but who, when conquered, were allowed to live freely as allies of Rome.

Although the Romans could be trusted to act mercifully, they could also be trusted to act decisively to defend themselves and their allies. Roman alliances were not just handshakes and friendly words. They were legally binding treaties. Even Rome's critics admitted that they painstakingly kept their word. It was this trustworthiness that would pull the Romans into an increasing number of conflicts. And it is this dynamic that explains why an isolationist people found themselves so often dealing with problems in faraway lands. The trust that they had established, the reputation that they forged, pulled them into an empire while simultaneously allowing them to deny that it existed at all.

A vivid example of this can be seen by simply opening up a Bible. In 161 BC the Jewish people were in a difficult fix. Their position was never too enviable, wedged as they were between the Hellenistic empires of the Seleucids in Syria and the Ptolemies in Egypt. But at that moment they found themselves on the bad side of the king of the Seleucid Empire, who was making plans to conquer Jerusalem. Although the Jews lived more than a thousand miles away from Rome, they had nevertheless heard of the Romans. In fact, they had heard quite a lot about them—not all of it correct.

> [They heard what the Romans] had done in the land of Spain to get control of the silver and gold mines there, and how they had gained control of the whole region by their planning and patience, even though the place was far distant from them. They also subdued the kings who came against them from the ends of the earth, until they crushed them and inflicted great disaster upon them; the rest paid them tribute every year. Philip, and Perseus king of the Macedonians, and the others who rose up against them, they crushed in battle and conquered. They also defeated Antiochus the Great, king of Asia, who went to fight against them with a hundred and twenty elephants and with cavalry and chariots and a very large army. He was crushed by them. (1 Maccabees 8:3–6)

All of that was true. But when it came to the Roman system of government, which was unusual, after all, the Jews were less clear. They believed that:

... not one of them has put on a crown or worn purple as a mark of pride, but they have built for themselves a senate chamber, and every day three hundred and twenty senators constantly deliberate concerning the people, to govern them well. They trust one man each year to rule over them and to control their land; they all heed the one man, and there is no envy or jealousy among them. (1 Maccabees 8:14–16)

Although this is a fair description of the Senate, except in the gravest emergencies the Romans did not give that sort of power to one man, even for a year. But the basic idea—that the Romans were not ruled by kings—was clearly understood in distant Jerusalem.

The leader of the Jews, Judas Maccabeus, decided to turn to the Romans for help. He had "heard of the fame of the Romans, that they were very strong and were well-disposed toward all who made an alliance with them, that they pledged friendship to those who came to them." (1 Maccabees 8:1) Even from the other side of the Mediterranean, Judas knew that "with their friends and those who rely on them they have kept friendship." (1 Maccabees 8:12) Here we see plainly the pulling principle at work. The Jews were threatened by a great power—one that the Romans had had problems with before. A Seleucid conquest of Jerusalem, furthermore, could threaten the balance of power in the East, which would itself be a danger to Rome's friends in Egypt. But none of this was important to Judas. All that he knew was that the Romans were strong, feared, and faithful to their friends. He wanted to be one of those friends.

Judas chose two envoys:

... and sent them to Rome to establish friendship and alliance, and to free themselves from the yoke; for they saw that the kingdom of the Greeks was completely enslaving Israel. They went to Rome, a very long journey; and they entered the senate chamber and spoke as follows:

"Judas, who is also called Maccabeus, and his brothers and the people of the Jews have sent us to you to establish alliance and peace with you, that we may be enrolled as your allies and friends."

The proposal pleased them [the Romans], and this is a copy of the letter which they wrote in reply, on bronze tablets, and sent to Jerusalem to remain with them there as a memorial of peace and alliance:

"May all go well with the Romans and with the nation of the Jews at sea and on land for ever, and may sword and enemy be far from them. If war comes first to Rome or to any of their allies in all their dominion, the nation of the Jews shall act as their allies wholeheartedly, as the occasion may indicate to them. And to the enemy who makes war they shall not give or supply grain, arms, money, or ships, as Rome has decided; and they shall keep their obligations without receiving any return. In the same way, if war comes first to the nation of the Jews, the Romans shall willingly act as their allies, as the occasion may indicate to them. And to the enemy allies shall be given no grain, arms, money, or ships, as Rome has decided; and they shall keep these obligations and do so without deceit. Thus on these terms the Romans make a treaty with the Jewish people. If after these terms are in effect both parties shall determine to add or delete anything, they shall do so at their discretion, and any addition or deletion that they may make shall be valid.

"And concerning the wrongs which King Demetrius is doing to them we have written to him as follows, 'Why have you made your yoke heavy upon our friends and allies the Jews? If now they appeal again for help against you, we will defend their rights and fight you on sea and land.'" (1 Maccabees 8: 19–32)

And so the Romans had gained a new ally—the Jewish people. It is striking, though, that although Rome was immensely powerful and the Jews distant and weak, the treaty is still one between equals. Indeed, it is the same sort of treaty that the Romans had made with their earliest allies in Italy centuries before. Then as now the treaty was taken so seriously that it was inscribed on bronze tablets and displayed for public view so that every Roman would understand his or her responsibilities. The immediate effect of the treaty is also made clear. The Jews were no longer just a small kingdom, but the allies of Rome. And so, as they had done many times before, the Romans sent word to the aggressor ordering him to cease attacking their friend or face the consequences.

An alliance with Rome had become a highly desirable thing—at least for those who feared their neighbors. As the African king Adherbal observed around 118 BC:

> I always believed my father's assurance that those who diligently cultivated your friendship were recompensed for the arduous task they had to perform by the enjoyment of unequalled security. He instructed us to seek the friendship of no one but the Roman people ... all the protection we could need, he said, would be given to us by our friendship with you; and if Fortune ever deserted the Roman empire, we must be prepared to fall with it. In the meantime, thanks to your own merits and the favor of the gods, you are great and prosperous, and the worldwide influence and dominion you have won make it easy for you to redress the wrongs done to your allies.

It was this trust in Roman faithfulness and strength that led to a rising number of appeals for aid from all over a dangerous world.

By the beginning of the first century BC it was dawning on the Romans that they had acquired something that resembled an empire. A similar realization is only now coming to Americans as they find themselves drawn into more and more conflicts, crises, and problems across the world. Nevertheless, both the Americans and the ancient Romans still held to the principle that their empire was a collection of free peoples, bound together for the common defense. Take, for example, the speech attributed to the Roman leader Sulla, who met with the all-but-defeated king Bocchus of Mauretania in 108 BC. The king had sided with Rome's enemy, but decided to change sides when a Roman victory became evident. Destroying Bocchus and his forces would have been child's play for Sulla. Instead, he accepted him as a friend and equal, telling him:

The Roman people have always preferred—even from those early days when they possessed nothing—to obtain friends rather than slaves, and have deemed it safer to rule by consent than by force. For you [Bocchus], no friendship is more advantageous than ours: in the first place, because the distance between us will minimize opportunities for discord, while not diminishing the effectiveness of our support; secondly, because we already have plenty of subjects, whereas neither we nor anyone else ever has enough friends.... Finally, let me impress upon you that there has never yet been a time when the Romans have allowed themselves to be outdone in generosity. I say nothing about what they can do in war—that, you have learned by personal experience.

Thus far we have heard plenty of good things about the Romans. No one should get the impression, though, that they were a nation of saints. Very often they did not live up to their standards. What makes a people trustworthy, though, is not simply their general faithfulness, but also how they respond when that faith is not kept. An empire can do what it wishes, yet an Empire of Trust must uphold that trust and, when it is violated, must act quickly to punish the guilty and provide restitution to the injured. We have already seen two occasions of violated trust in Roman history. The first occurred 280 BC during the Pyrrhic War when the Roman commander Decius and his men were sent to Rhegium to garrison and protect the town. Claiming that the leading men were planning to give the city to Pyrrhus, Decius had them killed and he and his men helped themselves to their wives. The response in Rome was to send new troops to Rhegium who restored the city to its citizens and arrested the guilty Romans. Decius committed suicide while his accomplices were beaten and decapitated in Rome.

At the beginning of this book we also witnessed the dramatic events at Locri. Having broken its alliance with Rome, Locri was captured and garrisoned by Scipio, who left Pleminius and a Roman contingent to hold it until the Senate decided its fate. But Pleminius and his men exacted their own vengeance for the treachery of the Locrians, who had betrayed the Roman people. They beat, raped, and killed many while stripping them of their goods. They even pillaged the sacred temple of Proserpine. The Locrians complained to the Roman Senate, which ordered the arrest of the accused Romans. They were brought back to Rome to stand trial and were subsequently executed for their crimes. In this case the Romans punished their own people for treating treacherously the Locrians, who had themselves treacherously allied with Hannibal to destroy Rome. Yet Pleminius and his men had broken trust, the lifeblood of the alliance. What they had done, as all the senators agreed, was simply un-Roman.

Those were not isolated events in Roman history. A similar incident occurred in Greece in 171 BC during the Third Macedonian War. Abdera, a city in Thrace, had sided with King Perseus against the Romans. When the city was surrounded by Roman forces under the command of Hortensius, the general ordered the people to provide him with money and provisions or face the consequences. The Abderans stalled, saying that they needed time to send envoys to Rome to discuss the matter. Hortensius had no patience for this sort of treachery. He stormed the city, beheaded the leaders, and sold most of the population into slavery. A group of Abderans traveled to Rome to stage a protest of sorts in front of the Senate House. They remained there for some time, weeping and wailing about their unjustified losses. When the Senate heard of their treatment they decreed it "disgraceful" and ordered the Roman consul in Greece to restore Abdera's freedom, make good its financial losses, and liberate those in slavery. They did all of this for a people who had betrayed them. Yet it was not the moral code of the Abderans that was on trial—but that of the Romans.

Throughout its subsequent history, critics of Rome and Roman power did not tarry long before bringing up these incidents of violated trust. We can see much the same thing today. Those who criticize American power are sure to list similar shortcomings in American history. Yet in both cases the standards that are violated are those of the Empire of Trust, not those of other empires or even of the accusers. The Macedonians or the Achaeans, for example, saw nothing wrong in their unprovoked attacks against their neighbors, but bitterly criticized the Romans for doing the same. Countries that today routinely use torture are vocal critics of the American detention of prisoners at Guantanamo Bay. Critics of the United States, both domestic and abroad, lay the blame for much of the world's ills at the doorstep of the United States. From their history of slavery to their treatment of the Indians, Americans are said have brought violence and injustice to the world. Yet, like the criticisms of Rome, these not only ignore the good done by the empire, but are based on a code of ethics that is itself unique to it.

Jean-François Revel, a French author who spent his life around these sorts of criticisms of American power in Europe, insightfully noted the paradox:

> It was [Europeans] after all who made the twentieth century the darkest in history; it was they who brought about the two unprecedented cataclysms of the World Wars; and it was they who invented and put into place the two most criminal regimes ever inflicted on the human race—pinnacles of evil and imbecility achieved in a space of less than thirty years. It is, again, Europe we must blame, at least partly, for the problematic legacy of colonialism in the Third World, for the impasses and convulsions of underdevelopment. It was the European nations— England, Belgium, Spain, France, and Holland, and belatedly and to a lesser degree Germany and Italy—who were bent on conquering and appropriating other continents. It won't do to bring up the extermination of the Native Americans or black slavery against the United States, for after all, who were the occupants of the future United States if not white colonizers from Europe? And from whom did these European colonists buy their slaves if not from European slave traders?

Yet this sort of reasoning is rare. It is more common simply to accuse the United States of willfully misusing its power. By responding to such accusations with apologies, payments, or resolutions both the United States and Rome further advertise their trustworthiness. This leads to further denunciations, but also a strengthening and expansion of alliance ties. In other words, the criticisms themselves help to further the growth of the Empire of Trust.

By now it should be obvious that for an Empire of Trust to remain healthy it must wield power in a predictable, responsible, and measured way. For the Romans this was built into their constitution, which did not allow military action until the enemy had rejected a peaceful solution. No such clause exists in the United States Constitution, yet American practice has been to define military actions carefully and to give plenty of warning before they occur. In recent years, the American invasions of Afghanistan and Iraq were preceded by a list of grievances against the states and an articulated course of action that could be taken to avoid invasion. Likewise, when Roman commanders were sent into foreign lands they were given precise geographic and temporal boundaries for their use of *imperium*, the legal ability to command troops. They were furthermore given a specific mission, which could only be altered with the consent of the people of Rome.

Consider the example of Flamininus, the commander of Roman forces in Greece during the Second Macedonian War (200–196 BC). After defeating Philip of Macedon and ejecting him from his conquests in Greece, Flamininus was urged by his allies to pursue Philip into his homeland of Macedonia, where he could be crushed completely. Flamininus refused. That was not the purpose of the war. He had come to liberate the Greek people, who had been attacked by Philip and his armies. His aim was to right a wrong, contain an aggressor, and, if possible, gain an ally. As Flamininus himself said, he had never "entertained the idea that Rome should wage war on Philip without any hope of reconciliation."

Now compare Flamininus' response to that of President George H. W. Bush during the First Gulf War in 1991. Despite the urging of many, Bush refused to allow the troops to press on to capture Baghdad and conquer Iraq, although they could easily have done so. He made this decision because the United States had predicated its actions upon the necessity of righting a wrong—Saddam's invasion of Kuwait—which Bush had famously said "will not stand." The United Nations mandate, furthermore, spoke only of the liberation of Kuwait, not the conquest of Iraq. Although Bush subsequently endured more than a decade of criticism for having failed to "finish the job," his choice was consistent with the predictable, responsible, and measured use of power crucial for building an Empire of Trust. Had the United States and its allies invaded Iraq in 1991 it would likely have gone well for them. There was a sizable opposition ready to help, as Saddam's massacre of some hundred thousand Kurds subsequently demonstrated. Yet pursuing such a course would have undercut the confidence that others put into the responsible and predictable use of American power.

Trust with power is not something that people give easily. It must be earned over a long period of time. By their responsible, sometimes merciful, and usually reluctant use of power, the Americans and Romans acquired sufficient trust among foreigners to be pulled into new areas, expanding the empire all the while. However, as they stretched their reach farther and farther abroad, they would be confronted with new shades of gray that threatened the predictability on which they had based that trust.

We have already seen a few of these shades of gray in Roman history. Remember, for example, the case of Saguntum, in which Romans worried over the nature of their obligations and, after the fall of the city, bitterly rebuked themselves for having failed to act sooner. Hoping to avoid a faraway engagement with Hannibal in Spain, the Romans ended up with a devastating war at home. Had they acted decisively to defend Saguntum, Hannibal would not have grown in power and the horrors of the Second Punic War might never have happened.

That was a hard lesson for the Romans and it affected the way that they approached another shade of gray, which cropped up only a little while after they had defeated Hannibal. In Chapter 6 we watched as a coalition of Greek cities asked the Romans to save them from King Philip of Macedon. But the request posed a problem for the Roman Senate. There was no doubt in the senators' minds that helping the Greeks was the right thing to do. But was it legal? The problem was that none of the Greek cities were allies of the Roman people—a concept foreign to the

Greek East. For Romans an ally, or *socius*, was legally bound to them at the hip. In the Greek East such alliances were rare and always temporary. Instead, Greek states would sign treaties of friendship, which meant that they would stay out of each other's way and might even offer help if the situation seemed to warrant it. Rome had signed a treaty of friendship with Egypt and the Aetolians in Greece. But was that enough? The Senate referred the matter to the fetial priests, who judged that friendship was sufficiently close to an alliance to allow Rome to enter a war to defend the Greeks. With little discussion, the Senate decided to do just that. In 200 BC they ordered the two consuls to take the Senate's verdict on the war to the popular assemblies for approval.

The people flatly rejected it. As an Empire of Trust, Rome was wrestling with a new shade of gray. For the Roman people, war was something to be avoided. They waged war when all other options had been exhausted and only to bring lasting peace. That is what they believed, and in most cases it was true. For the people, declaring war on Philip would have been an unwarranted and illegal action. None of the Greeks who asked Rome for aid were allies of the Roman people. Rome owed them nothing. Only months earlier the Romans had finished the long and exhausting Second Punic War. Now, as the troops were returning from Africa, the senators wanted to involve them in another war on foreign shores? No. Let the Greeks kill each other if they wished. This was not Rome's war.

The Senate's position was a difficult one, for it asked the Romans to look beyond immediate threats to themselves and their allies and to consider the long-term dangers to the confederation. It asked them to modify their isolationism in order to preserve what Rome had built. For that reason, the Senate's position was sure to be controversial, but the debate had to be joined. The consul Sulpicius addressed the Assembly, laying out the arguments for the Senate. They are arguments that will seem familiar to modern Americans. They were used to justify the United States' war in Iraq and much of the War on Terror. Because they call for war abroad in order to avoid war in the homeland, they are at once interventionist and isolationist. Listen to the words the consul Sulpicius delivered to the Assembly:

> You seem to be unaware, fellow citizens, that what you have to decide is not whether you will have peace or war; Philip will not leave you any option as to that. He is preparing war on an enormous scale both by land and sea. The only question is whether you will send the legions into Macedonia or wait for the enemy here in Italy. You have learned by experience in the recent Punic War, if not before, what a difference it makes which you decide upon. When Saguntum was besieged and our allies were imploring us for help, who doubts that if we had sent prompt assistance, as our fathers did to the Mamertines, we should have confined within the borders of Spain that war which, most disastrously for ourselves, we allowed through procrastination to enter Italy? ... If you had thought it too much to go to Africa you would still have Hannibal and his Carthaginians in Italy today. Let Macedonia rather than Italy be the place of war. Let it be the enemy's cities and fields that are devastated with fire and sword. We have learned by now that our arms are more potent and more successful abroad than they are at home. Go to the poll with the help of the gods, and confirm the decision of the Senate.

What Sulpicius was proposing was just as controversial in ancient Rome as it is in the United States. But the argument is the same. In order to defend the homeland, the state must not allow an enemy to grow strong enough to attack. It must act first, disrupting the enemy before the attack can occur. The current *National Security Strategy of the United States of America* puts it this way:

> The security environment confronting the United States today is radically different from what we have faced before. Yet the first duty of the United States Government remains what it always has been: to protect the American people and American interests. It is an enduring

American principle that this duty obligates the government to antici-
pate and counter threats, using all elements of national power, before
the threats can do grave damage. The greater the threat, the greater is
the risk of inaction—and the more compelling the case for taking an-
ticipatory action to defend ourselves, even if uncertainty remains as to
the time and place of the enemy's attack. There are few greater threats
than a terrorist attack with WMD. To forestall or prevent such hostile
acts by our adversaries, the United States will, if necessary, act preemp-
tively in exercising our inherent right of self-defense.

Or, to put it more succinctly, as President Bush did in his 2002 speech at
West Point, "We cannot defend America and our friends by hoping for
the best. We cannot put our faith in the word of tyrants, who solemnly
sign nonproliferation treaties, and then systemically break them. If we
wait for threats to fully materialize, we will have waited too long.... We
must take the battle to the enemy, disrupt his plans, and confront the
worst threats before they emerge."

Although more than two thousand years old, this strategy is now referred to as the "Doctrine of Preemption" or just simply the "Bush Doctrine." As in ancient Rome, it has attracted plenty of critics. Some accused
President Bush of squandering the trust that America had gained in the
world, acting as an emperor seeking foreign conquests rather than as a
defender of freedom. Such criticisms are to be expected and, indeed, are
evidence of the health of the Empire of Trust. The millions of people
around the planet who depend on the United States for peace and security can see clearly in American elections and in the American media how
controversial the question of preemption remains. Behind that controversy is an American isolationism that continues to see the use of military
force as an act of last resort. Knowing that the Americans themselves are
torn on the issue only further multiplies the reasons for trusting them
with overwhelming power.

It is at this point that a reader might object to the idea that the United
States has earned the world's trust with power at all. The rapid spread of
anti-Americanism and the frequent criticisms of world leaders who decry

American unilateralism suggest otherwise. So do international polls, like that conducted by World Public Opinion in 2007 in which 53 percent said that they do not trust the United States to "act responsibly in the world." How, then, can it be said that the United States is becoming an Empire of Trust when the people of the world distrust it so? We will return to this question in more detail in the next chapter. Here, though, it is important to keep in mind that trust cannot be gauged by what people say, but rather by what they do. The United States has a military power that is unmatched not only by any other country in the world, but by any other empire in history. The United States has the capability to lay waste any region or country on the planet within the space of minutes. And, in almost all cases, should it do so, it would be immune from counterattack. That unprecedented level of power in the hands of an irresponsible and untrustworthy state is not something to complain about in op-ed columns, assembly speeches, and public opinion polls—it is something to be genuinely feared. When that sort of fear is born, people and their states usually react in one of three ways. If they have the ability to construct a rival military force, they do so for their own protection. If they do not have that ability, they attempt to find powerful friends to help defend them. If they can do neither of those things they flatter, pay tribute, grovel—whatever it takes to appease the great power. As the reader may have noticed, there is a noticeable lack of groveling among the world's citizens to the magnificence of the American people. There is also no country or group of countries building a military force or organizing a military alliance that can rival the United States. Indeed, deployable military troop strengths have been declining worldwide, not increasing. These facts speak louder than words about the trust that the world places in America's responsible use of power.

Although the dynamic of trust pulls the empire into theaters farther and farther from home, that in itself only modifies the empire's isolationism. It does not end it. We can see this most clearly after the successful projection of power—in other words, after the empire has defeated its enemies. Because they are not Empires of Conquest, Rome and the United States had difficulty deciding what to do with conquests. The

Roman solution was to turn the enemy state into a new ally, usually with new leaders. In this way, the people could remain free and the Romans could withdraw their forces. For the Romans, a soldier in foreign lands was considered temporary. There were only three circumstances that would lead the Romans to establish a permanent military presence in a region: It was too primitive or disorganized to enter into an alliance (e.g., Spain, Corsica, Sardinia), it had repeatedly demonstrated that it was incapable of remaining peaceful (e.g., Macedonia, Campania, Carthage), or it had no desire to defend itself and asked for Roman troops (e.g., Sicily, Pergamum). As time went on, the number of regions that fell into one of these categories increased, leading to something that looked very much like an empire.

Americans still tend to see the deployment of their troops into foreign lands as an exception and temporary. But it is no longer either. During World War I American troops could invade Europe and then withdraw completely. But Americans were quicker to leave troops overseas than the Romans had been, doing so most dramatically after World War II. As conquered foes, Germany and Japan received permanent military garrisons. Even these were designed not simply to enforce the transformation of enemies into allies, but also to defend them against their powerful neighbors—particularly the Soviet Union. The fall of the Soviet Union led to a decrease in the number of American troops stationed overseas, yet not their withdrawal. Indeed, the U.S. military presence in Europe continues with new bases in Romania, Poland, and the Czech Republic. Despite this long-term foreign deployment of the American military, Americans still tend to view it as a temporary situation. Since 1945 there has not been an American intervention in a foreign country in which Americans did not demand an "exit strategy." And yet, in all but a few cases, American troops simply do not exit.

Secretary of State Colin Powell famously enunciated what he called the Pottery Barn Principle of American foreign policy: "If you break it, you own it." This is true. Because of the nature of American expansionism, in which regions are invaded precisely because they are dangerous and unstable, it is rarely the case that the troops can safely leave. Once the

Americans arrive, once the United States has become part of the conflict, there can be no withdrawal until the country is no longer "broken." To withdraw would be to break faith with America's allies in the struggle and thereby seriously erode the trust of other allies and the expectation among enemies that Americans will fight to win. That, of course, is precisely what did happen in Vietnam. The American withdrawal led not only to the fall of the South, but also to the killing fields of the Khmer Rouge. That, as well as the later American withdrawals from Lebanon in 1984 and Somalia in 1994, led enemies like al-Qaeda and Saddam Hussein to conclude that American leaders were hobbled by a public that accepted military action only when losses were minuscule.

But the conclusion was incorrect. Sticking with the Pottery Barn Principle, the United States did not "break" Lebanon or Somalia. Rather, American troops were there as part of a larger effort to referee a peace or provide humanitarian aid. There is no getting around the fact that the United States abandoned its allies in Vietnam. That is why it remains such a controversial subject. Just as the Romans argued for centuries about Saguntum, so will Americans agonize over Vietnam. But the argument itself is indicative of a self-criticism impossible for an Empire of Conquest and crucial for an Empire of Trust. Despite the tragedy of Vietnam, the United States continued to keep faith with all of the other regions into which its troops were sent. Americans may talk about exit strategies, they may believe that foreign deployment should be temporary, but the fact remains that American troops to this day are still in Germany, Japan, Italy, Korea, and virtually every other country that Americans "broke" while invading them. Americans remain because their withdrawal would put those countries at risk. As citizens of an Empire of Trust, Americans defend their allies.

From this perspective, the debate over American involvement in Iraq is instructive. Stripping away politics and simply looking at the events from a historical perspective, it would appear that the American conquest of Iraq went reasonably well. The country was captured, the enemy leaders were arrested and punished, a new friendly government was installed, and American troops established a permanent presence. All of this is standard procedure for an Empire of Trust. Given the instability in the region and the number of American enemies nearby it seems certain that there will be no obvious way to withdraw all U.S. troops in the foreseeable future. Just as American forces remain in other conquered countries, so it seems they will remain in Iraq.

Now let's put politics back into it. After all, America, like Rome, is a republic awash in domestic power politics. As isolationists, most Americans want to believe that their involvement in Iraq is temporary. They want to believe that the job will be finished and the troops will come home. The political opposition in the United States—at the time of this writing, the Democratic Party—was eager to appeal to this thwarted desire while at the same time attempting to neutralize any political benefits that would accrue to the president's party from a perceived victory in Iraq. And that's where things get strange. Democrats in Congress began arguing for a quick withdrawal from Iraq because, they said, the United States could not win the war, and therefore American lives and wealth were being wasted. On April 19, 2007, Senate Majority Leader Harry Reid announced that the war in Iraq was already "lost" and other Democrats urged an immediate withdrawal (or "redeployment") out of the region.

And yet, despite the controversy and wrangling, the fundamental dynamics that led the Romans and are leading Americans into the creation of an Empire of Trust remain unaffected by domestic politics. They work because they are built into the very nature of the people and their state. The push and then the pull that nourishes the empire's growth occur irrespective of who wins elections. The Romans fought fierce campaigns for political offices, yet none of the debates or elections stopped or even slowed the march of progress toward empire. The same is true today in the United States. It is a simple fact that no politician in Rome or Washington ever rocketed to power by promising the people defeat, insecurity, or depression. As a campaign issue, victory and prosperity beat failure and decline every time. Neither Americans nor Romans elect politicians who fail to protect their allies or uphold the integrity, honor, and trust of the people—or, if they should, would quickly vote them out of office at the first opportunity.

During the Cold War, both parties in the United States competed to be the toughest on resisting Communist expansion in the world. During the years of the Vietnam War the only presidential candidate to advocate retreat, George McGovern, was rewarded with the second largest drubbing in American political history at the hands of an already scandal-tainted Richard M. Nixon. (Nixon carried forty-nine states, including McGovern's home state of South Dakota.) But while McGovern promised defeat and withdrawal, Nixon promised "peace with honor." The same political calculus remains valid today. Although many Democrats insisted on an end to American involvement in Iraq, John Kerry did not advocate such a thing during his 2004 presidential campaign. Indeed, he advocated an increase in American power there, claiming to have the know-how to win the war. In so doing, he very nearly beat an incumbent president. That is something that has not gone unnoticed by presidential hopefuls in 2008. It is something that will never go unnoticed by aspiring leaders.

Within an Empire of Trust, the political party that is out of power serves an important purpose. In the American empire it generally criticizes the in-power party's foreign policy and, if politically safe to do so, the conduct of military actions. The partisan purpose of this is clear enough: to convince Americans that the country is going in the wrong direction or that an important mission is being botched. However, this has no effect on the dynamics of the empire's growth. For example, during the administration of President Bill Clinton, Republicans strongly opposed the idea of nation building. Most held to a hard-nosed insistence that the United States should act only in its own or its allies' security interests. President Clinton and his administration ignored the criticism, acting unilaterally to advance American interests and defend allies. Clinton unilaterally broke a United Nations arms embargo in the former Yugoslavia, sending weapons directly to the Bosnian Muslims. Likewise he refused to sign an international land-mine treaty because it would harm American military effectiveness. He unilaterally launched numerous military strikes against foreign countries such as Afghanistan, Bosnia, Iraq, Serbia, and the Sudan. President Clinton's secretary of state, Madeleine Albright, famously boasted that "if we have to use force, it is because we are America. We are the indispensable nation." She dismissed criticism of unilateralism, saying that America "stands taller and therefore can see further" than other countries.

As the out-of-power party, the Republicans strongly criticized all of these actions. They worried that the American military was so busy with nation building around the world that it no longer had the time or resources to act as a fighting force. George W. Bush ran on that idea. Just one day before the 2000 election he said, "I'm worried about an opponent who uses nation building and the military in the same sentence." Yet after his election, President Bush and most Republicans embraced nation building, embarking on it on a scale not seen since the end of World War II. They excused the change in policy by citing the new challenges in preserving American security and interests in a post-9/11 world. But that's the point. Over time, everything comes under those interests and security. And so the empire marches on.

After 2000 it was the turn of the Democrats, as the out-of-power party, to criticize the president for his interventionist nation building—particularly in Afghanistan and Iraq. Yet these criticisms have had and will have no effect on the empire's progress. Should a Democrat be elected president in 2008, he or she will face the same calculus with regard to American security that President Bush faced before. Withdrawing from Iraq would create a nightmare scenario so gruesome, so humiliating, and so dangerous to Americans that no politician or political party could withstand it. For that reason alone the new president will have to continue the Iraq occupation and attempt to reduce the violence. His or her party will support those efforts. With both major political parties then supporting the fact of the occupation there will be much less domestic criticism, and slowly, Americans will come to accept it—as they have done with all of the other ongoing American occupations around the world. It is not what they want, but short of becoming something they are not, they will accept it.

At this point it might be worthwhile to summarize these dynamics with a road map of sorts for the development of an Empire of Trust. (Follow along on Figure 1.) It begins with a mixture of environmental and innate characteristics that lead to a people having both military power and isolationism. These together lead to a desire to be left alone, which ultimately is thwarted by outside powers. The isolationist desire is then modified to include a desire for security and stability. It is at this stage that the state is pushing to expand its network of allies or friends, which in itself becomes an attempt to secure an ever-extended horizon. Allies find themselves fairly treated and well-protected. Enemies find themselves conquered and turned into free allies. Over a period of many decades, this leads to a growing feeling among foreigners that the "empire" can be trusted with power, even power over them. Having achieved this level of trust, the empire then moves into a phase in which the dynamics of growth are taken over by a pull from outside rather than a push from within. This occurs in two ways. In one, the empire's allies or friends are attacked, the attackers are defeated by the empire, and the defeated are enrolled as allies or friends. States that are consistently troublesome are then incorporated into the empire with permanent military garrisons. In the other, the empire receives an appeal for aid from a nonallied state threatened by its neighbor. It responds by allying with the threatened state and defeating the neighbor. Later, as the ally tires of providing for its own defense, it asks for and receives incorporation into the empire with a permanent military garrison. The end result is an Empire of Trust.

Now that we have explored what some of the dynamics *are* that led the ancient Romans and modern Americans into the establishment of empire, it is worth saying something about what they *are not*. From its beginnings, the people of the United States have seen their country as a "city on a hill" and a "beacon to the world." It is a place of freedom, opportunity, and hope set apart from a quarreling world. Until the twentieth

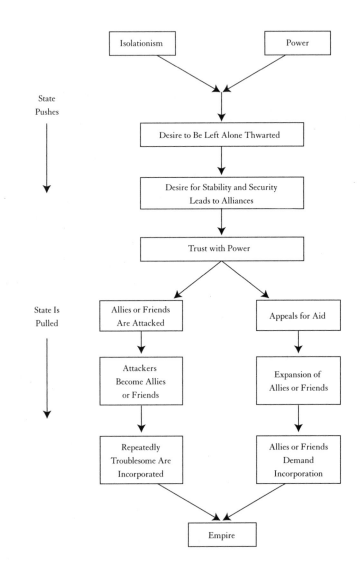

Development of an Empire of Trust

century, this perspective was part and parcel of American isolationism. Yet with the growth of American power in the late nineteenth and early twentieth centuries it began to be used as a justification for intervention. This is most visible in the American involvement in World War I, which was explained by President Woodrow Wilson as an attempt to "make the world safe for democracy." Wilson pointedly refused to make peace with a defeated Germany and Austria because they were ruled by emperors. Only when the autocrats abdicated and new democratic governments were declared did he accept an armistice. Wilson continued this crusade at the Versailles peace talks, where he insisted on "national self-determination" as the guiding principle. This missionary zeal continued through the decades and is still vibrantly alive today. As *The National Security Strategy of the United States of America* makes plain, "the United States will use this moment of opportunity to extend the benefits of freedom across the globe. We will actively work to bring the hope of democracy, development, free markets, and free trade to every corner of the world."

Although these noble words may be genuinely felt by Americans and their leaders, they have little to do with the dynamics behind the growth of the Empire of Trust. The United States did not acquire a reputation for the responsible use of power by spreading freedom. It did so by using that power predictably, responsibly, and in a measured way. In the modern era the United States has never intervened in any region strictly for the spread of freedom and democracy. Indeed, it has intervened in many areas where these factors were not a consideration at all. Hitler came to power legally, through a democratic government, yet Americans fought him just as vigorously as they did the emperor-god in Japan. Indeed, they allied with a brutal Communist dictatorship in the Soviet Union to do so. After Hitler's defeat, the Cold War battlefields were draped in ideological fog, but the struggle was one of power. The United States sought to arrest the growth of the Soviet Union because it was a threat to itself and its allies. Some observers have criticized President Bush for abandoning America's policy of promoting freedom and democracy in his invasion of Iraq. Yet that was never the motivating dynamic behind the war, whatever the president said or even believed. The United States invaded Iraq because, by its refusal to account for weapons of mass destruction, it was perceived as a security threat. If spreading democracy really drove American expansionism the president would have done better to invade nearby Cuba rather than distant and dangerous Iraq.

Although the missionary aspect of American culture does not drive the expansion of the empire, we should not conclude along with Robert W. Merry that all such idealism should be abandoned. Principles matter. And although the United States will never be able to vanquish every tyrant or free every soul, Americans are genuinely proud when they can vanquish and free a few of them as part of their defense of themselves and their allies. The image of the United States as a liberator is not a fiction, after all. But it is security, not liberation, that drives the progress of the Empire of Trust.

The Romans saw their own actions within a similar framework of liberation. In speech after speech, Cicero reminded his audience that Rome was a beacon to the world and a citadel for every nation and people. We have already seen how the Roman invasion of Greece to check the power of Philip of Macedonia and Antiochus of Syria was later bound up in the idea of the liberation of the Greek people. Livy tells us that when the Senate met after the war to discuss the future of Greece "it was resolved that the Macedonians and Illyrians should be free peoples, so that it might be clear to all the world that the arms of Rome did not carry slavery to the free, but on the contrary freedom to the enslaved."

Because the Romans had no king, they quickly gained a reputation for wanting to topple autocrats and tyrants of any sort. When Rome captured Macedonia, Polybius tells us, the people "had been delivered from the arbitrary rule and taxation of autocrats, and, as all confessed, now enjoyed freedom instead of slavery. And, thanks to the beneficent action of Rome, the cities were freed from serious civil discord and internecine massacres." Even in Palestine, Judas Maccabeus had heard that the Romans "have subdued kings far and near, and as many as have heard of their fame have feared them." When the great Roman poet Virgil summed up the historical purpose of his country he wrote:

But, Rome, 'tis thine alone, with awful sway,
To rule mankind, and make the world obey,
Disposing peace and war by thy own majestic way;
To tame the proud, the fetter'd slave to free:
These are imperial arts, and worthy thee.

Like modern Americans, ancient Romans saw themselves as liberators. And, like Americans, sometimes they were.

Both the Romans and the Americans achieved unprecedented levels of power because they steadfastly used that power for the defense of themselves and their allies and—this is crucial—because they did not want it in the first place. At the end of the road that both states were pulled along was a protected world of peace and security. Neither achieved that goal completely, but both came close—probably as close as is possible with human beings involved. Yet peace brought new problems and new threats to the health of the Empire of Trust. Those will be the subject of our next two chapters.

Chapter 8

Pax

Pax means "peace"—and the purpose of an Empire of Trust is to obtain that peace for its citizens. That is why it was created in the first place, and the desire to "secure the horizon" is one of the central dynamics that impels its growth. We have already seen that dynamic in action. The Romans secured Italy by bringing together a coalition of free allies in order to safeguard their homeland. Their reputation for the trustworthy use of military power then pulled them onto foreign shores, which in turn expanded their constellation of allies and greatly enhanced their empire's power. With greater power came more powerful enemies, who resented or feared the rise of the Romans. These were likewise defeated and turned into new allies. Similar dynamics have led to the development of an American Empire of Trust.

The question is: When is enough, enough? When does an Empire of Trust stop expanding?

The answer is simple: when the purpose of the empire has been fulfilled. The catalyst that repeatedly led to Roman expansion was an external attack or threat. It seems reasonable to assume that if the empire was no longer threatened by powerful neighbors—in other words, if that catalyst were removed—then the empire would cease expanding. And that is essentially what happened. By 146 BC the Romans were so powerful that they no longer had much to fear from outside powers. Although they did not directly control the entire Mediterranean, those states that remained outside of the empire—a collection of various kingdoms—recognized that Rome held all of the cards. Provided they did not disturb the peace, the Romans let them be. In the next century many of those kingdoms would drift into the Roman Empire—either willingly or not. Yet for all practical purposes the Romans were controlling them long before that. Although the empire would expand here and there after 100 BC, most of the expansion was intermittent, temporary, or small. As Edward Gibbon wrote in the eighteenth century, "The principal conquests of the Romans were achieved under the republic; and the emperors, for the most part, were satisfied with preserving those dominions which had been acquired by the policy of the Senate, the active emulation of the consuls, and the martial enthusiasm of the people."

Roman expansion did not slow and then stall in the first century BC because it had met its match on the battlefield. Quite the contrary, Roman military might would grow as the centuries passed. Rather, the expansion slowed because the empire's purpose was largely fulfilled. The Romans had managed to secure the horizon. And what a horizon it was! Stretching from Spain to Egypt, the Roman Empire had managed to bring peace and security to millions of people who had not known it before. Beyond that horizon were warlike people, but most of them were primitive, tribal groups, such as the Celts, Germans, or Arabs, who posed no danger to the legions. Others, like the Parthians, wanted no trouble with powerful Rome. And so began the *Pax Romana*.

When historians refer to the Pax Romana they usually mean the two centuries after 27 BC, during the reign of the Roman emperors. Yet that dating is used simply to avoid the civil wars of the first century BC. The real origins of the Roman Peace are in the second century BC, after Rome had eliminated all of its serious military rivals. It was then that they managed to bring an unprecedented peace and prosperity to the lands of their empire. History teachers like to remind their students that the Roman Peace was not peaceful. Yet, *Pax* does not mean universal peace—something that is impossible in human terms. Instead, it means that a general peace is maintained within the borders of the empire. For the first time in history, people living under the Pax Romana did not worry about an invasion of foreign armies. Indeed, for the citizens of the empire the very idea became absurd. New cities were founded in the empire with no thought at all for defense, since it was patently unnecessary. Nevertheless, war did continue intermittently on the borders and occasionally within the empire in areas of instability. Those were the areas in which insecurity was fought and kept at bay, away from the citizens of the Empire of Trust.

War—not peace—is the normal state of affairs in human history. In our own day, not only within the borders of the United States but in the lands of America's allies, war is almost unknown. For most people reading this book now, war is something that exists on a television screen or a newspaper article. It is scarcely more real than an entertainment show, video game, or crossword puzzle. Indeed, in the United States the news itself is packaged as entertainment. That is something that is truly remarkable. And it does not happen by accident. Yet for those of us born into such an extraordinary set of affairs it *seems* to be the norm. Peace has become the expectation, war the brutal interloper.

But it is an illusion. The stark, unvarnished truth is that humans have always fashioned weapons and always fought wars. Other primates do it too. In all of history's civilizations the leaders have been the warriors—or those with control over the warriors. Peace is an intermission, a time to prepare for more war. The idea that peace could become the norm did not develop until the seventeenth-century Enlightenment. It was then that some thinkers began to argue that humans had no natural state, but could instead be fashioned into peaceful creatures.

We are the inheritors of those ideas. We believe that the normal human condition is peace, periodically disrupted by war. That illusion is the product of a large and historically rare superstructure built to keep lasting peace in existence. Without the perfect functioning of that superstructure, peace disappears. Accustomed to peace and security, we are like people born and forever living in an air-conditioned, climate-controlled building, believing all the while that weather has been abolished. It hasn't. It's still out there. And if the air-conditioning ever breaks down we will discover just how hot it can get.

Much like Rome in 146 BC, the United States has successfully brought peace and security to its homeland and to its allies. Since the fall of the Soviet Union the United States—again, like Rome—no longer has any serious military rivals. Americans can no longer fathom the idea of a foreign country invading the United States or capturing American cities. It is beyond absurd—it is unthinkable. That is true peace and security. It is something that sets modern Americans apart from the large majority of people who have ever lived on Earth.

By the same token, the American Empire of Trust has brought peace and security to its allies. The empire requires that allies be both loyal and peaceful. Warfare between them is not allowed. Since no one ally—or even a collection of allies—has the military power to challenge the empire, the idea of disturbing the peace slowly becomes extinct. This occurred in antiquity and it is happening in a similar fashion today. Look, for example, at Europe. This is a region in which the brutal slaughter of warfare was brought to unprecedented levels. The countries and leaders of Europe waged nearly constant warfare for more than fifteen centuries. Even after the carnage of World War I had wiped out an entire generation of Europe's young men, as soon as a new generation was ready Europe again plunged itself into an even bloodier war that spread across the globe, claiming the lives of millions.

Since 1945 western Europe has been at peace. Is that because Europeans finally learned their lesson, beating their swords into ploughshares and foreswearing future wars? No. It is because the United States remained engaged in the region. American troops stayed there and the American people made clear that they would defend any NATO ally against any enemy. Like the Romans, Americans would not accept warfare between their allies. Everyone knew, and the NATO treaty made clear, that the United States would defend the attacked and punish the attacker. And since the power of the United States after the 1949 treaty was so much greater than any of the allies, the allies accepted the security of American promises at the expense of forfeiting their time-honored right to attack their neighbors. Today peace reigns in Europe for one reason—because the United States guarantees it.

Imagine if the United States and all of its people suddenly disappeared into a parallel dimension. What would happen next in Europe? For starters, France, Germany, Italy, and all of the other European countries would no longer be defended against possible enemies. They would have no choice but to defend themselves. One can imagine that the European Union would crumble within hours, since control over military forces would suddenly become crucially important. As one country began building its forces, other countries would necessarily follow suit. Although everyone would claim that their buildup was defensive, the instability and uncertainty would eventually lead some countries to come under the control of others. In the end, war would erupt. This is just a hypothetical, of course, but it is not one that requires too much imagination. It has already happened in Europe again and again from the third century until the twentieth. It is standard procedure not just in Europe, but between all states. But, hang on. Why was Europe at peace before the third century? Because the last Empire of Trust, Rome, made it so.

To achieve "Pax," an Empire of Trust must have achieved an extraordinary level of power. It must be able to guarantee to its inhabitants (including allies) peace and a high level of security against attack. As with the Pax Romana, the Pax Americana does not denote the end of all wars. But it does mean that peace and security predominate within the empire, while the empire's military forces fight to suppress or restrain instability on the frontiers. Although the Pax Romana was punctuated by various high-profile wars, that does not change the fact that overall it was a period of unprecedented peace. Nevertheless, during the rush of events it can sometimes seem as though the peace is unraveling. That is certainly true today. Opening any newspaper will reveal warfare and killing going on across the globe, but in parts of the world the Pax Americana is firmly established.

North America, western Europe, and Japan are clear examples. Since the fall of the Soviet Union, Pax has spread to include much of eastern Europe and perhaps even Russia itself. The growing power of the United States as an Empire of Trust will lead to the further expansion of Pax. This trend is already visible. Although we often assume that the world is becoming more violent, the reality is different. According to the "Human Security Report 2005" produced by the Human Security Centre at the University of British Columbia, the number of armed conflicts has been dropping steadily since the end of the Cold War. Civil wars, coups, interstate wars, and genocides have all declined rapidly. The only exception to that trend is international terrorism. However, the death toll from terrorism is minuscule, averaging only around a thousand deaths per year over the last thirty years. The Human Security Centre gives the credit for the decline in violence to the United Nations, remarking that "the single most compelling explanation" is that Cold War hostilities no longer restrain UN peacekeeping operations. For that reason, the report continues, outright warfare is concentrated in sub-Saharan Africa.

Yet, this analysis confuses the result with the cause. The UN can send negotiators or troops only because the United States ended the Cold War and subsequently acquired hegemonic power. If it was truly the UN that was responsible for the growing peace, then the continued warfare in Africa makes little sense. UN missions to Africa are numerous. In truth, it is American apathy for the region that allows it to continue to remain violent, provided that the warfare does not affect American assets or security. Just as the Romans had only a passing interest in Germans or Celts outside of their empire, so Americans tend to ignore a sub-Saharan Africa that, while frequently in a state of crisis, poses no security threat to the United States or its allies.

Has the United States reached the level of power that Rome had achieved by 146 BC? In other words, did the fall of the Soviet Union create a world in which there are no longer any serious external threats to the United States and its allies? And by "serious external threats" I do not mean acts of terrorism, which can be devastating and bloody, but which pose no threat to the survival of the empire. In order for the United States to have reached that level it would have to possess a military supremacy so overwhelming that no other foreign power could rationally expect to defeat or even challenge it. That is what the Romans had in 146 BC and it is the reason that even countries like Egypt had to accept Roman hegemony. It is only that level of military preeminence combined with a relationship of trust that can usher in a true Pax. Only when foreign powers recognize that they can never challenge the power of the empire will they eventually abandon attempts to do so.

Whether the United States has reached that level of military power today or not, it is nevertheless the policy of the U.S. government to acquire it. And it is doing so for the same reasons that the Romans sought it. In his 2002 West Point speech, in which the president laid out the "Bush Doctrine," he said:

> As we defend the peace, we also have an historic opportunity to preserve the peace. We have our best chance since the rise of the nation-state in the seventeenth century to build a world where the great powers compete in peace instead of prepare for war. The history of the last century, in particular, was dominated by a series of destructive national rivalries that left battlefields and graveyards across the Earth. Germany fought France, the Axis fought the Allies, and then the East fought the West, in proxy wars and tense standoffs, against a backdrop of nuclear Armageddon.
>
> Competition between great nations is inevitable, but armed conflict in our world is not. More and more, civilized nations find ourselves on the same side—united by common dangers of terrorist violence and chaos. America has, and intends to keep, military strengths beyond challenge, thereby making the destabilizing arms races of other eras pointless, and limiting rivalries to trade and other pursuits of peace.

It is here, in the intention to create and maintain American "military strengths beyond challenge," that Pax is born. It is precisely the way the Romans created and nurtured their own Pax. Put another way, *The National Security Strategy of the United States of America* states: "Our forces will be strong enough to dissuade potential adversaries from pursuing a military build-up in hopes of surpassing, or equaling, the power of the United States."

The question remains as to whether or not the United States has achieved this "Pax level" of power. In order to answer that question, let's begin with a few simple facts. There is today no power on Earth that has the capacity to launch an effective invasion of the United States. Although China or Russia may have large armies, neither has the means to transport them to America. Conversely, there is no country on Earth that the United States could not invade. For some years the military strategy of the United States has included the ability to project significant power anywhere in the world. For the most part it has achieved that goal. These facts, in and of themselves, represent an extraordinary disparity in power. This is not to say that the United States has the power to fight the world and win. It does not. Nor does it need it. An Empire of Trust only requires sufficient power to defend its allies and deter or punish aggression. In short, it must have "military strengths beyond challenge."

Based on the Roman model of alliances and expansion, we can speak of the American Empire of Trust as including all formal allies—those bound by treaty to the United States such as NATO countries, Pacific Allies, and the Gulf Cooperation Council—as well as informal or individual allies such as Israel, Mexico, India, Iraq, or Taiwan. If the American empire has achieved Pax, then these countries should be free from the danger of war. Although they may have internal problems, all of these countries must trust sufficiently in American promises and military might that they harbor no reasonable fear of invasion from outside. In order for this to be the case, their neighbors and potential enemies must know beyond doubt that an attack against them will not only fail but bring devastating penalties during an American response. So, to take one example, although China has the means, the will, and the historic justification to invade Taiwan (which the Chinese government considers to be a rogue state planted on Chinese soil), they have refrained from doing so because the response of the United States is not in doubt. By the same token, the economy of Taiwan remains robust because investors do not view the threat of a Chinese invasion as a serious one.

Defining the precise borders of the American Empire of Trust is difficult, just as it was for the Roman Empire in 146 BC. Certain areas were clearly within Rome's empire, others were not, others remained in a gray zone. Certain cities, regions, or kingdoms could depend on Roman support and defense, others hoped for it, and others clearly were outside of it. Today there are areas of our own world that are demonstrably not within an American empire. With the possible exception of South Africa, the United States seems to have little interest in defending sub-Saharan African countries from cross-border attacks. Beyond sub-Saharan Africa, there are other countries that have proven themselves to be hostile to the growth of American power and therefore remain outside of the empire. These include places like Syria, Iran, Libya, North Korea, and China and may or may not include Russia, which remains in a strategic state of flux after the Cold War. These countries are harshly critical of the United States. Russia's president Putin has chastised the United States for acting like an empire and even raised the specter of a new Cold War if American plans to install missile interception technology in eastern Europe were not abandoned. For their part, the leaders of Iran regularly refer to America as the "great Satan." Disagreements and insults, however, do not suggest American military weakness. After all, American allies engage in much the same behavior. Instead, they point to the character of the Empire of Trust, which allows dissent provided it does not disturb the peace. For all of their bluster, it is instructive that none of these countries beyond the empire's borders has engaged in any cross-border invasions of any kind since the end of the Cold War.

To complete our analysis of a modern Pax, we must include a factor that was absent in the ancient world: nuclear weapons. Unimaginable to the Romans, nuclear weapons substantially complicate the creation and preservation of Pax-level military supremacy. In order for the United States to maintain Pax for itself and its allies it must have the same preeminence in nuclear weapons that it has in conventional forces. In other words, it must have the clear and credible ability to launch nuclear weapons against any enemy on Earth with sufficient power to destroy it completely. It must also have no deterrent to the use of that power except its own restraint. That means that no other country in the world must have the ability to launch a nuclear strike against the United States with sufficient force to destroy it. This kind of nuclear hegemony is crucial, because it provides a final assurance that direct attacks against the United States or its allies will—one way or the other—be punished with extraordinary force. If, on the other hand, any state has the ability to destroy the United States with a nuclear attack, then the ability of the empire to protect itself or its allies is severely diminished. During the Cold War, the United States defended western Europe against a Soviet attack. Yet it could only do so by risking nuclear war—a war that would destroy the United States in the bargain. Americans were willing to risk oblivion for Europe, but the same was not true for most of the rest of the world. So, for example, when Soviet armies invaded Afghanistan in 1979, President Jimmy Carter could do little more than boycott the Olympics. Soviet nuclear arsenals were simply too great to issue ultimatums over an area that most Americans could not find on a map.

But that was during the height of the Cold War when the Soviets had nuclear arsenals of staggering size. What is the situation today? The so-called "Nuclear Club" of nations that have deployable nuclear weapons is small. Many are friends or allies of the United States. These include Great Britain, France, India, Pakistan, and (probably) Israel. These nuclear arsenals are tiny, though, and none of the countries has the ability to use them against the United States. There is a great deal of concern today about nuclear programs in North Korea and Iran. Both have attempted to acquire nuclear devices. Yet even if successful, they would only have the ability to threaten their neighbors—which is important, certainly, since those neighbors are American allies. But neither country has the technology to launch those weapons against the United States nor could they produce sufficient nuclear weapons to destroy it. On the other hand, should either country use these weapons against American allies the United States would respond. Since North Korea and Iran have a reputation for acting irrationally, that is a scenario that the American government seeks to avoid by denying them the weapons in the first place.

With its economy growing and the largest military on Earth, China seems to be a looming threat to America's Empire of Trust. In truth, it is not. Although China has a large army, its quality both in weapons and training is low. And, of course, China's army is powerless against the American homeland. China does have nuclear weapons, which it has been attempting to expand and modernize. According to the Department of Defense's 2007 *Annual Report to Congress: Military Power of the People's Republic of China*, the Chinese currently have twenty intercontinental ballistic missiles (ICBMs) that could theoretically reach the continental United States. The operative word here is *theoretically*. The rockets are generally unreliable, so it is not clear that they could deliver more than a few of them to the United States. Of course, a few nuclear blasts can certainly ruin your day, but it is insufficient to destroy the country. Furthermore, the American response would undoubtedly be the nuclear annihilation of China. In general, not a good trade-off.

In truth, it is very unlikely that the Chinese could launch such an attack at all. The nuclear warheads for China's ICBMs are kept in storage, away from the rockets themselves. As for the rockets, because they work on primitive liquid-fuel systems, they must be fueled up before they can be launched—a process that can take several hours. (Corrosion occurs twenty-four hours after liquid fueling.) All of this clumsy preparation would be plainly evident to American spy satellites, and so the missiles could be destroyed well before they left the ground. The Chinese have thus far produced two submarines capable of launching nuclear missiles. One sank. The other is in such poor repair that it no longer leaves harbor. At least for the foreseeable future, then, China has no obvious ability to threaten the survival of the United States.

This is not to say that China is no threat to America's allies or interests. Clearly it is. But China's strategy is not to build a military capable of defeating the United States. Instead, the Chinese are focusing on "asynchronous" attacks that would undercut the United States' ability to respond quickly to Chinese provocations overseas. These include knocking out American satellites and other technological infrastructure. By blinding and crippling the American behemoth, China hopes to have the means to retaliate against an American attack or strike a neighbor without

American interference. Behind this strategy lies an assumption that, if faced with a military fait accompli (such as a rapid invasion of Taiwan), the United States would not go to war with China. Whether or not the assumption and the strategy are valid, it remains that the Chinese lack the capability to significantly harm the United States at home.

That leaves Russia, the descendent of America's Cold War nemesis, the Soviet Union. In 1990 the Soviets had thirteen hundred ICBMs that could reach anywhere on the planet. Those, together with Soviet bombers and SSBNs (ballistic missile launching submarines), made up the largest nuclear arsenal in the world. Not only did the Soviets have the ability to lay waste to the United States, but they could do so even after withstanding a theoretical American first strike. Despite a smallish economy, the Soviet Union's enormous expenditures on the military—both nuclear and conventional—made it a powerful rival to the United States. Those were the days of MAD—Mutual Assured Destruction—in which both nations planned their military strategy around deterring a nuclear attack by maintaining the clear ability to utterly destroy the other country. It was dangerous. For decades the world stood only minutes away from nuclear holocaust. But it worked. The United States and the Soviet Union protected their core allies and jostled for position in the Third World, but managed to avoid a direct conflict between themselves.

Those days are gone. It is not cheap to be a nuclear superpower and the new, free-market Russia has other things it wants to spend its money on. Since the fall of the Soviet Union the Russians have devoted only a fraction of their wealth toward the upkeep of conventional and nuclear forces. To get a feel for the change, let's take a look at what is left in Russia of the old strategic triad—SSBNs, bombers, and ICBMs.

During the Cold War the Soviet Union had a large fleet of sophisticated submarines kept on regular patrols, armed with nuclear missiles, ready for the order to strike American forces or the American mainland at a moment's notice. In 1990 alone Soviet submarines completed more than sixty separate patrols. Today the Russians deploy only two patrols per year, sometimes. Their submarine fleet has been reduced to nine poorly maintained vessels, which spend most of their time in dock. Submarines are complicated devices. They require constant upkeep and their crews need frequent training. They are not getting it in Russia. Many Russian submarine tests, including one attended by President Putin in 2004, have failed spectacularly.

In order to maintain the long-range-bomber arm of the strategic triad a country needs to have well-trained crews and regularly maintained aircraft loaded with nuclear weapons ready to deploy at any time. During the Cold War the Soviet Union had its bomber squadrons scattered across the country at various bases and kept some of them in the air in case of surprise attack. Today it is a different story. Almost two-thirds of Russia's long-range bomber fleet has been scrapped. The remaining planes are kept on the ground at just two bases. They are by no means ready for rapid deployment. Training exercises are rare, maintenance is poor, and the warheads themselves are stored off base.

In 2007 the Russians began using some of these bombers to make a diplomatic point. Upset at American plans to install antiballistic missile technologies in eastern Europe, the Kremlin began sending a few bombers (probably without warheads) very close to American and NATO airspace, causing the allies to scramble fighter jets in response. With much fanfare, President Putin announced the resumption of "regular flights of Russian strategic aviation." Yet the number and quality of these missions have not been strategically significant. As the U.S. Department of State spokesman Sean McCormack, said, "If Russia feels as though they want to take some of these old aircraft out of mothballs and get them flying again that's their decision." Clearly these missions were meant to attract publicity, probably to convince Europeans that American actions in eastern Europe were threatening their own security. When the Soviets had real squadrons of bombers flying with real nuclear warheads they kept mum about their numbers and locations. They did not schedule press conferences to announce them. In any case, these limited Russian flights do not represent a serious threat to the United States.

What about the missiles? Exact figures are hard to obtain, but it appears that in 2007 Russia still had about 500 ICBMS—far more than China, but fewer than half what the Soviets had during the Cold War. Of those, fully 80 percent are already beyond their original service lives. ICBMs are complex machines that are difficult and expensive to maintain. The Russians are apparently unwilling or unable to maintain an arsenal anywhere near the size they had during the Cold War. They have already announced plans to reduce their ICBM levels by an additional one-third, but the cuts are likely to be even greater. Most analysts believe that by 2010 Russia will have only 150 missiles or fewer.

Has the United States similarly reduced its nuclear and conventional arsenals since the end of the Cold War? In a word, no. With the collapse of Soviet power, the United States now has unquestioned mastery of seas. While Russian and Chinese subs are anchored in ports, American SSBNs have been significantly modernized and equipped with much more accurate and more powerful Trident II nuclear missiles. The United States currently deploys around forty nuclear submarine patrols per year, only slightly down from Cold War highs. As for bombers, American B-52s are now equipped with nuclear-armed cruise missiles, which are invisible to Chinese and Russian radar systems. B-2 stealth bombers can now evade even the most sophisticated foreign radars. They can literally attack anywhere on earth at will. Although American ICBM arsenals have declined slightly, the Minuteman missiles have been upgraded for accuracy and power. In short, the United States has a *more* powerful nuclear arsenal in 2008 then it did during the Cold War.

It is this amazingly lopsided set of circumstances that has led Keir A. Lieber and Daryl G. Press to conclude that the United States either currently has or is about to have "nuclear primacy"—the ability to launch a first strike anywhere in the world without fear of retaliation. That is important. Nuclear primacy ultimately makes the United States unassailable, since any serious saber-rattling risks an American first strike. Given the pitiful state of Russian or Chinese radar, satellite, and weapons technologies, Lieber and Press assert that the United States could destroy all the nuclear weapons of those countries before they had a chance to respond. Since a first strike from Russia (or China, if that were possible) would almost certainly not destroy the United States, and would therefore not stop the destruction of the launching country, there is even less reason to pursue it. Indeed, nuclear weapons with the capability of reaching the United States become a liability, since they invite attack, particularly in times of tension with America or its allies. MAD no longer exists. "Assured Destruction" still exists, it is true. But there is no longer anything "Mutual" about it.

Taking all of this together, it appears that the United States has either achieved its stated goal of "military strengths beyond challenge" or that it is very close. Such a goal has its critics, both at home, among the allies, and in other states. But it is and will remain a fact of life. Some American liberals may consider the policy to be intolerable arrogance. Some American conservatives may consider it to be dangerous internationalism. But it has happened all the same. It is the direct result of an American desire for security at home, coupled with an international desire for American protection abroad. American military supremacy makes the United States and its allies safe in a way that they have not been safe before. It produces a Pax that is infinitely preferable to the alternative.

Let's look again at the Roman example. One of the results of the Pax Romana was a significant decrease in the military levels of the regions that were part of the empire. The Romans required some level of support for the legions, but local military forces, in most cases, could remain local. Roman allies continued to have their own armies even after they had become part of the confederation. Yet because of their membership in the Empire of Trust, the need for those armies slowly disappeared. Rome not only defended them from aggressors but forbade them from attacking their neighbors. As a result, states like Athens, Sparta, Pergamum, Rhodes, and others ended up with militaries much smaller than at any pervious time in their history.

If the American Empire of Trust has reached this level of Pax, we should expect to see a similar decline in the size of foreign military strengths. We have already seen the decline in the Russian military. What about elsewhere? One place to start might be NATO—the most powerful alliance in the world. Powerful it may be, but the military strengths of its non-American members have been declining for years. Indeed, things have become so bad that on June 14, 2007, Secretary of Defense Robert Gates complained during a NATO meeting that "only a fraction of the alliance meets the standard of spending at least two percent of GNP on defense." He was not exaggerating. *The 2004 Statistical Compendium on Allied Contributions to the Common Defense* (the latest publicly available) shows that the only NATO countries to meet the minimum 2 percent GNP treaty requirement are the Czech Republic, France, Greece, Norway, Poland, Portugal, Turkey, the United States, and the United Kingdom. The countries of Belgium, Canada, Denmark, Germany, Hungary, Italy, Luxembourg, the Netherlands, and Spain have militaries too small to meet their treaty obligations.

It is worth remembering that these are percentages of economies much smaller than that of the United States. For example, although France has met the NATO minimum requirement, it nevertheless spent only $45 billion on its military in 2003. During the same year the United States spent $384 billion—almost nine times more than France. When we look at the allies' respective shares of the total alliance effort the contrast becomes even starker. U.S. military spending accounts for almost 70 percent of the total NATO military spending. Sixty percent of all ground combat troops, 70 percent of all naval combat tonnage, and 65 percent of all combat aircraft capability are contributed by only one of the NATO allies—the United States. With regard to spending on major equipment and research and development, the United States carries 73 percent of the load for NATO. The United Kingdom, France, and Germany provide a *combined* share of 17 percent, leaving the other 10 percent to be split up among the thirteen remaining allies. This is an alliance in the image of ancient Rome. It consists of the empire's troops and materiel accompanied by the token assistance of those it has promised to defend.

The reason for this disparity has nothing to do with the various countries' ability to create large militaries. It has everything to do with their *desire* to do so. In 1939 Belgium had an army larger than that of the United States. Today Belgian active duty military personnel number around 40,000. The United States has 1.5 million. In 1945 Great Britain emerged from World War II with a navy of 900 vessels. Today it has fewer than 35. And there is even talk about abolishing the Royal Navy altogether! The reason? Without a navy, the British will not have to respond to American requests for help in patrolling the world's oceans. In 2004 German defense minister Peter Struck announced a restructuring of Germany's 250,000-strong military. Thirty-five thousand would be trained for foreign interventions as part of a coalition—i.e., to endorse (or not) American operations. Seventy thousand would be designated for peacekeeping—i.e., to endorse (or not) the end of an American operation. The rest would be "support"—i.e., government projects at home. None were designated for the defense of Germany.

I am focusing here on Europe because it is there that we can most dramatically witness the demilitarization that accompanies Pax. Not very long ago European countries had built the largest and most lethal military forces in history. Today it is difficult to imagine any European country having the ability to put up much of a fight against a determined aggressor. It is not a question of economic means. The combined economies of Europe exceed that of the United States. This has led some Europeans to call for the building of a military that would "balance" American hegemony. As we saw earlier, there are several reasons that this is unlikely to happen. The primary one, though, is that it is eminently unnecessary. Europeans enjoy unprecedented peace because of the American military. If the EU were to build a powerful new military, it could only be seen as a rival to the United States. It would require Europeans to funnel massive resources into building a force that would actually make them *less* safe. And who would control it? No one in Europe trusts anyone else to hold that much military power, except the Americans. And they trust the Americans for a very simple reason: because Americans have responsibly kept the peace for decades. It is that trust which prompts Europeans to continue to reduce the size and quality of their militaries, thus allowing the Empire of Trust to hold hegemonic power.

Although non-American military strength will continue to decline within the Empire of Trust, it will not disappear entirely—at least not for a very long time. Militarily less significant, the native forces of the allies still do perform important functions. They can be used to do public works and to maintain order within their countries. They are good for parades. But most importantly, by their presence they can endorse or not the military actions of the empire. They preserve the idea that the actions of the Empire of Trust are those of a coalition. That is something that both Americans and their allies want to believe.

As those history teachers are still reminding us, the Pax Romana did not bring an end to all wars. The Pax Americana will not either. There will always be wars, either outside of the Empire of Trust or in the gray zone along its borders. Not everyone likes the empire. In fact, many do not. But because of the empire's extraordinary power, no one can seriously expect to defeat it. Foreign powers throughout the ancient world and our own discover that they are defined by their relationship to the empire. Warfare does not cease. But the extraordinary imbalance in military strength leads to conflicts increasingly taking place within the politics of the empire, with events on the battlefield designed to win political, rather than military, victories.

We saw this dynamic at work during the Second Macedonian War (200–196 BC), in which Philip pinned his hopes for victory on dragging out the war. Realizing that he could not win militarily, he planned to bore or tire the Romans enough that they would withdraw their forces from Greece. Knowing that the war had been unpopular in the streets of Rome, Philip tried to use that political fact to his own advantage. Unfortunately for him, Flamininus was able to achieve military victory before popular opinion demanded a withdrawal.

In the decades that followed, it became increasingly clear across the Mediterranean world that the real avenue to power was not so much on the battlefields but in the streets and forums of Rome. Foreign rulers, particularly those in smaller kingdoms, began to seek support from the Romans. The coveted title "friend of Rome" carried with it an implicit threat, that Rome would defend not only the kingdom but also the king. It could also bring Roman bases and foreign aid. The sons of foreign kings and elites were increasingly sent to Rome for their education—not just to learn their subjects but to learn Roman ways and language, and to forge connections that would benefit their kingdoms later. In the 170s BC King Ariarathes IV of Cappadocia sent his son and heir to Rome for his education. So did Charops, the ruler of Epirus. In 167, Nicomedes, the heir of the kingdom of Bithynia, came to Rome for schooling, while in 153 the future kings Attalus III and Demetrius II of Syria were in Rome for the same purpose. And these are just a few cases that we know something about. Undoubtedly many more foreigners at lower levels of the ruling classes came to Rome too. They did so not because Rome was a beacon of education or high culture, but because an understanding of the Roman language, government, and customs was crucial to success. The same is true today. The children of the world's elite flock to American universities to acquire their education. They are looking for the same things that their ancient counterparts sought in Rome—knowledge, and knowledge of the empire.

As more and more kingdoms became allies and their leaders "friends of Rome," the politics and warfare of those kingdoms became a franchise store of Roman politics. Put another way, foreign politics began to exist within the larger framework of Roman politics. The result was a wave of foreign lobbyists in Rome who did their best to persuade politicians to support their causes. Naturally, this led to accusations of corruption. Gaius Gracchus once told a Roman audience that so much foreign money had been spread around concerning the passage of a particular piece of legislation that those who argued against it were doing so for money from King Nicomedes III of Bithynia, while those who argued in favor of it were paid by King Mithridates V of Pontus. Those who were undecided were the worst, he said, because they were taking money from both kings.

To illustrate this dynamic more clearly, let's take a look at one example—the Jugurthine War. Although this was a real war, it was fought at a time when Rome's military supremacy was such that her enemies could only hope to win by exploiting Roman politics and popular opinion. The war occurred in Numidia, a kingdom in what is now northeastern Algeria. It was a spin-off state, carved from the spoils of the Second Punic

War. The first king, Masinissa, was a Carthaginian general who had switched sides to help Scipio Africanus defeat Carthage. As a reward, Rome let him keep the territories his armies controlled, which he formed into the kingdom of Numidia. Masinissa was a "friend of Rome" who remained loyal until his death in 148 BC at the age of ninety. He left Numidia under the control of the Roman general Scipio Aemilianus, who was charged with dividing it among Masinissa's three sons. As it happens, this was an easy job, since only Micipsa lived for very much longer.

King Micipsa of Numidia assisted Scipio with the final defeat of Carthage in 146 BC. Out of those lands, Rome created the province of Africa, which neighbored Numidia. The relationship between Rome and Numidia remained close. Like other foreign kings, Micipsa made certain to have his heirs and kinsmen educated in Rome, and he was himself a frequent visitor. When Micipsa died in 118 BC he left three heirs—Hiempsal, Adherbal, and Jugurtha. The plan had been for the three to split Numidia, but Jugurtha had other ideas. He sent some of his men to a house where he knew that Hiempsal was staying. They broke in, ransacked the place, and ultimately found the prince in the maid's quarters, cowering in a closet. They hacked off his head. In retaliation, the other heir, Adherbal, mustered some forces and attacked Jugurtha. Adherbal was defeated. He fled to Roman Carthage and then finally back to Rome itself, leaving Jugurtha with control of Numidia.

At first Jugurtha was jubilant in his victory. But, as Sallust tells us, "when he had leisure to reflect on what he had done, he began to be afraid of the reaction of the Roman people." Jugurtha sent agents and lobbyists to Rome to spend freely among senators and other opinion makers. He knew that Adherbal would be seeking Roman support and he wanted to make certain that Rome stayed out of Numidia. When Adherbal came to appeal his case to the Roman Senate, Jugurtha had his supporters there as well. Adherbal cast his own expulsion from Numidia as an insult to the Roman people. He told the senators:

> The kingdom from which I have been expelled is the kingdom that was given to my ancestors by the Roman government.... It is your

gifts, gentlemen, that have been wrested from me. It is you who are insulted in the wrong done to me.

Jugurtha's supporters retorted that it was Adherbal who had attacked Jugurtha, not the other way around. Having lost on the battlefield, Adherbal was simply whining to the Senate about his own failures. Jugurtha, they insisted, remained a loyal friend of Rome. The senators should let no one convince them otherwise.

The important point for us here is that this dispute between two royal claimants of Numidia was being fought in the Senate House of Rome. This was a natural by-product of Rome's military supremacy and the dynamics behind the Empire of Trust. In this case, the Senate decided to send a ten-man commission to Numidia. It listened to both sides and then dictated a division of Numidia. Adherbal was given the capital, Cirta, as well as the surrounding lands. Jugurtha was given the rural western districts. Things remained calm for a few years, but in 113 BC Jugurtha began sending raiding parties against Adherbal, hoping to provoke him into launching an attack, which would formally break the Roman peace. Adherbal did not oblige, so Jugurtha finally invaded, claiming that Adherbal was plotting against his life. He had good success, capturing most of Adherbal's kingdom and laying siege to the capital. Adherbal managed to get word to Rome, where he again put Rome's prestige and trustworthiness at the center of his appeal:

> For more than four months I have been besieged by his [Jugurtha's] army, and it avails me nothing that I am a friend and ally of the Roman people ... and that you have passed decrees in my favor.... It is plain, however, that Jugurtha is aiming at something more than my downfall. He cannot hope to obtain my kingdom and at the same time keep your friendship; and which of the two he sets more store by, no one can fail to see, since he began by murdering my brother Hiempsal and then drove me from the kingdom of my fathers. How much notice he takes of the warnings of your ambassadors, my parlous condition

shows. What is there left that can influence him save only the force that you can bring to bear on him?

The whole business between Jugurtha and Adherbal was itself becoming entangled in Roman political struggles between aristocrats and the populist groups known as Populares. Populares leaders claimed that the fat-cat elites in Rome had been bought off by Jugurtha, while Rome's true friend, Adherbal, was being hung out to dry.

To forestall these complaints, the Senate sent a high-level commission, led by Marcus Scaurus, the leader of the Senate, to Utica, which was the capital of the Roman province of Africa. They ordered Jugurtha to appear there at once. He obeyed. They then demanded that he raise his siege of Cirta and promised severe penalties if he refused. But Jugurtha believed that he had sufficient clout in the Senate to keep those penalties from materializing. He also knew that the Germans were attacking Italy from the north, something that was much more pressing for the Romans than this squabble in Africa. With the news cycle about to change in Rome, Jugurtha was sure he could take Cirta without repercussions. Shortly thereafter, that is just what he did. After capturing the city he tortured Adherbal to death and ordered the execution of all men with arms in their possession. Although he may not have known it, that included a large number of Italian expatriots living in Cirta. When the people of Rome learned of the slaughter of their own people they were outraged. The news cycle swung back to Jugurtha.

The Senate was under enormous pressure to retaliate. Jugurtha responded by sending lobbyists with plenty of money to keep the whole mattered bottled up in committees and resolutions. The plan, as Sallust tells us, was to have the matter "drag on until all public resentment had evaporated." This time, though, it didn't work. The Senate dispatched an army under the command of the consul Lucius Calpurnius Bestia to wage war against Jugurtha. Bestia and his troops landed in Numidia in 111 BC, but it was not much of a war. Jugurtha surrendered and got an exceptionally lenient peace that allowed him to keep almost everything.

He believed he had sufficient support in the Senate to get the consul's decree confirmed, but the matter once again became mired in Roman domestic politics. The Populares insisted that Jugurtha had bribed Bestia and key senators in order to get his way. By the actions of the Senate and aristocrats, they argued, "the Republic had been put up for sale." Since Jugurtha had surrendered, the assemblies ordered him to come to Rome and testify before a commission. They demanded that he name names, telling them precisely whom he had bribed and when.

Jugurtha dutifully traveled to Rome under a guarantee of safe passage. He knew very well how Rome worked, and he planned to work it to his advantage. At once he began spreading money around town. He was even able to bribe a tribune, who summarily closed the corruption inquiry before Jugurtha was forced to testify. A few weeks later it was discovered that Jugurtha had hired a Roman hit man to kill one of his Numidian rivals, who was also in Rome at the time. That was too much. The people in the streets were boiling with rage, both at Jugurtha and their government. Utilizing his safe passage, Jugurtha decided to return to Numidia. As he departed he is supposed to have said that Rome was "a city for sale and ripe for destruction, if it ever finds a buyer."

More Roman troops were sent to Numidia to prosecute the war. Unable to defeat the Roman military, Jugurtha continued his policy of buying friends, exploiting political divisions in Rome, and attempting to bribe the Roman military commanders sent to fight the war. He also planned to tire out the Roman people by fighting small skirmishes and then retreating. He hoped, like Philip of Macedon almost a century earlier, that the Romans would become bored or frustrated and go home. The Jugurthine War dragged on year after year, and all the while it remained a political football in Rome. The end did not come until 106 BC, when Jugurtha was at last captured, returned to Rome, and executed.

The Jugurthine War reveals much about how wars are fought in a time of Pax. Unable to defeat the empire, enemies wage war on the battlefield only as one component of a larger strategy to achieve victory within the politics of the empire itself. There is no doubt that Rome had the military might to defeat a small power like Numidia. Yet Jugurtha used his knowledge of Rome to win political battles that he hoped would end the war and give him what he wanted. To do so, he not only had to buy political influence but also to convince the Romans that he was their friend, or not important, or just too troublesome to bother with. But winning a military victory against Rome was so far outside the realm of possibilities that it was never even attempted.

There are at least a few similarities between this situation in Rome at the end of the second century BC and in the United States today. As a republic, America has in some measure played out all of its wars in the halls of Congress, or the political stump, or the editorial pages of America's newspapers. Yet in recent decades, even when American soldiers are not directly involved, local wars and crises frequently come to the United States to be fought with words. Consider the role played by the United States in brokering peace and establishing settlements in the Middle East. Not only do administration officials deal with these problems, but numerous members of Congress regularly travel abroad to listen to constituencies. Back at home, leaders and lobbyists from all over the world converge daily on American politicians to make their cases.

Like Jugurtha, many modern foreign governments and interests realize that they can win in the empire's political and popular arenas what they could never achieve on the battlefield. Foreign wars and foreign policy are all part of everyday politics in the United States. That provides an enormous incentive for foreigners to do all they can to affect those politics in their favor. Although laws were enacted in the 1970s to stop foreign contributions to American political parties and candidates, these have not always been effective. Like Jugurtha, foreign leaders find ways to circumvent or avoid the laws. In 1996, for example, there were the high-profile cases of Maria Hsia, Charlie Trie, and Johnny Chung (among others), who were accused of funneling money from the government of China into the Democratic Party. The scandals quickly became part of regular political wrangling in 1998 and beyond, as Republicans accused the Clinton administration of handing over sensitive satellite technology to the Chinese in return for the illegal campaign contributions. The republic, they argued, was for sale.

Spreading money around the capital remains a good way for foreign powers to try to get what they want from the empire. War is to be avoided, since it is impossible to defeat the empire's military forces. But when war does happen, the strategies of Philip of Macedon and Jugurtha are still quite viable. That is because the demise of all serious military rivals means that *none* of the empire's wars are ever fought for survival. The strategy of the empire's enemies, then, is to convince their politicians or people that the war is no longer worth fighting. This can be done in many ways, all of which include drawing out the conflict with low-level fighting. At the same time, the enemy attempts to convince the politicians and people of the empire that the war is lost, or foolhardy, or useless, or just very, very tedious. As we have seen in this and earlier chapters with regard to Rome, this enemy strategy stirs up quarrels among domestic political parties, who square off on the question of continuing the war or withdrawing.

Here again the examples of this phenomenon in recent American history are plentiful. The most obvious is the war in Vietnam. By dragging it out year after year the North Vietnamese were able to create both fatigue and frustration among the American people. When these were coupled with the social dynamics at work in the newly affluent baby-boom generation, frustration was transformed into civil unrest. The war became a political issue—not over the strategy of winning, but the wisdom of losing. War opponents in the United States argued that the American military was killing men, women, and children in the jungles of Southeast Asia for no good reason. The antiwar protests that erupted across America led the North Vietnamese negotiators in Paris to conclude that they need concede nothing in order to achieve an American withdrawal. General Vo Nguyen Giap is reported to have remarked that the North Vietnamese did not win the war on the battlefield but on the streets of San Francisco and Chicago.

The same set of factors can be seen at work in Iraq as well. Although the United States toppled the Iraqi government and replaced it with a friendly one, an insurgency of opposition groups continued to attack American forces. These militants did not believe that they had the military power to defeat the United States. They plainly did not. As of this writing, a little over thirty-six hundred American troops have died in Iraq during the four years since the American invasion. From a purely military perspective, a wartime casualty rate of less than a thousand troops per year would normally be considered good news. During the nine years of the Vietnam War more than fifty thousand American troops were killed. During the four years of American involvement in World War II four hundred thousand U.S. soldiers died. From the perspective of military strategy and history, American fatalities in Iraq remain remarkably small (albeit no less tragic).

The militants in Iraq knew this well enough. They were there on the ground, after all. But they also believed that the war could be won in the American political arena. Like Jugurtha, their job was to convince Americans that the war was lost, futile, or tiresome. They knew that killing an American soldier with a roadside bomb would have no impact on the battlefield in Iraq, but it would have a powerful impact on the news cycle in the United States. For the militants, each dead American was a CNN story, an op-ed piece, a political speech. Racking up additional dead brought additional disheartening news for the empire's population. In this, America's enemies were following a time-tested strategy. Although they might not be familiar with ancient Rome, they knew modern American history well enough. What had worked in Vietnam, they believed, would work again in Iraq. The Americans would become angry, frustrated, disillusioned, or bored and they would abandon their cause.

Were they right? According to an ABC News/*Washington Post* poll taken in July 2007, 59 percent of Americans believed that the United States "should withdraw its military forces from Iraq in order to avoid further U.S. military casualties, even if that means civil order is not restored there." That number grew steadily from just 23 percent who agreed with the statement when the war began. Clearly, the Jugurthine strategy still works. Nevertheless, it seems certain that the United States will remain in Iraq for the foreseeable future. The bloodbath that would ensue after an American withdrawal would be blamed fully on the president who ordered it. According to a 2007 report from the left-leaning

Brookings Institution, "the only thing standing between Iraq and a descent into a Lebanon- or Bosnia-style maelstrom is 140,000 American troops." If that were to happen, the report continues,

> we should expect many hundreds of thousands or even millions of people to die with three to four times that number wounded.... Of course, an Iraqi civil war will be even more painful for Americans to bear because, if it happens, it will be our fault. We will have launched the invasion and then failed to secure the peace, a failure that will have produced a civil war. For years to come Iraqis, Americans, and indeed most of the world will point their fingers at the U.S. government.

And they would be right to do so. Not only would the United States have broken faith with its friends in Iraq, but the abandoned country would become a haven for terrorists emboldened by their victory over the American "crusaders." The political damage to the president who ordered such a thing and to his or her party would be so devastating that it is difficult to believe that it would ever be seriously considered.

The benefits of living under Pax are undeniable. For that reason, Pax has a way of naturally drawing others toward it. It creates, in other words, a tug—strongest among those closest to the Empire of Trust yet still affecting those on its frontiers. Over and over again we have seen how smaller states appealed to Rome for aid, asking to become integrated into their alliance system. The same is true for the United States today. Eastern European countries have clamored for membership in NATO, which would place them firmly under American protection. Although Russian officials have rebuked and threatened them for their willingness to do so, these countries have accepted American troops and military installations. In May 2007 the Romanian Parliament voted 257–1 to allow the United States to establish a military base in their country. Ordinary Romanians celebrated the decision, pointing to America as their one beacon of hope during the days of Soviet control.

If the development of the American Empire of Trust is at all similar to that of its Roman predecessor, we should expect this "tug" to continue as more countries seek closer relationships with the United States. But that is only the earliest manifestation of this tug. As the empire continues to grow in strength, the tug becomes stronger, almost like a gravitational field pulling everything toward its center. When that level is reached, other states and peoples seek not just to become allies or friends but to be directly incorporated into the empire itself. For the Romans this meant the annexation of territories and their reorganization into provinces. We saw this happen in Sicily after the First Punic War, but the gravitational pull of Rome's Empire of Trust later became so great that by the second century BC wars were not required at all.

Let's illustrate this with a few examples. In 133 BC King Attalus III of Pergamum died. Kings do that. But what they don't do—what they had never done before—is leave their entire kingdom to foreigners. Attalus so trusted Rome with the care of his people and their lands that he bequeathed the rich territories and cities of Pergamum to the Roman people. The kingdom was subsequently organized into the Roman province of Asia. Unusual, yes. But the gravitational tug of Rome's Empire of Trust had become so great that it was literally causing rulers to hand their states over to the Romans without any prompting whatsoever. Indeed, in most cases, the Romans were uninterested in accepting the gifts, since they preferred allies to provinces. In 96 BC King Ptolemy Apion left his kingdom of Cyrene to the Roman people. The Romans tried to ignore it, although eventually they sent officials to administer the kingdom. A few years later, in 88 BC, Ptolemy Alexander I left all of Egypt to the people of Rome. Once again, the Romans declined the gift, installing instead other friendly Ptolemaic kings. In 74 BC King Nicomedes II bequeathed his kingdom of Bithynia to the Romans. And these are just a few cases. It is striking, though, that despite the Romans' desire to limit their overseas involvement, it was the overseas kingdoms that came to them.

It was not only the kingdoms on the periphery of Roman interest that responded to the tug of the Empire of Trust. Even those near the core found themselves pulled further toward the center. At the beginning of the first century BC Rome's oldest allies in Italy began to demand full citizenship as Romans. They no longer wanted to be part of separate states. For more than a century all decisions of importance to them had occurred in Rome, not in their local governments. They wanted to be part of those decisions. They wanted the same right to vote and hold office in Rome that the Romans had. In short, they want to *be* Romans. The Romans refused. Allies were one thing, citizens quite another. So, in 91 BC the Italian allies formed their own coalition and actually waged war against Rome *in order to become Romans.* Astonishing, but true. The Roman legions eventually won the "Social War," defeating the allies on the battlefield. But the Italian allies had made their case. Shortly after the war they were granted full citizenship as Romans.

Over the subsequent decades and centuries this tug of Pax continued to draw more people closer to the Empire of Trust. Enemies became friends; friends became allies; allies became citizens. Indeed, by the time of Christ, most Roman citizens were not Italian at all. A great many could not even speak Latin! But they had the same rights as anyone else in Rome. When St. Paul, a Jew from Tarsus, was arrested in Jerusalem he avoided a flogging and demanded a trial in Rome. Those were his rights as a Roman citizen. A few centuries later, in AD 212, the process was complete. *All* free inhabitants of the lands of the Roman Empire were granted full Roman citizenship. The gravitational tug had finally brought everything to its center.

The American Empire of Trust is still too young for anything like that. Nevertheless, it is possible to see the earliest manifestations of it. Since the end of the Cold War there has been an increasing interest worldwide in American elections. Many foreigners see them as having a direct, even overriding, impact on their own lives. Within the past ten years some Europeans have even suggested that it is unjust that they have no voice in America's government. On August 17, 2000, George Monbiot wrote in the Manchester *Guardian*:

> Everyone on earth should be allowed to vote in American elections. All the major decisions about the future of the world are now brokered by the United States. Only the US has the power to provoke a world war. Only the US can re-engineer the global economy. As the Trans-

atlantic Economic Partnership—which is quietly "harmonising" our laws with those of North America—demonstrates, Washington now exercises more control over the lives of British people than Westminster.

That was not just hyperbole. During the 2004 presidential election in the United States the *Financial Times* noted that for the first time in history every country in the world had been polled on the election, as if it were for the president of the world rather than simply one country.

If the 2004 election had been worldwide, John Kerry would have won in a landslide. Poll after poll showed that George W. Bush was deeply unpopular among the international "electorate." As Election Day approached there was a palpable frustration among many Europeans that they had no voice at all in the decision. Ken Dubin, a political scientist at Carlos III University in Madrid, told *The New York Times* in May 2004, "People say, 'I'm very frustrated that I can't vote in the U.S. elections, because these are the ones that affect my way of life more than anything else.'"

Responding to this frustration, the editors of the *Guardian* wrote an important editorial, called "My Fellow Non-Americans," just one month before the 2004 presidential election. In it, they told their British audience that:

> Certainly, the actions of the US impact on our lives in overwhelming ways; British political life may now be at least as heavily influenced by White House policy as by the choices of UK voters. And yet, though the US Declaration of Independence speaks of "a decent respect to the opinions of mankind," you don't, of course, have a vote. You can't even donate money to the campaigns: foreign contributions are outlawed. And you're unlikely to have the chance to do any campaigning on the ground. All you can do is wait and watch: you're powerless.

In order to influence the election, the editors urged their readers to write to the voters of Clark County, Ohio—a crucial swing area that would have an important impact on the election—urging the residents to vote for the candidate of the reader's choice—which they acknowledged would be John Kerry. The *Guardian* readers did so, by the thousands. The effort failed. Clark County residents resented the idea that foreigners would seek to influence American elections. Like the Romans of 100 BC they wanted allies, not foreigners acting as citizens. The editors of the *Guardian* quickly realized that their "Operation Clark Country" was backfiring, feeding into a suspicion among some Americans that Kerry was running to be president of Europe rather than America. "Yikes!" replied the editors, and they called the whole thing off. But the damage was done. George Bush won Clark County (which Gore had won four years earlier) and went on to win Ohio and the presidency.

When the 2004 election results were announced there was a real sense of exasperation among many Europeans—and not just the readers of the *Guardian*. London's *Daily Mirror* famously ran the cover headline "How can 59,054,087 people be so DUMB?" and then just below that: "U.S. Election Disaster, pages . . ." Smoldering at the election outcome, many Europeans pinned their hopes on the Congressional midterm elections in 2006. When the Democrats won big, capturing both houses of Congress, French citizens were packed into bars hailing the election results with whoops and cheers. More than two hundred Socialist members of the European Parliament called the result "the beginning of the end of a six-year nightmare for the world."

It is safe to say that few American bars will be filled with cheers or boos over election results in Paris, London, or anywhere else in the world for that matter. Although every European, and almost every soul on planet Earth, can name the president of the United States, a great many Americans cannot name a single foreign leader. Americans are not stupid—they just don't care. The American president directly affects the lives of an increasingly large segment of the world's population, while other world leaders do not. That is why in 2008 the BBC World Service beams to its global audience the show, *Election 2008: America's Decision—Your Business*. That is why all European news outlets covered closely not only the 2008 election, but even the primaries in each state. As *USA Today* noted on January 9, 2008, "You'd think they were electing their own president the way Europeans are following the U.S. presidential primaries this year."

In the decades to come, the drumbeat of calls for foreign involvement in American elections will increase. Like Rome's Italian allies, the Europeans will be the first to demand the right to vote in American elections (as some of them are already doing). Americans, like Romans, will continue to resist. But the gravitational tug of the Empire of Trust will continue apace. At some point, perhaps not during the lifetime of anyone reading this, but at some point it seems likely that American citizenship will indeed be extended to America's closest allies.

Before ending our discussion of Pax, something should be said about the role this will have, indeed is already having, on culture and language. Although the Romans greatly admired Greek literature and culture, they nevertheless insisted on the use of Latin for all practical purposes. Throughout the Roman Empire all communications, treaties, contracts, or any other legal document had to be written in Latin. Roman ambassadors always spoke Latin and used translators, even when they could speak Greek perfectly well. It was *illegal* to speak any language other than Latin in the Senate House. In lightly civilized western Europe, Latin quickly displaced the native Celtic languages. That is why today the areas of the continent that were part of the Roman Empire still speak Romance languages—the language of the Romans. There Latin conquered, just as the legions did.

But in the heavily populated and highly sophisticated Greek East, it was a different story. Latin may have been used for business or government, but it was Greek that remained the language of refinement, high culture, and good manners. Long before the Roman Empire fell, the Latin language died in the East, surviving only in the backward West. Why did Latin win the West but lose the East? In the West, Latin was the language of power and prestige. In the East, Greek kept that position. The sophisticated East remained the factory of high culture in the ancient world—and all of that culture was in Greek. The best plays, histories, philosophy, music, everything—it was overwhelmingly Greek. The

Romans had something that resembled high culture, to be sure, but in the main it was little more than a Greek knockoff. The Romans were very good at winning wars, keeping order, and building things, but they were all thumbs when it came to producing culture.

That is one way in which the Romans and the Americans are very, very different. Americans are cultural innovators in a big way. A unique American culture has spread across the world, where it not only dominates, it smothers. There are few places on Earth where one cannot pop into a theater to see an American movie, turn on the radio to listen to American rock, or look around a street to see American blue jeans. It may not be high culture, but it is ubiquitous culture and that's enough. And with all of it comes English.

It was not so long ago that French was the language of high culture in the world. I remember as an undergraduate student my French teacher proudly telling us that French was the world's truly indispensable language. No matter where you roamed in the world, he said, you could always do a little *"parlez-vous français"* and find yourself sufficiently understood. And he was quite right. As a young man, I used French across Europe and the Middle East and found it to work wonders. It was, quite literally, the lingua franca. But no more. French has become the leather punch in one's Swiss Army knife of spoken languages—obviously sharp, but with no clear purpose. Today only one blade is necessary: English. When a Frenchman or German or Italian or Spaniard travels to a country in which he does not speak the language, he no longer uses French. He speaks English. English is the first foreign language taught in virtually all schools in the world. It is the worldwide language of finance, science, computers, aviation, and, yes, culture.

This naturally upsets Europeans—and particularly the French, who see their once-mighty language drowning under a wave of English. Unlike Greek, the French language has no good way to defend itself against the empire's tongue. In France the Académie Française works hard to preserve French, even coining new words for new technologies. Yet this is the sort of artificial resuscitation usually reserved for not-quite-dead languages such as Gaelic in Ireland or Latin in the Vatican. It is a symptom of decay that will likely accelerate as time passes. This is not to say that French or any other European language will disappear entirely. It won't. But in the coming centuries each will become more like the various European dialects that still survive today—spoken at home, cherished for its history, but simply not used in polite society.

And yet, the decline of French is particularly ironic, for that most beautiful of languages is the very one that was planted in France by the last Empire of Trust—the Romans.

Chapter 9

_____

Fights Around the Dinner Table of Empire

It was a day of nasty partisan fighting on Capitol Hill. Rowdy protestors had surrounded the area while representatives tried unsuccessfully to schedule an already delayed vote. The stakes were too high and the rancor too bitter to permit agreement on even a simple roll call. One side was demanding sweeping reforms; the other insisting on preserving tradition and stability. Both were engaged in plenty of finger-pointing, accusing the other of endangering the people and the rule of law. Tensions on the Hill had never been higher.

That was the scene in Rome in 133 BC. Capitol Hill was the city's highest and most revered of the seven hills that made up Rome. Of course, Washington, D.C., has a Capitol Hill, too, named after the Roman one, and which has seen its own share of political fights. But not like this. In 133 the Popular Assembly was convening in the open air to vote on an extraordinarily controversial measure. As the voice of the people of Rome, the Assembly was the constitutional basis of all power. Yet in the past the people had always deferred to the Senate, the revered body of Rome's greatest and most respected men. Not today. And perhaps not anymore.

The problem was one of politics. Rome's growing affluence had swelled the city's population to unprecedented levels. What had once been a modest city-state with a committed citizenry was now a massive metropolis dotted with slums, the unemployed, and more than a few gangs.

Floods of working-class and middle-class people had descended on Rome in search of opportunities—or just to be close to the halls of power. As a result, the lower classes in Rome were now more numerous and potentially more powerful than ever before. That fact had not escaped the notice of aspiring Roman politicians. In the Senate, which had long been the de facto seat of power, a two-party system began to take shape. The Optimates, who had a firm control over the Senate, defended tradition and moderation. The Populares, on the other hand, were the out-of-power party. Excluded from positions of authority in the Senate, Populares leaders turned instead to the people, seeking to energize the Popular Assembly and the increasingly vocal urban population in order to acquire political power. Despite their name, the Populares were not commoners themselves. They were typical blue-blood elites, members of some of the oldest and richest families in Rome. But they saw a way to advance their own political interests by serving (or posing) as the champions of the people against the rich, aristocratic Optimates.

That is what led to the ruckus on Capitol Hill. One of the Assembly leaders, the tribune Tiberius Gracchus, had recently ridden a wave of popularity in Rome by championing a land reform bill that would distribute state property to common citizens. But he had passed the measure without consulting the Senate, something almost unheard of in the history of the Republic. In order to do that, he had engineered the forcible removal of a colleague tribune from the Assembly—another unprecedented step. And to make matters worse, he was now giving speeches across the city in which he claimed that the rich elites in the Senate were out to kill him. To defend himself, he cobbled together a bodyguard of freedmen (former slaves) who generally took care of crowd control and busting heads.

And there was quite a crowd to control that day in 133 BC. Tiberius' supporters loudly demanded passage of his latest initiative, which was really all about him. Tiberius wanted the Assembly to appoint several of his own family members to official positions of great authority. But there was more. He also wanted the Assembly to reelect him as tribune—something that had not been done for centuries and may well have been illegal.

Tiberius insisted that it was necessary. You see, in Roman law no one, no matter his position, was allowed to lay hands on a tribune. They were legally sacrosanct. Tiberius claimed that the moment his term of office expired, his aristocratic enemies would arrest him or murder him. For his own safety, he argued, he must remain tribune. Besides, who better to defend the people's interests against the fat cats in the Senate than he?

Not everyone in the Assembly or among the onlookers agreed with Tiberius or his plan. Many judged him to be a political opportunist who was using the mobs in a bid to seize ultimate power and overturn the Republic. Romans, like Americans, were allergic to the idea of concentrated power. The Roman Republic was founded on the rejection of kings. And Tiberius Gracchus was starting to look a lot like a king in the making. Protesters and opponents of Tiberius shouted him down, trying to stop an Assembly vote on a measure that they believed was plainly illegal. The clamor was deafening—so loud that it was difficult for anyone to make himself heard. Thinking that the meeting might erupt into violence, Tiberius and his men armed themselves with sticks, which they hid beneath their clothing. The stage was thus set for a new kind of Roman politics.

What happened next is still unclear. Apparently Tiberius made a sign of some sort to his people in the crowd. The sign—whatever it was—included bringing his hand up to his head. His supporters later claimed that he was letting them know that he believed his life was in danger. Some historians have suggested that it was a sign for his ruffians to start strong-arming the opposition in order to eject them or at least get them to quiet down. Whatever it was, some observers took it as a sign that he wanted the Assembly to crown him king of Rome. One of them sped toward the nearby Temple of Trust, where the Senate was assembled. There the senators were discussing what should be done with an Assembly in chaos. The witness burst into the temple and excitedly told the senators what he had seen. Tiberius Gracchus, he insisted, was using the people to make himself king.

Immediately, a cry of protest rang out among the senators. Even Tiberius' supporters could not defend this, if it were indeed true. The tribune had already used the power of the Assembly to overturn tradition and precedent. They would not let him use it to overturn the Republic as well. The high priest of Rome, Pontifex Maximus P. Scipio Nasica, rose from his seat and turned toward the attending consul, P. Mucius Scaevola. He demanded that the consul use the military against Tiberius and his supporters before it was too late. If Tiberius managed to legislate himself a crown, it would be he who commanded the troops, not the consul. But Scaevola remained seated, refusing to budge. He replied that he would never use violence against a Roman citizen unless he had been duly convicted of a crime. If Tiberius managed to convince the Assembly to vote him a crown, or a new term of office, or any other measure that was unconstitutional, Scaevola affirmed that he would not recognize it as valid. But he would not break the law in order to save it.

That was not the answer that the *pontifex maximus* wanted to hear. Red-faced, he turned to the Senate and said in a loud voice: "Since, then, the chief magistrate betrays the state, those who wish to preserve the law follow me!" Solemnly, he covered his head in the style of an officiating pontifex and walked out the great door of the Temple of Trust. Many of the senators followed him, filing past the still-sitting consul. As they approached the Assembly they stepped into a sea of chaos that was rapidly degenerating into a brawl. Some of the senators stooped down to pick up the sturdy legs of broken benches that had been smashed in the disorder. Shocked to see the toga-clad senators marching toward them, the crowd began to scatter. With his supporters fleeing, Tiberius had only his loyal bodyguard. It was not enough. The senators and their attendants fell upon Tiberius and his men, pummeling them with their makeshift clubs. Tiberius tried to run, but a senator grabbed him by his toga—the defining garment of his class. Frightened, Tiberius tore off the toga, speeding away in just his tunic. He did not get far. Two senators caught up to him at the magnificent Temple of Jupiter Capitolinus. There they clubbed him to death. His bloody corpse was left there, mangled and broken, beneath the brooding statues of the ancient kings.

Things had changed in Rome. The Romans had always had their differences. That is the essence of a republic. But they had dealt with those differences with respect and always within the rule of law. By 133 BC respect was becoming a rare commodity in Roman politics. With regularity, Tiberius had insulted the Senate, even refusing to allow it to perform its time-honored function as an advisory body. For their part, many senators referred to Tiberius as a ruthless tyrant whose aim was to overturn the state and restore the days of monarchy. At last, the rhetoric became so heated that law itself was dispensed with and blood began to flow. Romans were killing Romans.

What caused the change? What led to this level of hatred, division, and strife among the Romans? Ironically, it was the direct result of Rome's unprecedented peace, prosperity, and security. In other words, the new and bitter disputes that erupted among the Romans were themselves another product of Pax.

No blood has yet flowed on America's Capitol Hill, but the Pax Americana is still young. Nevertheless, the Cold War had hardly ended before the partisan rancor in the United States began to rise. This is not to say that Americans have not always fought like cats and dogs in the political arena of their Republic. But in the 1990s, when the country had reached unprecedented levels of prosperity, peace, and security, the "politics of personal destruction" seemed to come suddenly to the fore. In 1991 the Supreme Court nomination hearings for Clarence Thomas took place amid a poisonous partisan atmosphere. Rather then assessing the nominee's credentials or qualifications, the Judiciary Committee of the Senate was reduced to asking questions such as "Did you ever say in words or substance something like 'There is a pubic hair in my Coke?'" and "Did you ever use the term *Long Dong Silver* in conversation with Professor Hill?"

It was the turn of Republicans during the years of the Clinton administration—the first full presidency after the fall of the Soviet Union. At the urging of conservatives, a sexual harrassment suit was filed against President Clinton by Paula Jones. During sworn depositions, the president was asked about other sexual affairs, including one that he had recently had while in the White House. He lied about it under oath. When this was discovered, the Republican-controlled Congress impeached

Clinton—only the second president in American history to achieve that infamy. It was President Clinton himself who coined the term *politics of personal destruction*, insisting that his opponents were trying to win through smear and slander what they could not win at the ballot box.

Setting aside the merits of the specific case, there can be no doubt that the course of the Clinton impeachment was animated almost exclusively by a hard-knuckled political struggle. In 1974 President Richard Nixon resigned the presidency because his own party, the Republicans, refused to support him if he were impeached. Nixon had disgraced the presidency, they said, and he deserved to go. But in 1998 it was a different story. Although the Democrats in Congress drafted a censure of President Clinton stating that he had "violated the trust of the American people," and "dishonored the office they had entrusted to him," they still walked out of Congress when the impeachment became final. Many of the same Democrats went to the White House, where they applauded Vice President Gore when he declared that the man who they believed had dishonored the presidency would "be regarded in the history books as one of our greatest presidents." The subsequent impeachment was a show trial. Every Democratic senator had made up his or her mind before it began. When the vote was called, not a single Democrat voted for conviction.

What is interesting is not whether the evidence warranted President Clinton's conviction, but the fact that throughout the entire affair it was political divisions, not truth or law, that mattered. No group of Democratic senators went to the Oval Office to serve notice to the president that they would not defend a man who had "violated the trust of the American people." Quite the contrary, every one of them—every single one—defended him. They did so not because they believed that he was innocent. Their censure document makes plain that they did not. They did so because they did not believe that disgracing the office of the presidency was sufficient reason to remove from office a member of their own party. And so, in the Senate of the United States of America, a question regarding the rule of law was put before the assembled—and the vote went down along party lines.

As the new millennium dawned in the United States, it was greeted with much chatter about a "nation divided" along a "red state/blue state" fault line. A flood of articles were written about these two different worlds—one peopled with wealthy, educated, liberal, coastal elites and the other with working-class, NASCAR-watching, flyover country, conservative trogs. And it is true that the two sides are hardly on speaking terms. Red staters tune in to Fox News and Rush Limbaugh and get their "print" information from the Drudge Report and the blogosphere—with a few still reading *The Wall Street Journal* or *The Washington Times*. The blue staters tend to hold with the establishment outlets like CNN, NPR, *The New York Times,* and (occasionally) network news shows, although they, too, have Internet resources like MoveOn.org. This division naturally breeds a caricature of one's counterparts. Rush Limbaugh, who has built the most successful radio show in America, refers to his political opponents as "environmentalist wackos," "libs," and "feminazis." On the left, a cult of Bush hatred reached obsessive levels. Liberal organizer Cindy Sheehan referred to the president as (among other more colorful things) an "evil maniac," a "fuehrer," and a "terrorist." *The New Republic*'s Jonathan Chait boldly wrote, "I hate President George W. Bush. There, I said it. I think his policies rank him among the worst presidents in U.S. history. And, while I'm tempted to leave it at that, the truth is that I hate him for less substantive reasons, too." Columnist Robert Novak has written that those on the political left have developed a hatred of the president "that I have never seen in forty-four years of campaign watching."

How is it that Pax brings about such internal division? The answer is as old as history. Humans are social animals. They naturally form themselves into groups. By their nature, groups have defining features that exclude others. That is what makes them a group. If I want to join the West End Bridge Club but have no idea how to play bridge and no desire to learn, well, let's face it—I'm not getting in. Even groups that insist that they are "inclusive" or "welcoming to all" have features that separate them from other people and other groups. For example, the Unitarian Universalist Association is known for its tolerance and acceptance of all faiths, traditions, and cultures, yet they would certainly decline to extend membership to Nazis or white supremacists. All groups define themselves not only by who they are but, just as importantly, who they are not. Those definitions become stronger, more deeply felt, when the group itself is under attack or threatened in some way.

States are just big groups of citizens. Like smaller groups, they define themselves by a set of criteria for membership (birth, language, et cetera) that by implication define nonmembers (otherwise known as foreigners). A tightly knit state will naturally be one in which the citizens share common beliefs and in which each citizen possesses a shared feeling of responsibility for the well-being of that state. This does not come about through happy talk or altruism. It frequently happens in opposition to others. A small city-state with powerful neighbors will normally have fewer internal divisions, because the citizens are bound together in their attempt to survive. As we have seen, the ancient Romans were fused together by a rejection of kings and a desire to preserve their city and culture against outside threats. They remained a closely knit group so long as they continued to have powerful outside enemies—so long as the collective focus of their lives was the defense and preservation of their society.

To one extent or another, the same might be said of almost every group of citizens that make up a state. It was certainly the case with Americans, who audaciously built theirs in direct opposition to Britain and even wrote a Declaration of Independence to explain that opposition to the world. Since then, Americans have seen themselves as a City on a Hill, set apart from a warring, degenerate, or immoral outside world. Enemies helped to sharpen that definition. In the early years, the British and some tribes of Indians served well enough. Later, during World War I, the autocrats of Europe took that role. But nothing helps to bind a state together better than a direct attack by a foreign foe. Pearl Harbor transformed an America wallowing in the depths of the Depression and determined to stay out of "foreign entanglements" into a unified, determined nation of patriots. That one attack did it. It defined in the starkest terms the difference between "us" and "them." And the "them" was hostile, foreign, and just plain bad.

For years I lectured to college students about the effect that Pearl Harbor had on Americans at the time. I told them how young men, just like those slouching in my very classroom, who thought the world could go hang itself in 1940 suddenly lined up at army induction centers after the Japanese Empire struck. I don't think they believed me—and I admit that I found it a bit hard to swallow myself. But then came the even more lethal attacks of September 11, 2001. And it happened again. Enlistments in the military soared. Patriotism was no longer a dirty word. All Americans felt closer to their fellow citizens than ever before. That happened because the attacks brought into sharp relief the fact that all Americans, no matter their race, creed, or politics, were the targets of a shared enemy.

You may have seen the television commercial that aired around the one-year anniversary of September 11. On a black screen appeared the words: "On September 11, terrorists tried to change our lives forever." The scene then faded to a residential neighborhood, each and every house proudly adorned with an American flag. And then the words: "They succeeded." It was a good commercial. And it's true. By attacking the United States, the terrorists managed to paper over the divisions in American life and politics, binding all Americans together—at least for a time. The feeling of unity remained strong for several years. But then no further attacks came. The enemy seemed to melt away. A few high-profile terrorist plans were uncovered, but the lack of any further attacks led more and more Americans to conclude that the threat was just not very grave. And without the threat, the dynamics that had bound Americans so closely together gave way to those that bound them together into smaller groups, such as red states and blue states. The dire threat to America was no longer al-Qaeda, but Bush, or the liberals, or someone else altogether.

Many centuries ago, the Romans had a similar experience. After the murder of Tiberius Gracchus divisions in Roman politics and society continued to deepen—and for the same reasons. The lack of any serious threat to the republic, along with extraordinary wealth and prosperity, created an environment in which groups were formed *within* the state in opposition to other internal groups. The stakes were not the survival of the state or the continued prosperity of its citizens. Those things were so well established that they were no longer in question. Instead, the objectives were power, money, and prestige within the empire. The battlefields that mattered were no longer on faraway shores, but in the forums, Senate House, and courts of Rome itself.

If peace and prosperity are the twin bearers of fierce internal divisions, then the Romans believed that their problems began with the prosperity—not the peace. Before they had emerged as the only remaining superpower, the Romans had already begun to enjoy the prosperity that comes with empire. Some of it was in the form of war booty, but that was only the most visible source. Much more important was the expansion of foreign markets, to which Roman businessmen began to flock. As the Romans stabilized their world, they also boosted their economy and the economies of those around them. Then as now, business loves stability and hates uncertainty. And the Romans had created plenty of stability.

Looking back almost two centuries, the Roman author Livy believed that the beginning of destructive internal divisions in his country could be dated to 188 BC, when the conquest of Asia Minor brought the Romans into direct contact with the extravagent riches of the East:

> [Thus was] brought into Rome for the first time bronze couches, costly coverlets, tapestry, and other fabrics, and—what was at that time considered gorgeous furniture—pedestal tables and silver trays. Banquets were made more attractive by the presence of girls who played on the harp and sang and danced, and by other forms of amusement. And the banquets themselves began to be prepared with greater care and expense. A cook, who used to be regarded and treated as the lowest menial worker, was rising in value. Indeed, what had been a servile job came to be looked upon as a fine art. Even still, what existed in those days was scarcely the germ of the luxury that was still coming.

Livy was right. Rome's affluence and wealth were growing and dramatically affecting the lives of its citizens. By 171 BC commercial bakeries had opened in Rome. That may not sound overly indulgent, but baking had always been the special duty of the Roman wife. It was something done at home, at the hearth, the reserve of Vesta. No more. Roman women were liberating themselves from the hearth, preferring instead to purchase their bread—or send their servants out to do so.

Growing affluence in Rome naturally drove a hunger for the finer things. Greek artists found a ready market for their wares in the homes and streets of the Romans. So, too, did Greek tutors and philosophers, who were mobbed by young Romans who sought their countercultural wisdom. Those young Romans, the heirs of a new affluence undreamed of by their parents, had an appetite for the new, the refined, and the exotic. Their elders did not. At least not at first. In 161 BC the Senate went so far as to expel all the philosophers from Rome. But it didn't last. As a new generation came of age and moved into their parents' positions of power, they brought with them their refined tastes. And the same would happen with their children, and their children, and so on.

The most vocal critic of prosperity and its effect on the fabric of Roman society was Cato the Elder—a respected senator and a man of great wealth himself. Cato was convinced that Greek learning, Greek ways, and Greek philosophy were extinguishing the noble Roman spirit. He frequently declared "in the tone of a prophet or a seer, that Rome would lose her empire when she had become fully infected with Greek culture." It was this fear that led the Senate in 154 BC to order the builders of a new theater in Rome to cease and desist from their project. The senators saw in the theater a conduit of Greek culture—a place not only for staging Greek plays but for Romans to become addicted to the pleasures of Greek life.

The change that was occurring among the Romans was noticed by outsiders as well. Polybius, a Greek who lived in Rome after the Third Macedonian War and who had the opportunity to observe Romans and their culture over the course of many years, was surprised by how much the culture—particularly among the young Romans—had changed.

> Some of [the young Roman men] had abandoned themselves to love affairs with boys and others to consorting with prostitutes, and many

to musical entertainments and banquets and all of the extravagance that they entail. In these respects, they had been quickly infected with Greek weaknesses during the war with Perseus. So great in fact was the permissiveness and hedonism among the young men, that some paid a talent for a male lover and others three hundred drachmas for a jar of caviar. This aroused the indignation of Cato, who said once in a public speech that it was the surest sign of deterioration in a republic when pretty boys fetch more than fields, and jars of caviar more than plowmen.

It was not just wealth that was changing the Romans, but peace and security as well. Polybius saw that too:

It was then that this inclination to extravagance declared itself, first because [the Romans] thought that now after the fall of the Macedonian kingdom their universal dominion was undisputed, and second because after the riches of Macedonia had been transported to Rome there was a great display of wealth both in public and in private.

Pliny, writing almost two centuries later and with 20/20 hindsight, agreed. It was in the second century BC, he insisted, that Rome was beset by wealth and unquestioned supremacy in the world. As he put it, "By fatal coincidence, the Roman people at the same time both acquired a taste for vice and obtained a means of gratifying it."

Polybius had no doubt about the effect all of this was having on the Romans. Although he had earlier praised them for their honesty, he saw in his own time that bribery and corruption was seeping into Roman civic life.

If I were dealing with earlier times, I would have confidently asserted about all the Romans in general that none of them would engage in such a thing; I speak of the years before they undertook wars across the sea and during which they preserved their own principles and practices. At the present time, however, I would not venture to say this of all of them.

241

Although a sophisticate of the luxurious Greek East, Polybius nevertheless mourned the passing of Roman virtues that had built their Empire of Trust. Hard work, thrift, moral integrity, piety ... these, he believed, were drowning in a sea of riches, luxury, and peace. There was nothing to be done. Indeed, Polybius considered the process itself to be inevitable.

> That all things are subject to decay and change is a truth that scarcely needs proof; for the course of nature is sufficient to convince us of this. There are two ways in which every state is liable to decay: one is external factors and the other is a growth of the state itself.... When a state has weathered many great perils and subsequently attains supremacy and uncontested sovereignty, it is evident that under the influence of long established prosperity, life will become more extravagant and the citizens overly fierce in their rivalry regarding office and other objects of desire. As these problems continue increasing, the beginning of the change for the worse will be due first to the love of political office and the disgrace that comes with obscurity, and second to extravagance and proud displays of personal wealth.

It was not the elites who were responsible for this state of affairs, Polybius argued. Rather, it was the Roman people themselves. Polybius predicted that, puffed up with pride because of their own new wealth and status in the world, the people would demand more of everything and gladly hand over limitless power to those politicians who promised it. Instead of leaders who conscientiously looked after the health and welfare of the Roman state, the people would elect those who made them feel good or showered them with gifts. Political pandering, not judicious wisdom, would become the basic qualification for Roman office.

> And for this change the people will be responsible. On the one hand they will think they have a grievance against those leaders who seem stingy, and on the other hand, they will be puffed up by the flattery of those campaigning for office. Stirred to fury and swayed by passion,

the people will no longer consent to obey or even to be the equals of the political class, but will demand the lion's share of power for themselves. When that happens, the state will change its name to the finest sounding of all, freedom and democracy, but will change its nature to the worst thing of all, mob-rule.

Since the Roman state outlived Polybius by some sixteen centuries, we can reasonably conclude that his prophesies of doom were a bit premature. Indeed, future centuries would witness the Roman people becoming *less* powerful, not more. But Polybius was not alone in his predictions. A curious thing about a time of Pax is that it produces a bumper crop of people claiming that the whole thing is about to collapse. It seems that the stronger and more secure the Empire of Trust becomes, the larger the market for prophecies of its destruction. Perhaps it is just boredom among the citizens. Or perhaps it is a response to a human need for adversity and challenge in an age in which those had been all but abolished. Whatever the case, it was difficult to go broke telling the Roman people that their empire, their culture, and their way of life were sick and ready to die.

Since these predictions did not come true, few have survived. But some have. In most cases, the culprit was the declining morality of the Romans, fed by peace and prosperity. The Romans, it was said, had turned from their old ways and become a people no longer worthy of empire. This was a particularly popular argument among the Romans themselves. Livy, for example, writing at the time of Rome's greatest opulence and power, published his history so that his countrymen could:

> follow the decay of the national character, observing how at first it slowly sinks, then slips downward more and more rapidly, and finally begins to plunge into headlong ruin, until it reaches these days, in which we can bear neither our diseases nor their remedies.... Wealth has brought avarice in its train, and the unlimited command of pleasure has created in men a passion for ruining themselves and everything else through self-indulgence and licentiousness.

Sallust, a Roman politician and writer in the first century BC, was just as downbeat as Polybius before him and Livy after him. He extolled the good old days of Roman values:

> Virtue was held in high esteem. The closest unity prevailed and avarice was a thing almost unknown. Justice and righteousness were upheld not so much by law as by natural instinct. They quarreled and fought with their country's foes; between themselves the citizens contended only for honor. In making offerings to the gods they spared no expense; at home they lived frugally and never betrayed a friend. By combining boldness in war with fair dealing when peace was restored, they protected themselves and the state.

All that changed, Sallust tells us, after Rome emerged as the lone superpower. It was then that the morality of Romans unraveled.

> To the men who had so easily endured toil and peril, anxiety and adversity, the leisure and riches which are generally regarded as so desirable proved a burden and a curse. Growing love of money and the lust for power which followed it engendered every kind of evil. Avarice destroyed honor, integrity, and every other virtue, and instead taught men to be proud and cruel, to neglect religion, and to hold nothing too sacred to sell. Ambition tempted many to be false, to have one thought hidden in their hearts, another ready on their tongues, to become a man's friend or enemy not because they judged him worthy or unworthy but because they thought it would pay.... Poverty was now looked on as a disgrace and a blameless life as a form of disorder. Riches made the younger generation prey to luxury, avarice, and pride. Honor and modesty, all laws divine and human, were alike disregarded in a spirit of recklessness and intemperance. To someone today familiar with mansions and villas built so magnificently that they seem to be towns unto themselves, it is instructive to visit the old temples built by our god-fearing ancestors. In those days piety was the ornament of shrines; glory, of men's dwellings.... I need not remind you of some recent

projects that no one but an eyewitness would believe—how private citizens have leveled mountains and paved the seas for their building operations. Such men, it seems to me, have treated their wealth as a mere plaything: instead of making honorable use of it, they have shamefully misused it on the first wasteful project that occurred to them. Equally strong was their passion for fornication, guzzling, and other forms of sensuality. Men prostituted themselves like women, and women sold their chastity to every comer. To please their palates they ransacked land and sea. They went to bed before they needed sleep, and instead of waiting until they felt hungry, thirsty, cold, or fatigue, they preempted their bodies' needs with self-indulgence.

Like other Roman writers, Sallust believed that it was also Rome's unquestioned supremacy in the world that further degraded its spirit. In this light, the final defeat of Rome's old enemy Carthage, in 146 BC was actually bad for the Romans.

Fear of enemies preserved the good morals of the state. But when the people were relieved of this fear, the favorite vices of prosperity—license and pride—appeared as a natural consequence. Thus the peace and quiet which they had longed for in time of adversity proved, when they had obtained it, to be even more grievous than the adversity. For the leaders started to use their positions, and the people their liberty, to gratify their selfish passions, every man snatching and seizing what he could for himself. So the whole community was split into political parties, and the Republic, which hitherto had been the common interest of all, was torn asunder.

The Romans were not the only ones predicting their demise. Foreigners also got into the act. We can see this in the *Sibylline Oracles*, a collection of prophesies that purported to come from the priestesses of Apollo, but were actually written with a strong Jewish influence beginning in the mid-second century BC and continuing until roughly the fourth century AD. Unlike the original Sibylline Books, the Oracles were published and widely read across the empire. Unconcerned with the effects of security and prosperity, the Oracles claimed that the empire would collapse simply because the Romans were bad people and they had done bad things. For example, the Roman victories in Asia Minor were, for the Oracles, a good reason to see their empire dismembered:

> As much of tribute as Rome did receive
> Of Asia, even thrice as many goods
> Shall Asia back again from Rome receive,
> And her destructive outrage pay her back.
> As many as from Asia ever served
> A house of the Italians, twenty times
> As many Italians shall in Asia serve
> In poverty, and numerous debts incur.
>   O virgin, soft rich child of Latin Rome,
> Oft at thy much-remembered marriage feasts
> Drunken with wine, now shalt thou be a slave
> And wedded in no honorable way.
> And oft shall mistress shear thy pretty hair,
> And wreaking satisfaction cast thee down
> From heaven to earth. . . .

It goes on like that, but you get the idea. The wickedness of Rome would cause it to founder and then "stretched prone among the burning ashes, it shall slay itself."

There was indeed a vibrant market for telling Romans that their empire was doomed. Although few such works survive, there is one that deserves special mention. Like so many others, this one would have been lost—except that in this case it was written by early Christians and became part of their sacred writings. It can be found in the last book of the Bible, the Book of Revelation. Written at some point in the late first century AD, probably at Ephesus, it uses symbolic language throughout. Nevertheless, it makes no secret of its prophesy of the impending fall of Rome.

It begins, like the Oracles, by referring to Rome as a woman (although in this case a harlot):

> Then one of the seven angels who had the seven bowls came and said to me, "Come, I will show you the judgment of the great harlot who is seated upon many waters, with whom the kings of the earth have committed fornication, and with the wine of whose fornication the dwellers on earth have become drunk." And he carried me away in the Spirit into a wilderness, and I saw a woman sitting on a scarlet beast which was full of blasphemous names, and it had seven heads and ten horns. The woman was clothed in purple and scarlet, and adorned with gold and jewels and pearls, holding in her hand a golden cup full of abominations and the impurities of her fornication.... When I saw her I marveled greatly. But the angel said to me, "Why marvel? I will tell you the mystery of the woman, and of the beast with seven heads and ten horns that carries her.... This calls for a mind with wisdom: the seven heads are seven hills on which the woman is seated; they are also seven kings, five of whom have fallen, one is, the other has not yet come." (Rev. 17:1–4, 7, 9)

Plain enough. Rome, built on seven hills, was wealthy and in bed with the kings of the world. The referenced seven kings are the Julio-Claudian and Flavian emperors. Chapter 18 of Revelation follows with an extended description of Rome's doom. First, an angel comes to announce it (18:1–3), then a voice from heaven calls out the Christians "lest you share in her plagues."

> Since in her heart she says, "A queen I sit, I am no widow, mourning I shall never see," so shall her plagues come in a single day, pestilence and mourning and famine, and she shall be burned with fire, for mighty is the Lord God who judges her.... And the merchants of the earth weep and mourn for her, since no one buys their cargo any more, cargo of gold, silver, jewels and pearls, fine linen, purple, silk

and scarlet, all kinds of scented wood, all articles of ivory, all articles of costly wood, bronze, iron and marble, cinnamon, spice, incense, myrrh, frankincense, wine, oil, fine flour and wheat, cattle and sheep, horses and chariots, and slaves, that is, human souls.... "Alas, alas, for the great city. . . ." (Rev. 18:7–8, 11–13, 16)

Leaving aside the beef that the Christians of Asia Minor had with the imperial cult (something that did not exist during the earlier centuries we are considering here), it is worth noting that a great many of those Christians were Roman citizens themselves. The Book of Revelation was predicting the violent fall of their state. In that respect, though, it fit well into a much larger genre of literature that Romans of the Pax had long enjoyed reading.

America's hegemony is still young. Nevertheless, there is no shortage of articles and books predicting its imminent collapse. In just the past five years their numbers have increased, and there is no reason to believe that the trend will reverse. Quite the contrary, as the Roman example makes plain, it is a natural by-product of Pax. To take a few recent examples, almost at random:

- Charles A. Kupchan, *The End of the American Era* (2002): American hegemony is a temporary fluke, destined to fade away in the next decade or so. The European Union, perhaps followed by China, will become the new superpower and the United States should start handing over power now so as to avoid conflicts later.
- Emmanuel Todd, *After the Empire: The Breakdown of American Order* (2002): Although the United States had its moments, such as after World War II, it is now a broken-down old empire that is strutting about the world stage because it happened to be around when the Soviet Union imploded. Pathetically, it manufactures pseudocrises like Iraq and Afghanistan to make itself seem powerful. What it fails to see, though, is that the truly great powers, namely Europe, Russia, and Japan, will soon push the United States out of their way.

- Chalmers Johnson, *The Sorrows of Empire: Militarism, Secrecy, and the End of the Republic* (2004): The American republic is doomed by its own imperialism. President Bush assumed a dictatorial control over the country, just as the Roman emperors did long ago. But this sort of swaggering adventurism will only be tolerated for so long. It merely invites the rest of the world to unite against America.
- Walden Bello, *Dilemmas of Domination: The Unmaking of the American Empire* (2005): The United States has drastically overreached. Its economy is in peril, its forces stretched too thin, and its actions have unleashed a smoldering hatred across the world. The empire is doomed.
- Noam Chomsky, *Hegemony or Survival* (2004): The United States has been seeking a world empire for the last fifty years. It is not a force for stability but for unrest, exploitation, and international indignation. Soon the world will have had enough and will strike back—indeed is already doing so. As the title suggests, either the United States ceases its drive for domination or it will not survive.
- Patrick J. Buchanan, *Day of Reckoning: How Hubris, Ideology, and Greed Are Tearing America Apart* (2007): "America is coming apart, decomposing, and ... the likelihood of her survival as one nation ... is improbable.... For we are on a path to national suicide."
- Chalmers Johnson, *Nemesis: The Last Days of the American Republic* (2007): America is still doomed. Things haven't gotten better since my last book.

There is no shortage in our bookstores of jeremiads predicting the ruin of America—each one competing for sales in a world of security and prosperity that a stable Empire of Trust provides.

Roman society began to turn inward, dividing itself along new lines, precisely at the time when the Romans had achieved everything they had ever wanted. After centuries of struggle, they had secured the horizon and ushered in a new era of security and prosperity. That, in turn, produced new generations of affluent Romans who found their enemies not across the seas, but across the Forum. Political rivalries became fierce—so fierce that they strained the fabric of the Republic. But not the Empire of Trust. Whatever controversies took place in the Senate or Assembly, they had virtually no impact on the lives of the people who lived under Roman protection. Prophesies of impending Roman doom became popular—and could even be used as tools in political struggles—but they were a symptom of the Empire of Trust's success, not its failure.

It is not surprising, then, that we can detect the same turn inward in the United States as well. As with the Romans of the second century BC, it will ebb and flow based on the level of foreign threat. Although not a threat to Rome, enemies like Carthage, Corinth, or Numidia provided the Romans with an opportunity to put aside their differences—at least for a time. The same is true in the United States today. While the unity of post-9/11 America may have faded, all of the country's leaders agree that al-Qaeda is bad and should be fought. If the country should be threatened again, unity will reappear. But because of the hegemony of America's Empire of Trust, those threats will remain small.

And yet, just because there are gaggles of authors predicting America's demise does not mean that they are not onto something. Livy, Sallust, Pliny, and others saw real changes in their world that they deplored and that they blamed on Rome's new affluence and power. Could a republic survive when civic virtue was in dramatic decline? Their experience suggested that it could not. It was not the Empire of Trust that was at stake, nor the Pax Romana that it brought. Those were established and would remain secure for centuries. It was, instead, the republican form of government and the moral virtue of the people that were in peril. The rise and fall of Tiberius Gracchus was a vivid demonstration of that peril. Do the same dangers await America? We will take up that question in the last chapter.

In the meantime, there is one other matter to be discussed.

Chapter 10

The Threat of Terrorism

The scene: a busy market in Jerusalem. Crowds of people move from shop to street to square—all going about their business in one of the world's most fascinating cities. Gaudy tourist curios compete with ripe fruit and fresh vegetables for shoppers' attention and all of them are poked and prodded before any deal is made. Laughter can be heard here and there as old friends meet or new ones are made.

And then come the screams. Across the square an explosion of panic erupts as frightened people push to get away from the danger. Shouts and cries fill the air. Everything is confusion. The authorities rush in, trying to calm people and secure the area. When at last some measure of order is restored, when the people have finally been pushed back to the edge of the market square, all that is left are the corpses. At least a dozen of them lie strewn across the ground, drenched in blood. They were killed while they talked, while they laughed, while they poked and prodded. More death in the streets of Jerusalem. More terrorism in the holiest of cities.

Such a scene was as common in first-century Jerusalem as it is today. We tend to think of terrorism as a relatively new phenomenon, a product of the modern age. It is not. It is ancient. First-century Palestine had an abundance of terrorists—perhaps even more so than today. They were organized into various groups, each with a different radical agenda, occasionally working together yet just as often fighting among themselves. Religious belief is what animated all of them, just as it still does today.

But those ancient groups were not composed of Muslims. No such religion existed, five centuries before the birth of Muhammad. Instead, the terrorists roaming the streets of the ancient Middle East were Jews. Some extremists called themselves Zealots—a loose term used to denote a variety of different terrorist groups. Among the most feared terrorists were the *sicarii*. The specialty of these killers was to enter a crowded area, like a marketplace or forum, position themselves strategically, and then quietly draw from their cloaks their trademark curved daggers. With stealth, these sharp blades noiselessly pierced the clothing of the victim, sliding up and under the rib cage. A moment later the dagger was again concealed and the victim, as surprised as anyone else, collapsed to the ground. The *sicarii* were often the first to raise the alarm, accusing others of guilt, calling for the authorities, or just running wildly about in mock panic. With the killing finished, the terrorists returned to their safe houses to plot their next attack.

The *sicarii* sometimes targeted important leaders. Indeed, among their first victims was the Jewish high priest. Yet, like all terrorists, they were not that particular about whom they killed. What mattered was that they killed—efficiently and unpredictably. And they would continue to kill until they got what they wanted. Josephus, a Jewish leader who lived in Jerusalem at the time, remembered that "more terrible than the crimes themselves was the fear they aroused, every man hourly expecting death, as in war." That is what terrorism is all about.

Terrorism is a subject very much on the minds of people today—and with good reason. The attacks of September 11, 2001, were the most successful in a long series of terrorist strikes, planned and executed by radical Muslims and targeting not just the United States but the West itself. In that, the Islamists (radical Muslims) recognize a unity that is itself the Empire of Trust. Built by the United States, it encompasses Europe and other American allies around the world. The Islamists want to kill that empire.

Why? That is a question that has exercised many minds since 9/11. Almost immediately after the attacks, America's editorial pages asked the desperate question "Why do they hate us?" Many of the answers offered since then have been so politically charged as to be almost useless. American liberals often conclude that the terrorists are a reaction to Western imperialism or exploitation, which have plunged the once great culture of Islam into a backwater of poverty and despair. In other words, it is the West—and particularly the United States—that is to blame. It is society—in this case global society—that has caused terrorism. Of course, this argument is itself a retread of similar ones used to explain high violent crime rates among young black men, high obesity rates among the poor, or even the high default rate among "subprime" borrowers in the American mortgage market. Blame falls on the powerful, who force the less powerful to do bad things.

Conservative answers to the question have not been much better. The most common is that terrorists hate our freedoms. They despise a world where people may choose their own lifestyle, their own job, their own religion. They hate a culture where women are free, where liberty is valued, and where democracy is a cherished way of life. In other words, they hate everything that is good about Western culture because it is the antithesis of their own. They attack, because Western culture is a threat to their own. Because given a free choice, no one would choose bondage over freedom. The "Islamofascists," as some conservatives describe them, seek to preserve a dictatorial way of life by waging war against liberty.

Because I have spent much of my life studying the history of medieval Christianity and Islam—and the intersection of the two during the Crusades—I have done my share of media interviews in the years after 9/11. The most common question I receive is "How did the Crusades lead to the modern terrorist attacks?" This, of course, is just another way of asking, "How did we cause terrorism?" The short answer is that the Crusades had nothing at all to do with 9/11. "Why, then, do the terrorists hate us?" is the usual follow-up. Here is my answer.

Islamists have an essentially medieval perspective on their religion, the world, and their place within it. They truly live in the past. Their gaze is fixed on Islam in the Middle Ages, when it constituted not just a faith but an empire ruled by divinely appointed caliphs—an empire that spanned the known world. They remember the glories of Muslim kingdoms that patronized the arts and scholarship and looked with pity on the backward, dirty, and weak Christian West. They reflect with pride on the might of the Ottoman Empire, which encompassed virtually the entire Muslim world and came very close to conquering the Christian one. Those great achievements occurred in a time when Islam was not just a way of living a holy life, it was a way of governing a state. Islamic law, the *Sharia*, dictated how a ruler must rule, how a government must work, how wars must be fought. That was a crucial component of Islam that defined it for centuries.

From an historical perspective, the great Muslim empires, like the Mamluks or the Ottomans, were simple Empires of Conquest. But they were not animated solely by a desire for more stuff. Behind their conquests lay the idea of *jihad*. Arabic for "struggle," jihad remains a requirement for all Muslims. Part of the struggle is an internal one, against evil desires or sinful ways. Yet part of it is external as well, directed against unbelievers and the enemies of the faith. Medieval Islamic thought divided the world into two parts: the *dar al-Islam*, or the Abode of Islam, and the *dar al-harb*, or the Abode of War. The *dar al-Islam* was that part of the world living under Sharia. It was ruled by Muslim leaders and populated largely by Muslims, although Jews and Christians were tolerated provided they submitted to Islamic law. The *dar al-harb* was the part of the world not under the Sharia. In other words, it was where infidels and unbelievers lived under their own laws. It was called the Abode of War for a good reason—because it was the proper place for Muslims to wage war. In that way, the Muslim nation (or *Umma*) would continue to expand across the world, thus eliminating the *dar al-harb* altogether and, thereby, the need for war.

Obviously, this is a medieval perspective that worked well for an expansionistic Empire of Conquest. Modern Islamists still hold it dear. The answer to the question "Why do they hate us?" is that we have turned the divine plan on its head. Rather than the Umma expanding, it is the infidel Empire of Trust that expands. Since the growth of the *dar al-Islam* occurs only through the actions of God and his people, it stands to reason that the growth of the *dar al-harb* must be the work of Satan and his minions. It does not matter whether the Empire of Trust brings increased levels of peace, prosperity, or security. That is irrelevant, for it does so in violation of the divine will. Islamists hate that.

Osama bin-Laden, the al-Qaeda leader behind recent attacks on Americans, has made no secret of his grievances. Indeed, he published them on February 23, 1998, long before the dramatic attacks of 9/11 took place. In his Declaration of Jihad he called "on every Muslim who believes in Allah and wishes to be rewarded to comply with Allah's order to kill the Americans and plunder their money wherever and whenever they find it." Why? Because the infidel American troops were stationed in Saudi Arabia, the holy land of Muhammad and Mecca.

> ... for over seven years the United States has been occupying the lands of Islam in the holiest of places, the Arabian Peninsula, plundering its riches, dictating to its rulers, humiliating its people, terrorizing its neighbors, and turning its bases in the Peninsula into a spearhead through which to fight the neighboring Muslim peoples.

Bin-Laden went on to argue that American troops in Saudi Arabia were actually Christian holy warriors sent to conquer Islam. The truth is that U.S. forces were sent to Saudi Arabia in 1991 to *defend* it from what appeared to be an impending attack by Saddam Hussein in the run-up to the First Gulf War. In other words, American troops went to Arabia to preserve the Muslim holy sites from conquest, not to destroy or pollute them.

That is not how bin-Laden and other radical Muslims view matters. The American presence in Saudi Arabia is an attack on and a humiliation to the Islamic world. Allah does not want infidels in his holy land. And so, to remove them, bin-Laden launched a jihad that would ultimately result in the horrific attacks of 9/11.

That was only the first step. After the removal of the Americans from Arabia, the divinely ordained expansion of the *dar al-Islam* must begin again. In a video message to the American people released on September 6, 2007, Osama bin-Laden made this point clearly. He had nothing to say about Arabia at all, focusing instead on the war between al-Qaeda and the United States.

> There are two solutions for stopping it [the war]. The first is from our side, and it is to continue to escalate the killing and fighting against you. This is our duty, and our brothers are carrying it out, and I ask Allah to grant them resolve and victory. And the second solution is from your side. It has now become clear to you and the entire world the impotence of the democratic system.... I invite you to embrace Islam.... it will achieve your desire to stop the war as a consequence, because as soon as the warmongering owners of the major corporations realize that you have lost confidence in your democratic system and begun to search for an alternative, and that this alternative is Islam, they will run after you to please you and achieve what you want to steer you away from Islam. So your true compliance with Islam will deprive them of the opportunity to defraud the peoples and take their money under numerous pretexts, like arms deals and so on.

In other words, bin-Laden has offered to stop the war if the United States will surrender to Islam. This is simply a long-winded way of saying "submit or die," a choice that Islamic empires routinely gave to their conquered foes during the Middle Ages. The Islam of Osama bin-Laden is one of medieval conquests in which the events of the last five centuries are simply irrelevant.

But they are not irrelevant. The meteoric rise of the West happened, and despite modern prophecies to the contrary, the West is not going away. More to the point, the American Empire of Trust cannot be defeated with medieval measures. Indeed, the strategies employed by al-Qaeda thus far have proven to be utter failures. While Americans were content to deal with terrorism with half measures or as a law-enforcement issue before 9/11, the attacks on U.S. soil transformed them into a nation at war. The result was the American conquest of Afghanistan and Iraq. In other words, because of al-Qaeda's actions there has been a substantial *increase* in the number of U.S. troops in the medieval *dar al-Islam*.

Even Saudi Arabia saw a doubling of its American military presence. The terrorists' strategy, therefore, was not only ineffective, it was monumentally counterproductive.

Has this led the terrorists of the world to hang up their suicide jackets and convert their cells into quiet prayer groups? No. Has it led to a switch in strategy, one that might not be so catastrophic for their objectives? No. Around the world Muslim terrorists continue to train, to fight, and to blow themselves up in a war against the Empire of Trust. They do so because they truly believe that God demands it of them and that He will ultimately give them victory. By its nature, religious terrorism does not obey conventional battle plans. It cannot, because the cornerstone of its strategy is divine intervention.

During its history, the United States has met a few enemies that have threatened the survival of the country. The terrorists are not among them. That does not mean that the War on Terror is not a serious business. It is. But it is not a life-and-death struggle. In 2001 the United States suffered more than thirty-five hundred deaths from terrorism—a record, due to the 9/11 attacks. Although every one of those deaths was horrible, they did not make a dent in an American population of some three hundred million. More than forty thousand Americans die in auto accidents every year—the equivalent of a passenger jet blowing up every other day. Tragic, yet not a threat to the republic. The simple fact is that the terrorists, while individually dangerous, are just too weak to threaten the survival of the United States. They cannot win their jihad. The powerful Muslim Empires of Conquest that they evoke did not succeed by taking potshots at civilian populations. They had elite, powerful armies that won major engagements. Yet they have long ago crumbled into dust.

The United States must fight the War on Terror because, as an Empire of Trust, it must defend its citizens and allies. That is the mechanism by which it builds trust and thereby peace and security. Religious terrorism, however, poses a difficult problem for it. By its nature, an Empire of Trust proceeds on the assumption that others will act in a rational manner. Enemies, when defeated, will surrender. Allies, when called upon, will contribute. Trust, once established, will lead to peace. All of this, though, is predicated on the idea that, given a choice, people will choose peace and security over violence and chaos. But what if they do not? Americans can insist until they are blue in the face that their troops in Saudi Arabia, which are physically separated from the people of that country and far from the holy sites, are there to help, not to harm, the Muslim world. They can point to the way in which the same American military has saved thousands of Muslims from extermination in the former Yugoslavia. It does not matter. The terrorists believe that God does not want infidels in Arabia. God does not want them in the *dar al-Islam*. And God, with the help of His people, will expel them.

Critics of the War on Terror have begun to deem it an "endless war" that is being used purely as a means of grabbing power and advancing domestic political agendas. It is not endless. Nothing is. But how it will be waged is a matter of great importance. Here the experiences of history's other Empire of Trust, the Roman Empire, can offer some guidance. Like Americans, the Romans had a difficult time understanding the religious terrorism of their day. Yet, as their power grew, they, like Americans, became its target. But not right away. Indeed, the Romans did not have to address this problem until several centuries later in their history—after they had passed into a new era when emperors oversaw the Empire of Trust.

Why did Jewish terrorists target the Romans? That is a simple question with a complicated answer. The basic aims of ancient Jewish terrorists were similar to those of modern Muslim terrorists. First, they wanted the Empire of Trust out of their God-given lands. Second, they wanted to continue God's plan to spread their religion and their Law to the whole world. Both groups of terrorists—the ancient and the modern—looked back to an idealized golden age in which their religion and its state were at the pinnacle of their achievement. They refused to accept any world in which that was not still true. In this respect, both groups were prisoners of their own past.

Like the United States in Arabia, the Romans did not ask to be in Jewish lands. They had made a treaty of alliance with the Jewish state in 161 BC, more than a century before the first Roman troop placed a boot in the region. As we saw earlier, the Jewish leader, Judas Maccabeus, sent envoys to Rome to request an alliance and Roman aid. He had recently led a popular revolt against King Antiochus IV of the aging Seleucid Empire. The Palestine region, including Jerusalem, had been under Seleucid rule since about 200 BC. Although at first the Jews had been allowed to retain their customs (many of which seemed positively bizarre to the Greeks), Antiochus began to have second thoughts about that policy. Jews of the Diaspora lived across his empire, the Romans' empire, Egypt, the Parthian Empire, and many other places as well. Everywhere, they constituted close-knit communities that shunned outsiders and were themselves connected to a web of financial assistance to the Jewish Temple back home. Because of the antiquity of their religion and laws, Romans and Greeks tended to make special provisions for the Jews. For example, they were usually freed from military duty and not required to do business or appear in court on the Sabbath. They were given separate city neighborhoods and later even allowed to convene their own courts.

Antiochus considered both the autonomy and the dispersion of the Jews to be a danger to his kingdom. He rescinded the special privileges, outlawed circumcision, and put a statue of Zeus in the Holy of Holies of the Temple. That is what led Judas Maccabeus, a member of a priestly family, to forcibly eject the Greeks from Jerusalem and subsequently reconsecrate the Jewish Temple. The Jewish world rejoiced and Judas became a national hero. The event is still commemorated by Jews today in the celebration of Hanukkah. But Judas knew that Antiochus and his armies would be back, which is why he quickly appealed to Rome for aid. The Romans willingly gave it, forming an alliance and sending word to Antiochus that he should back off.

Not much else is known about that war. Roman aid seems to have taken the form of diplomatic and economic support for the Jews. By 142 BC, though, Simon, who had succeeded his brother, Judas, was able to push the Seleucid Greeks completely out of the region and establish an independent Jewish state centered on Jerusalem—something that had not existed for more than four centuries. The Romans not only congratulated the Jews, they wrote to all of their neighbors, reminding them that the Jews were Roman "friends and allies" and that they "should not seek their harm or make war against them and their cities and their country, or make alliance with those who war against them."

The relationship between the Romans and the Jews was off to a very good start. That is apparent throughout the First Book of Maccabees, which speaks in very approving tones of the Romans. And no wonder. With Roman help, the Jews had managed to restore their ancient state. It was a time of great rejoicing for all Jews, no matter where they lived. The restored government in Jerusalem was a theocracy—led by God, through his priests. At the top was the high priest, who was assisted by a council of elders (sometimes called the Sanhedrin). Simon appointed himself high priest—a controversial move, since it was generally believed that a high priest must be a descendent of Aaron, the brother of Moses. But it was allowed for the moment. It did not hurt things that Simon's family was very good at expanding the Jewish state. With Roman help Simon's son, John Hyrcanus, was able to remove the Seleucids again and thwart a planned Egyptian attack. He then went on the offensive, attacking the Samaritans (those estranged cousins of the Jews) and conquering Galilee and Idumaea, where he forcibly converted many thousands to Judaism.

By the beginning of the first century BC a new and powerful Jewish state had been born. Yet problems lay below the surface. The Jews had done quite well for themselves by currying favor with Gentiles, particularly the Romans. But this did not sit well with more conservative Jews, who yearned for the past glories of the Jewish state. God alone ruled the Jews, they believed. The Jewish God, Yahweh, was not just a jealous God, he was the *only* God. This was a tenet of Jewish faith not much liked by other peoples, but the Jews stuck by it resolutely. In the ancient world, one might worship a particular god or set of gods, but that did not imply that different gods did not exist. Quite the contrary, the prosperity of those who worshipped other gods was proof enough of their existence. The Jews rejected this reasoning, insisting that their God alone was real. Many Jews believed that God would use them to bring His glory and power to the whole world. Most assumed that this would entail the creation of a worldwide kingdom, with the Chosen People at its head. Clearly, the restoration of the Jewish state was a first step toward that. The interference of Romans or any other Gentiles, even when it was beneficial, was resented by those Jews who awaited these events.

Yet many Jews in Palestine and across the Diaspora disagreed with this approach to the Gentiles. So-called "Hellenized Jews" were well-educated, usually wealthy men and women of the world. They appreciated Greek culture and Roman ways and saw no reason why these should be incompatible with Judaism. The days of David and Solomon were long past, they argued, although they naturally hoped for a return to that greatness at some point in the future. In the meantime, the Jews should not only embrace the "modern" world, but seek to spread the Jewish faith within it. And they had some success in that respect. Affluent Romans and Greeks (like affluent Americans today) were always in the market for a new religion with ancient credentials (even if its antiquity was manufactured). Judaism was clearly ancient and there is plenty of evidence that Jewish proselytizers brought in a good crop of converts. They also made a lot of friends. "God fearers" were Gentiles who believed in the Jewish God and would even support and attend synagogues, but were not willing to be circumcised, keep kosher, or adhere to other requirements necessary for full conversion.

The division between the Hellenizers and the conservatives was one that would plague the Jews for centuries. Were the Hellenizers collaborators and traitors, as the conservatives often claimed? Or were they simply realists seeking cooperation with people of other cultures and faiths? Were the conservatives closed-minded antiquarians or radical extremists, as the Hellenizers argued? Or were they true believers who refused to compromise God's law for the sake of the world? These are the sorts of questions and divisions that similarly plague Muslims today. Most Muslims who live outside the Middle East—and many who live within it— believe that there is no contradiction between embracing Western ways and living life as a pious Muslim. Many others, though, insist that Western culture is simply incompatible with Islamic law and therefore must be rejected.

Not surprisingly, the powerful and wealthy families of the Jewish high priests and elders became decidedly Hellenized. This was not just a reaction to affluence but a strategic necessity, since only through close relations with Rome could a relatively weak Jewish state hope to survive. Among Jewish conservatives this did not sit well. It was bad enough that the high priest was not of Aaron's blood, but to have a pro-Gentile in the office was intolerable. Things got so bad that the Pharisees led a revolt against the priestly government in 94 BC, although it was eventually put down. Nevertheless, the situation remained dangerously unstable. In the 60s BC another civil war erupted between two brothers, John Hyrcanus II and Aristobulus, both heirs to the high priest position. The Jewish state was becoming a cauldron of violence and chaos.

Provided it did not harm their other allies, the Romans were content to let the Jews fight whatever civil wars they liked. But this particular civil war was dropped right on their doorstep—because their doorstep had just recently moved. The last remnants of the Seleucid Empire had become so troublesome and dangerous that the Roman general Pompey brought his legions to Syria to restore order. In 63 BC, with little fanfare, he ended the dynasty and annexed the territory for Rome. Just to the south of Syria the Jewish civil war was raging. Both warring brothers rushed to Pompey, seeking his support. The general tried to ignore the problem, yet in the end found himself forced to make a decision. The Jewish state was a Roman ally. It was appealing for aid against an enemy. The question was, which of the brothers was the ally and which the enemy?

Pompey decided to support John. In a flash, Aristobulus became the candidate of the extremists. He fled to Jerusalem and prepared for a siege. Pompey and John brought up their combined forces and demanded Aristobulus' surrender. He refused. Within the city the religious factional lines between the Jews were strained to the breaking point. Street fighting broke out, causing many deaths even before the Roman forces entered the city. Once inside, securing Jerusalem was no easy matter, but in time Pompey's troops managed it. While inspecting the city, Pompey and his staff entered the Temple. They were looking for enemies, since the Temple precincts were a fortification of sorts. But Pompey was also curious. Everyone had heard of this strange place where Jews sacrificed animals to a God with no name and no image. Although the Jewish Temple was built on the plan of other pagan temples, it did not have a great cult statue in its inner sanctum. Instead, the Ark of the Covenant was kept there, reserved solely for the eyes of the high priest himself. Pompey was probably unaware of all that. In any case, he confidently walked through the Temple right into the Holy of Holies, looked around, and then left. He did not touch the Temple Treasury and, when he later learned that his mere presence had polluted the Temple, apologized and asked the priests to do whatever ceremonies were necessary for its purification.

And so, for the first time, Roman troops were in Palestine. They did not come as conquerors but in response to a request for aid. Almost immediately they saw how unstable the situation was. There were too many factional groups, too much bad blood among the Jews themselves. In an attempt to stabilize the region, Pompey granted freedom to non-Jewish cities and regions that had recently been conquered by the Jews, reducing the high priest's state to ancient Judaea and Galilee. Recognizing the importance of Jerusalem to all Jews, Pompey also made John the point person for Jewish matters throughout the Roman Empire. Before leaving, he established a tax to defray the costs of maintaining a permanent Roman military presence in Syria and Palestine.

Although this was of great importance to the Jews, most Romans did not pay much attention to it. In general, the Romans did not spend time thinking about the Jews who lived among them. They were generally considered to be an odd sort, who apparently did not like people very much since so many of them kept to themselves. Resting on the Sabbath seemed like an excuse for laziness, not eating pork a foolish choice, and circumcision a perversion. But outside of Palestine the Jews did not cause trouble, so they were tolerated. The Romans respected the antiquity of the Jewish faith—much older than Rome itself—and so they were willing to make provisions in order to avoid giving offense.

Nevertheless, the Jewish homeland remained a place of unrest as dynasties and religious groups squared off against one another. Over the following decades, the Romans responded with a number of different initiatives to bring peace to the region. They tried dividing it up into small republics, a tactic that had worked well in Macedonia. It did not work in Palestine. Galilee especially became a hotbed of insurrection and terrorist groups. The area was beset by a kaleidoscope of competing factions, religious groups, and agendas that made it a place of violence, fear, and instability. Increasingly, Jews began talking about a Messiah who would remove the Gentiles from the Holy Land and usher in a new Golden Age. The Romans tried repeatedly to find a solution to the violence among the Jews and their neighbors, but nothing worked. The problem, which the Romans could not understand, was that Palestine was filled with warring people who each had God on their side. Something had to give. And it did so almost every day.

Some measure of stability was brought to the region under King Herod the Great. A Hellenizer par excellence, he acquired the position because of his service to and contacts in Rome. As is plain enough in the New Testament, the Jews did not think much of Herod or his heirs. They considered him to be a Hellenized, pro-Roman toady. And he was. But he was also a brilliant administrator able to bring plenty of Gentile money into the kingdom. With those funds he turned Jerusalem and the other cities of the region into showplaces. It was Herod who paid for the renovation of the Temple, an expansion of extraordinary size and beauty. The number-two man in the Roman Empire, Marcus Agrippa, even visited Herod in 15 BC and made an offering to the Jewish God in the Temple's Court of the Gentiles. It was a rich—and rare—moment of Jewish and Roman friendship and cooperation.

The first Roman emperor, Augustus, was pleased with Herod's successes but troubled by his methods. In order to keep power in the serpent's nest of Jewish politics, Herod could not shirk from intrigue or ruthlessness. He had already ordered the execution of many of his own family members, which disgusted the princeps of Rome. Augustus once remarked that in Herod's palace it was safer to be a pig than a son. What Herod had forged through blood and persuasion, his family could not maintain. Almost immediately after his death the Jewish kingdom again erupted in fighting. Galilee, Judaea, and the streets of Jerusalem were filled with factional warfare and terrorist attacks. Augustus was exasperated. This was the height of the Pax Romana, a time in which peace, security, and prosperity reigned throughout the Mediterranean world. Why was Palestine a place of warfare and strife? At last, after seventy years of Roman attempts to bring peace to the Jewish state, the Roman government gave up. In AD 6 Augustus annexed the kingdom, making it the new province of Judaea. A governor was sent to administer it with command over several Roman contingents to keep the peace. Problem solved.

Or at least that had always solved the problem elsewhere. Not in Judaea. Indeed, the problem only worsened. This is the world into which Jesus Christ was born. The New Testament provides numerous examples of the strained relations and competing interests of the time. Jesus was pointedly asked by the Pharisees whether it was lawful to pay the tax to the Romans. Many Jews held that it was not, since it made one complicit in the continuation of Gentile rule over the Jewish people. Yet to refuse would be to break the law of Rome. Jesus' solution, to "render unto Caesar what is Caesar's," both approved the payment of the tax and asserted its irrelevance. The crowds who followed Jesus frequently hailed him as the Messiah or the king of the Jews. Such claims were not uncommon in this age. The deserts saw many Messiahs. But the Gospels insist that Jesus did not claim to be a conquering king. As he told Pontius Pilate, the Roman governor, "My kingdom is not of this world." Whatever he claimed, Jesus was executed in an atmosphere of competing Jewish and Roman interests that led ultimately to the cross.

Although it was now a Roman province, the Romans tried to maintain a government run largely by the Jews. Roman governors stayed in the coastal city of Caesarea Maritima, where they could stay in touch with the Roman world and stay out of religious strife in Jerusalem. Governors came to the holy city only when trouble broke out or they were expecting it. So, for example, Pilate came to Jerusalem during Passover, because that was when the city's population swelled with pilgrims and tensions were often high. Jesus' royal entry into the city on an ass could not have escaped Pilate's attention, for it was precisely the sort of thing he was there to prevent. Pilate and the other governors of Judaea were constantly beset with problems of unrest, exacerbated by terrorist groups like the Zealots and the *sicarii*, as well as bands of insurgents that roamed the countryside. In short, the place was a mess.

The problem became worse in AD 40 when the mentally unstable emperor, Caligula, decided that he was a god and ordered his statue to be put in a holy place of honor in all of the cities of the empire. Most cities already had a temple of the imperial cult, so the order did not cause too much trouble—except in Jerusalem. Caligula insisted that he would make no exception for the Jews. He ordered the Roman governor of Syria, Petronius, to have a colossal statue made and erected in the Jewish Temple. Petronius did as he was commanded, although he let the sculptors know that he was in no rush to receive delivery. He knew that the emperor's "gift" would lead to a bloodbath in Judaea when the Jews refused to accept it. Furthermore, Jews across the empire, thousands of whom were Roman citizens, were appalled at the idea. In Alexandria, which had the largest Jewish community outside Palestine, a delegation of Hellenized Jews, each one learned in Roman ways, was sent to Rome to convince Caligula to rescind the order. Philo of Alexandria, who was one of the envoys, provides a fascinating and detailed account of his meeting with the emperor, which took place while he was inspecting a new palace construction on the Esquiline Hill. Philo and his companions failed to change Caligula's mind, but it did not matter. The following year the emperor was murdered by his own bodyguard.

Many Jews considered the death of Caligula to be an act of God. But the emperor's actions convinced many Jews outside of Palestine, including many Hellenized Jews in the big cities of the Roman Empire, that Rome was an enemy of their faith. Like some Muslims in Western countries today, ancient Diaspora Jews began to suspect that the policies of their country entailed the desecration of their ancestral homeland and the destruction of their faith. These sentiments became so virulent in Alexandria that the Jews of the city, who constituted a third or more of the population, took up arms and attacked their Gentile neighbors. It was only with difficulty that Roman authorities were able to restore order.

The new emperor, Claudius, rescinded all of Caligula's policies toward the Jews. Claudius was a scholar who quite admired the Jews both for their history and their beliefs. But he would not tolerate Jewish attacks on Roman citizens. In a rare surviving papyrus letter from Claudius to the Jews of Alexandria, the emperor makes plain that the Romans' patience with the Jews was wearing thin. He insisted that they must be tolerant of others, just as the Romans had been tolerant of them. Shortly thereafter, Claudius sent a general letter to all Jews of the empire, assuring them of his support and friendship, but warning them that they must not "behave with contempt toward the gods of other peoples."

In an attempt to appease the Jews, Claudius restored the independence of the Jewish state. He handed over the entire province to his Jewish friend and supporter Herod Agrippa, who now became the king of the Jews. Roman administration and troops were removed in the hope that this would quiet the region. At first it seemed to work. Herod Agrippa ruled piously and well, and terrorist activity declined. Although Hellenized, Herod Agrippa did his best to prove that he was as devout as any other Jew. To that end, he ordered the persecution of the new Christian sect that had taken root in Jerusalem and elsewhere. The Apostle James, son of Zebedee, was arrested and executed. Peter, the leader of the Christians, was also arrested, although he later escaped, according to the New Testament, with the help of an angel. Herod Agrippa ruled for only a few years, dying suddenly during Victory Games that he sponsored to celebrate Claudius' conquest of Britain. The Christians naturally saw the hand of God in Herod Agrippa's demise.

Claudius mourned Herod Agrippa, but he did not think that his son Julius Marcus Agrippa II, was ready at the tender age of seventeen to take on the powder keg that was Judaea. Instead, he gave the young man a small neighboring kingdom and jurisdiction over religious observances in Jerusalem. As for the rest, he restored Roman provincial control. A governor returned and so did the Roman troops. For many Jews, this action constituted a reversal of the proper course of history. From that moment on, the level of terrorist activities in Judaea and across the empire sharply increased. The extremists would not accept the presence of Romans in the Promised Land. As for the Romans, like modern Americans in Iraq, they had no interest in sending their sons to stop these people from killing each other. But the alternative was to allow a dangerous religious extremism to spill beyond the borders of Judaea, infecting much of the empire, including Rome itself. Besides, the Romans had a natural optimism that led them to believe that they could bring peace and security to almost everyone.

How bad had things become in Judaea? We probably know about only a fraction of the terrorist incidents that occurred in the years after AD 44, yet even these are numerous enough. To give a few examples:

- A Jewish insurgent leader in the city of Peraea took the name of Hannibal—the great enemy of the Romans—and attacked the non-Jewish population of the city, including many Romans. The Roman procurator of Judaea, Cuspius Fadus, was forced to restore order and subsequently executed Hannibal.
- A Jewish prophet, Theudas, attracted multitudes to the River Jordan, claiming that he would lead them across when God parted the waters as he had done for Moses. Once again, the Roman authorities restored order.
- During Passover of AD 49 a riot broke out in Jerusalem when one of the Roman troops stationed there was thought to have made an obscene gesture toward the Temple. The city fell into chaos and the damage was horrible. The Roman procurator, Ventidius Cumanus, sent in additional troops to restore order, which led to mass panic among the rioters and the deaths of many people killed in the trampling.
- A few years later a Jewish pilgrim in Galilee was killed by some Samaritans. Led by the insurgent leader Eleazar ben Dinai, the Jews put together a large force at Jerusalem to exact vengeance. The Roman procurator attempted to stop the brewing war and to defend the Samaritans, but was only partially successful. Fighting continued in

pockets across the region. Indeed, Eleazar and his terrorist insurgents remained active for several years, before a new Roman procurator, Antonius Felix, finally captured him. But that did not put an end to the insurgency or the terrorism.

And these problems were not just limited to Judaea. The same violence was occasionally mirrored in the cities of the empire. Claudius became so worried about the problem that he expelled many Jews from the city of Rome, although they did not stay away for very long.

Sicarii were killing randomly in the streets and markets of Jerusalem. The countryside in Judaea was alive with insurgents, rival terrorist bands, and religious extremists. The whole place was on the verge of complete collapse. The Roman procurator, Felix, had to contend almost daily with "deceivers claiming divine inspiration, who schemed to bring about revolutionary changes by inducing the people to act as if possessed and leading them out into the desert on the pretense that God would show them signs of approaching freedom." A Jewish prophet from Egypt, claiming to have been chosen by God to lead the Jews to victory over the Romans, gathered many thousands of supporters and marched on Jerusalem itself. The ragtag army assembled on the Mount of Olives and prepared to attack, apparently believing that God would bring down the walls at the Egyptian's command. Felix brought up a contingent of Roman troops and dispersed the rebels, but the mysterious Egyptian escaped. For many years he, too, remained a rallying point for terrorists and insurgents.

When Gessius Florus arrived as the new Roman governor in AD 64 he found a region in chaos. Aside from the usual terrorist activities, there were prophecies floating around that God was ready to give the Jewish people victory over the Roman Empire. The absurdity of such a possibility did not bother the extremists, who now numbered in the tens of thousands. But it did bother pro-Roman Jews like Agrippa II. The king traveled to Jerusalem, where the word on the Jewish street was *war*. Florus had upset the people when he demanded that they pay back taxes with the riches of the Temple Treasury. Now, they believed, was the time to strike Rome. Now was the time to defeat the Gentiles.

Horrified at what he saw, Agrippa gave an impassioned speech to the people of Jerusalem in which he begged them to reconsider. His words, which were remembered by Josephus, who was there, are important. In them, Agrippa laid out the reasons why a war against the Romans was not only unjustified but irrational. He began by arguing that the Jews had no just reason to declare war against the Roman people.

> I grant that the ministers of Rome are unbearably harsh; does it follow that all the Romans are persecuting you, including Caesar? Yet it is on them that you are going to make war! It is not by their wish that an unscrupulous governor comes from Rome, and western eyes cannot see the goings-on in the east. It is not easy in Rome even to get up-to-date news of what happens here. It would be absurd because of the trifling misdemeanors of one man to go to war with a whole nation, and such a nation—a nation that does not even know what it is all about!

He then urged his fellow Jews to think about who they were attacking. Was it, he asked, reasonable to believe that they could defeat the vast Roman Empire?

> Where are the men, where are the weapons you count on? Where is the fleet that is to sweep the Roman seas? Where are the funds to pay for your expeditions? Do you think you are going to war with Egyptians and Arabs? Look at the far-flung empire of Rome and contrast your own impotence. Why, our forces have been beaten even by our own neighbors again and again, while Roman arms have triumphed over the whole world! And even the world is not big enough to satisfy them; the Euphrates is not far enough to the east, or the Danube to the north, or Libya and the desert beyond to the south, or Cadiz to the west; but beyond the Ocean they have sought a new world, carrying their arms as far as Britain, that land of mystery. Why not face facts? Are you richer than the Gauls, stronger than the Germans, cleverer

than the Greeks, more numerous than all the nations of the world? What gives you the confidence to defy the power of Rome?

Agrippa then ridiculed their professed desire for liberty. Liberty from what? he asked. The Romans had brought such peace and security that even the most freedom-loving and ferocious people in the world were content to live within their empire, watched over only by small Roman garrisons. Agrippa took his listeners on a tour of the Roman Empire, comparing the greatness of ancient peoples who willingly accepted Roman hegemony with the Jews who rejected it. The Greeks, for example, who fought against the massive Persian Empire and every form of tyranny,

> who surpass every nation under the sun in nobility and fill such a wide domain, and yet they bow before the fasces of a Roman governor, as do the Macedonians, who have a better right than you to demand their liberty! And what of the five hundred cities of Asia? Do they not, without a garrison, bow before one governor and the consular fasces?

Even the Mediterranean Sea, he reminded them, which was once infested with pirates, was now kept safe by a mere forty Roman warships.

Agrippa concluded his address by urging the Jews to turn away from their false prophecies and dreams of divinely ordained victories. God favored the Romans, he said, not the Jews who thirsted for their blood. The Romans could be merciful, but not when provoked like this. An attack on the Romans would bring a response—and it would be both terrible and irresistible. Through tears Agrippa begged the assembled Jews not to wage war against the Romans.

> Pity your wives and children, or at least pity your mother city and its sacred precincts. Spare the Temple and preserve for your use the Sanctuary with its sacred treasures. For the Romans will no longer keep

their hands off when they have captured these, since for sparing them up until now they have received no thanks at all.

When Agrippa had concluded his speech the response of his listeners was direct and to the point. They threw stones at him. He left the city and returned to his kingdom.

The attack came in August AD 66. It began with the provocative announcement of Eleazar, the captain of the Temple guard, that he would no longer allow foreigners or sacrifices for foreigners to occur there. In effect, this meant that the Jews would no longer be praying for the Roman Empire. The high priest, Matthias, protested this action, which caused Jerusalem to split apart into two warring factions. Matthias and his supporters fled to the upper city, where they holed up in the fortified palace at the Jaffa Gate, supported by a small detachment of Roman soldiers. The rest of the Roman troops were stationed at the Antonia fortress, which overlooked the lower city and the Temple. Eleazar ordered his people to attack. They brought fire and sword to the upper city, killing many and destroying much. After two days of fighting they captured the Antonia fortress and massacred the Romans inside. It had begun.

As news of the violence in Jerusalem spread, the killing was mirrored across the region and then the empire. A popular Jewish insurgent leader, Menahem, the son of the famous terrorist Judas the Galilean, led a surprise attack on the fortress of Masada, killing all of the Romans within and capturing their weapons. He then marched on Jerusalem, where he challenged Eleazar for leadership of the new Jewish state. He allowed the high priest and his men to flee Jerusalem, although the Roman soldiers in the fortified palace held out, watching what they could not prevent. Eleazar defeated Menahem, whom he later captured and tortured to death.

Unable to take the Jaffa Gate fortress, Eleazar offered to allow the Roman soldiers to leave the city peacefully, provided they surrendered their weapons. Their commander, Metilius, agreed. At the appointed hour the Romans marched down the stairs and into the open area, where they drew up their ranks. In an orderly fashion, they submitted their helmets, armor, and weapons to Eleazar. Then they made an about-face and began marching toward the open gate. They never got there. As soon as their backs were turned, Eleazar ordered his soldiers to cut them down. The unarmed Romans began shouting, protesting that they had kept their part of the bargain and calling on the Jews to do the same. It had no effect. They were all killed. Only Metilius begged for his life. Weeping and trembling, he promised to do anything the Jews asked. Eleazar ordered him to convert to Judaism and accept circumcision. Metilius obeyed. With that, Jerusalem and the surrounding territory was cleansed of the Romans.

The Roman world responded with outrage. Patience for the perpetual unrest in Judaea was already running low. Now it was gone completely. Jews of the Diaspora were put in a particularly difficult bind. Like western Muslims after 9/11, Diaspora Jews sympathized with their coreligionists, but few would condone this sort of slaughter. And yet, in some places in the Middle East, Jews celebrated the massacre of the Romans. Several cities with large Jewish populations saw open warfare between them and their Gentile neighbors. In places like Alexandria, Caesarea Maritima, Caesarea Philippi, Tyre, and Ascalon, the Jews had the worst of it, with many thousands killed. In other places like Sebaste, Gaza, Anthedon, Gaba, and the Decapolis it was the Jews who won out, massacring many Gentiles.

The official Roman response came from the governor of Syria, Cestius Gallus, who led a full legion down into Judaea, crushing insurgent groups and finally arriving at Jerusalem itself. The citadel, however, held out and when winter approached Cestius was forced to withdraw to the coast to resupply. Along the way, Jewish forces harassed his army, scoring impressive victories in the disordered Roman retreat. By the time Cestius arrived in Caesarea Maritima, six thousand more Roman soldiers lay dead on the fields of Judaea. That was the last straw. More anger swept through the empire, all of it directed against the Jews. In Damascus the population poured into the streets killing Jews wherever they could find them.

In Judaea, though, the mood was jubilant. They had ejected the Romans, and when a legion had come to retaliate, they had defeated that too. Any doubts that they were waging a holy war against God's enemies were now dispelled. But there remained a great deal of doubt over who should lead this war. The deserts and mountains were soon filled with Messiahs, each claiming to be the divinely appointed leader. There was almost no unity or organization in the region as various extremist and terrorist groups splintered away from each other and then coalesced again. The only constant was bloodshed as Jews continued to kill Jews.

Outside of Palestine, affluent Hellenized Jews did their best to smooth things over with their fellow Roman citizens. It was not an easy sell. Josephus, who turned out to be the most visible apologist for the Jews, argued that much of the blame rested with Florus, the Roman governor, who had notoriously mistreated the Jews under his jurisdiction. Terrorism could not be condoned, of course. But, Josephus maintained, it was bad Roman policy that had led to the revolt. Similar arguments are posited today to explain Islamist terrorism. It is sometimes said that American policies in the Middle East have bred religious extremism. This argument transfers agency to the Empire of Trust, making everyone else a passive victim. It is not a very interesting or satisfying argument. It also ignores the fundamental dynamic that drives religious terrorism—religion. First-century Judaea had economic and political problems, that is true. But so did other parts of the empire. Why did Judaea alone spill its own and others' blood? Modern Muslim countries also have economic and political challenges, but no more so than countries in Africa or Latin America. Why have they produced deadly anti-Western terrorism? Both groups of terrorists were driven by a belief that God was on their side and an equally strong conviction that the Empire of Trust, because of its expansion, was the enemy of God. This in turn convinced them that they were at the center of an epic struggle between good and evil that must be fought and which they could not lose.

Emperor Nero, who was in Greece at the time of the Jewish revolt, shared the outrage of his countrymen. The Jews had been respected and given privileges across the Roman Empire. Was this how they repaid such kindness? Nero appointed a senator, Vespasian, as the new governor of

Judaea with orders to crush the rebellion. Vespasian picked up two legions in Antioch and then marched south, where he rendezvoused with his son, Titus, who brought up another legion. And more forces were on the way. The Jewish king, Agrippa II, who had begged the people of Jerusalem not to attack, sent cavalry to assist the Romans. Even the Parthians, longtime enemies of Rome, sent archers. Altogether Vespasian commanded some sixty thousand troops. This was the Roman equivalent of "shock and awe."

Vespasian's forces quickly captured Galilee, although Roman forces continued to have problems with insurgents who hid in the cities and melted into the mountains. He then moved down the coast and across the Jordan, restoring everything to Roman control. His final objective was Jerusalem. The hope was that by isolating the capital he could convince the Jewish leaders there to surrender and thus spare the ancient city.

But Jerusalem was in no state to surrender. Indeed, it was in no state to do much of anything. Torn apart by factional warfare, it was a city literally separated into armed camps. Even the Temple was divided. Assassinations and kidnappings occurred daily. Galilean terrorists even became experts at dressing up as beautiful women in order to seduce powerful enemies and assassinate them. In AD 68 a coalition of terrorist groups—mostly Zealots—massacred thousands of moderate Jews still left in the city. The whole place was drunk on messianic prophecies, certain that God was ushering in a new age or perhaps bringing about the end of the world. Either way, there was no room for moderates—or Romans.

Vespasian and his armies prepared to put a stop to it. But, just at that moment, in June AD 68, Nero was murdered. The Roman Empire spent the next year paralyzed by the "Year of Four Emperors" (AD 68–69). When it was all over Vespasian himself had become the new emperor in Rome. That was good news for Vespasian but even better news for the Jews of Palestine, for it had kept Vespasian and the empire busy with their own problems back home. In AD 66 King Agrippa II had told the people of Jerusalem that they were fools to attack Rome. And yet, here it was three years later and still the independent Jewish state survived. Legions had come and gone and still God's chosen people held out. Of course, the "state" was little more than a stew of competing factions, but there was no getting around the fact that the prophets and Messiahs seemed to be onto something. Across the Roman Empire, Jews began to feel more confident in the future of the Jewish state, sending more money for the defense of Jerusalem. The Passover of AD 69 saw strong attendance as Jews across the world flocked to a Jerusalem free of Gentiles.

But the Romans had not surrendered. In May 69 Titus returned with a massive force and laid siege to Jerusalem. He went about his task methodically and carefully. He hoped that by taking down one wall at a time he could convince the inhabitants to make peace. There was also the fact that the internecine warfare within the city was doing some of his job for him. Josephus, who had gone over to the Roman side early in the war, was with Titus during the siege. He would regularly go out to the walls of the city, shouting to the defenders, begging them to make peace with the Romans.

> You obdurate fools! Throw away your weapons, take pity on your birthplace at this moment plunging to ruin. Turn around and gaze at the beauty of what you are betraying—what a City! What a Temple! What gifts from all the Gentile world! Against these will any man set the flames? Does any man wish these things to pass away? What better deserves to be kept safe than these, you inhuman, stony-hearted monsters! If the sight of these things leaves you unmoved, at least pity your families, and let each man set before his eyes his wife and children and parents, so soon to perish by famine or the sword.

Like Agrippa II three years earlier, Josephus was answered only with insults and a shower of rocks.

Jerusalem, with its many walls and fortresses, fell little by little to the Romans. It was difficult and deadly fighting because it not only required house-to-house warfare, but also navigating the labyrinth of underground passages that honeycombed the city and into which many terrorists had fled. In July 69 the Romans captured the Antonia Fortress and the following month the Temple was taken as well. In the scuffle a fire broke out that leveled the great, majestic building of King Herod. Titus claimed that it was an accident. Whatever the case, the Temple was never rebuilt. For all practical purposes, the Jewish Revolt was over.

The initial Roman reaction to the Jewish attacks was not unlike that of Americans to Islamist terrorism. They were angry and bewildered. Why had Jews attacked those who had helped them, or at least ignored them? From the Roman perspective the Jews had failed to act rationally or with honor. They had abandoned their alliances and turned against the Romans, who had been their friends. Just as Americans asked "Why?" so the Romans wrestled with the same question. With the Jews defeated, Titus gave voice to the answer that the Romans had finally settled on:

> There is only one answer. You [Jews] were incited against the Romans by Roman kindness itself. First we gave you the land to occupy and set over you kings of your own race; then we upheld the laws of your fathers, and allowed you complete control of your internal and external affairs; above all, we permitted you to raise taxes for God and to collect offerings, and we neither discouraged nor interfered with those who brought them [to Jerusalem]—so that you could grow richer to our detriment and prepare at our expense to make war on us! Then, enjoying such advantages, you flung your abundance at the heads of those who furnished it, and like beasts you bit the hand that fed you! ... [My father] ravaged Galilee and the outlying districts, giving you time to come to your senses. But you took generosity for weakness, and our gentleness only served to increase your audacity.... When the whole Empire had come to us for protection, when all its inhabitants were enjoying the blessing of peace ... [you] rose up against us. You sent embassies beyond the Euphrates to stir up a revolt; you rebuilt your city walls; there were faction-fights, rival party chiefs, civil war—just what we should expect from men so depraved!

As Erich Gruen has correctly noted, in the eyes of the Romans the Jews' greatest crime was ingratitude. They had taken Roman gifts and repaid them with injury. The Romans, Titus believed, *were* to blame—first by giving the Jews special treatment and then by responding to their attacks with appeasement. That policy was at an end.

The Romans were slow to find a solution to the problem of religious terrorism and extremism because it simply did not compute within the context of their Empire of Trust. They had pacified the known world with a simple formula—that a life of peace and security under Roman supervision is better than a life of chaos, fear, and bloodshed any day of the week. That is why, as Agrippa had said, the Spartans and Athenians—the most freedom-loving people in the world—lived peacefully under Roman government with only token forces stationed nearby. But years of terrorism, which finally broke out into an attack on the Romans, brought the matter to its head. The conquest of Jerusalem was joyously celebrated in Rome. The Arch of Titus near the Forum still bears witness to that victory today.

Whether by deliberate plan or by stumbling into it, the Romans had settled on a strategy to deal with religious terrorism: The religion itself must change. Judaism as a theocratic state would cease to exist. The time for such things had passed. Judaism would have to be modernized to accept a different world. No longer would it have a capital, or a high priest, or a king, or anything else that other religions in the empire lacked. Jerusalem would simply be another city; Judaea another province. The Jews could retain their privileges, but those would no longer include tax collecting for the support of the Temple. There was no Temple, no sacrifices, not anymore.

And slowly, very slowly, Judaism did change. With the priests gone, the Pharisees stepped into the gap. A moderate Pharisee, Johanan ben Zakkai, established a refugee settlement at Jamnia on the coast. There he began a Jewish school. The teachers, or rabbis, there laid the foundation stones of a new rabbinic Judaism, without animal sacrifices, but with a dedication to the reading and living of the Law and the preservation of the Jewish people and faith. It was here that Jews began to see the state—

even a Gentile state—as something ordained by God. In the years that followed, Jews began to see synagogues and schools as the new centers of their faith, sending money back to Judaea to support those, rather than the lost Temple.

But these were only the seeds of the solution. To change a religion, particularly one as ancient and resilient as Judaism, takes time—lots of time. In the years after the destruction of the Temple the immediate response among most Jews was a smoldering resentment against the Romans. Many thousands of them throughout the empire still prayed for a messiah who would destroy the Romans and usher in a new world based on the Chosen People. The Romans kept a close watch on messianic movements because they knew from experience of their danger. Terrorism and insurgencies did not stop completely, but the Romans dealt with them, and they remained vigilant.

It would be more than forty-five years before another major Jewish attack was launched against the Romans. In AD 115 the emperor Trajan led a large number of Roman forces against the Parthian Empire. He eventually conquered it, thereby extending the Roman Empire into Mesopotamia (modern Iraq and Kuwait). Taking advantage of the redeployment of troops, Andrew, a Messianic leader in Cyrenaica (just west of Egypt), organized large popular armies of Jews. At his command they attacked the local authorities and began spreading bloodshed wherever they went. Their purpose was nothing less than the extermination of Gentiles and the creation of a new Jewish state. According to Dio:

> They would eat the flesh of their victims, make belts for themselves of their entrails, anoint themselves with their blood and wear their skins for clothing; many they sawed in two, from the head downwards; others they gave to wild beasts, and still others they forced to fight as gladiators. In all 220,000 persons were killed.

Although this is clearly an exaggeration, the archaeological record does confirm that the devastation was immense.

Not content with Cyrenaica, Andrew and his armies then invaded

Egypt. They were joined by thousands of Jews from Alexandria. These terrorist bands roamed the countryside at will, murdering Romans and Greeks by the thousands. In Alexandria the violence was astonishing. This was not a revolt, but a revolution in which the participants truly believed that they were preparing for a new world order. It spread by word of mouth to Cyprus, where a rival Messiah took up the challenge, organizing his own army. He attacked and captured the capital city, Salamis, killing (again according to Dio) more than 200,000 Romans and Greeks.

Although these casualty estimates are too high, the death toll was nonetheless staggering—easily more than the number of Americans lost in all acts of Islamist terrorism to date. The Roman response was swift. Trajan sent his general Quintus Marcius Turbo with legions and a fleet to crush the terrorists. Within a year it was done. The Jewish community in Cyprus was exiled and Trajan decreed that henceforth no Jew was ever to set foot on the island. As the Romans counted their dead, it certainly did not feel as if they had found a solution to religious extremism in their empire. Indeed, it seemed to have become much worse.

The new emperor, Hadrian, inherited the continued problem of Jewish insurrections and violence. Like Titus (and probably most Romans), Hadrian believed that Jewish hatred of the Romans was the result of Roman policies that had indulged or appeased them. The Jews were members of the Roman Empire. They should start acting like it. It was time, Hadrian believed, that they learned some toleration themselves. To that end, although Hadrian kept all of the old Jewish privileges on the books, he refused to extend additional ones. This became a problem when he reiterated the long-held Roman prohibitions against bodily mutilation. Hadrian ruled that since castration was specifically forbidden—even to slaves—it must also follow that circumcision was illegal. He made no provisions for the Jews.

The emperor also decided to rebuild the ruined province of Judaea. At great expense, Jerusalem was rededicated as Aelia Capitolina. When finished, this new, modern city would, he hoped, be a beacon of prosperity, learning, and security to the people—all the people—of Judaea.

Hadrian may have expected that these measures would help to modernize Judaism, making it less dangerous, less separatist, and more tolerant. Just to be sure, though, he stationed another legion in Judaea. This Roman "surge" was meant not only to deal with unrest, but to counter the large number of low-level insurgencies that had been continuing in Judaea for years.

The dramatic makeover of Jerusalem quashed the last hope of Jews everywhere, who still dreamed of its restoration. In desperation, various religious groups in Judaea began to organize around one charismatic leader, Simeon bar Kosiba. Yet another messiah. The ninety-year-old rabbi Akiba ben Joseph, the leading Pharisee at Jamnia and the most respected leader in the Jewish world, surprised everyone by proclaiming that Simeon was indeed the Messiah who would lead the Jews to victory over the Gentile world. And so, once again, the Jews of Palestine went to war with the empire. Hostilities broke out in AD 132 when the new Messiah led his forces to Jerusalem, which he easily captured. Simeon may have attempted to restore the old priesthood and he certainly began offering sacrifices on the site of the ruined Temple. To prepare the way for the new order, he decreed that henceforth no uncircumcised man would be allowed to enter Jerusalem. Letters found in Dead Sea caves describe the vision that Simeon and his followers shared. They truly believed that they were living at the dawn of a new age in which Israel was rising up to defeat the kingdoms of the world. Simeon's followers, called "the Brothers," were both devoted and fierce.

Little is known about the war itself. Hadrian sent eight legions to Judaea and probably joined them himself. The much anticipated new age crumbled to dust and blew away. As the Romans defeated Simeon's forces and recaptured Jerusalem, the remaining Brothers went into hiding to wage guerrilla warfare and plan further acts of terrorism. For the next several years Roman forces were busy ferreting the insurgents out of their holes. Simeon himself was captured and executed in AD 135. Thousands of Jews who took part in this latest revolt were rounded up and sold into slavery. Thousands more died of starvation or at their own hands. A disgusted Hadrian changed the name of the province from "Judaea" to

"Syria-Palestine," thus erasing any association of the land with the Jewish people.

As for Aelia Capitolina, it was finally finished—and it was indeed a magnificent city. But it was one without a trace of Judaism. Indeed, Jews were forbidden to come within sight of it. Without Jerusalem, the epicenter of Jewish religion and culture shifted to Galilee. There the Jews had no choice but to accept a world in which cities did not shun images simply because Jews lived there. It took time—time for new generations to be born and grow up, generations that had never known a Jewish state, a high priest, or a king of the Jews. And so in that manner, after so much killing and destruction, Judaism turned itself toward the synagogue and the family. The Temple and priesthood became artifacts of history, still cherished but no longer the hoped-for foundation of a restored Jewish theocracy.

Subsequent emperors relaxed Hadrian's ban on circumcision. Rebellions, insurrections, and terrorism appeared on a small scale here and there over the next few decades. But by AD 200 they were rare. It was not easy, but the Romans had managed to modernize Judaism and largely extinguish its radical elements. No longer a threat, the Romans left Judaism in peace. And so it remained.

What lessons can we draw from ancient Rome's war on terror? First and foremost we must recognize that the root causes of the problem are not economic, social, or political—they are religious. The Romans attempted an array of solutions to put an end to Jewish terrorism and violence in the Middle East. These included giving the Jews a free hand in local governance, garrisoning the region, withdrawing from the region, politically dividing it, politically uniting it, and, of course, throwing money at it. All of these efforts served only to produce among Jewish extremists an even greater hatred of the Romans and a stronger determination to kill them. The Jews of the Roman Empire were no worse off than any other people that had come under Roman control. Judaea was not governed more harshly than other Roman provinces. Quite the contrary, the Romans did their best (without always succeeding, of course) to make special provisions for the unique culture and laws of the Jews.

None of that mattered. That is because Jewish terrorism, insurgency, and rebellion flowed directly out of a particular interpretation of Jewish religious beliefs. An Empire of Trust is based on the assumption that it is acceptable for one state to have hegemonic power over others because it has established a reputation for using that power in a predictable, responsible, and measured manner. It was not that the Jews did not trust the Romans. Indeed, they had sought out an alliance with them and even asked them to help settle their own civil war. But many thousands of Jews had come to believe that the Romans should not have any power—hegemonic or otherwise. From their perspective, the rise of Rome was contrary to God's plan for humanity. It fell to them, therefore, to wage holy war against the Romans.

None of the Jewish attacks against the empire in the first and second century AD made one ounce of strategic sense. Jewish military assets were minuscule when compared to those of the Roman Empire. Messianic movements or urban terrorism that sought to exterminate all Gentiles were even more senseless. Yet they were senseless only within a worldly calculus. From a supernatural perspective they made eminent sense. That is why so many people engaged in them. They believed that they were doing the will of God and that He would give them victory by vanquishing their foes. They believed that they had the ultimate weapon—divine favor.

Modern Islamist terrorism flows from a similar source. Like first-century Jewish extremists, modern Islamists believe that they are engaged in a holy war against an empire that should not exist. Just as Allah gave victories to the Muslim empires of the Middle Ages, so, they believe, he is calling them to restore Islamic greatness, to reinstate Islamic law, and to spread Islam across the world. The rise of the West in the sixteenth century interrupted the expansion of Islam as a faith and an empire. The rise of the United States has, from the Islamist perspective, only made things worse. Islamists view the extension of American power and culture as a direct attack on the Umma—the Islamic "nation." It does not matter if Americans bring greater peace and security. They are infidels and the growth of their empire is contrary to God's plan.

Terrorism is not an economic issue. Although there is much poverty in the Middle East, there is also much wealth. Every one of the 9/11 terrorists was from an affluent Middle Eastern family. They were educated, intelligent, and privileged. The same is true of Osama bin-Laden as well as his lieutenants. It is not about money, or opportunity, or the "legacy of colonialism." It is about a religious perspective that was acceptable a thousand years ago but makes no sense any longer. The Romans faced the same problem with the Jews of their time and it was only when they recognized the religious character of the problem that they began to grope their way toward a solution.

Second, we must pay close attention to the constituencies of the Muslim Diaspora. Like the first-century Jews, Muslims today are concentrated in their ancestral lands but are also spread out across the world. Although they share a common faith, their perspectives and experiences are dramatically different. Islamist terrorism and the ideas behind it put an enormous strain on Diaspora Muslims and the fault lines that appear are similar to those that occurred among Jews two thousand years ago. Islamists are the most visible, but we must remember that they are a minority of the faithful, representing only one extreme of a continuum of Muslim approaches to the modern world. On the other side are secular Muslims, who, like Philo of Alexandria, believe that their religion should be "a personal faith, not a political doctrine." For example, in the March 5, 2007, St. Petersburg Declaration of the Secular Islam Summit, the Muslim participants called on "the governments of the world" to:

- reject Sharia law, fatwa courts, clerical rule, and state-sanctioned religion in all their forms; oppose all penalties for blasphemy and apostasy, in accordance with Article 18 of the Universal Declaration of Human rights;
- eliminate practices, such as female circumcision, honor killing, forced veiling, and forced marriage, that further the oppression of women. . . .

Like the "Hellenizers" of ancient Judaea, Muslim extremists today see the "Secularists" as traitors to the faith.

These tensions are keenly felt by the Muslim majority in the middle, those between the two poles of opinion. Just as first-century Jews of the Diaspora supported and watched Jerusalem and the Holy Land, so Muslims today are understandably concerned, not just with Mecca, but the entire Middle East. The vast majority of Muslims today are opposed to acts of terrorism, yet many are also sympathetic with the complaints of the terrorists. That puts them—and the Empire of Trust—in a difficult spot. It means that by the nature of the religious Diaspora, the extremism of the homeland will manifest itself abroad. Terrorists will be (and are) everywhere. Yet the empire must not alienate the moderates—be they Hellenizers or Secularists—by associating them with the enemy. It is a tricky, yet necessary, task. The Romans were hit hard by Jewish terrorism, yet they continued to have Jewish members of the Senate. It was when they cracked down on all Jews, friend and foe alike, that they exacerbated their problems.

Third, Americans need to accept that the War on Terror is going to be a long one. The Romans fought theirs for more than a century before seeing a light at the end of the tunnel. Even the Cold War will seem short by comparison. Yet there is no alternative to fighting it both at home and abroad. Whether or not Islamist terrorism was present in Iraq before the American invasion, it is there now. As their tapes and press releases make plain, al-Qaeda and other terrorist groups consider Iraq to be the front lines in the war against the United States. Americans would naturally prefer not to have their troops stationed in a faraway land attempting to keep peace between rival bands of terrorists, insurrectionists, and bandits. The Romans felt the same way. Yet Roman attempts to remove or reduce their military presence in Judaea always led to more violence, chaos, and instability. In the end, they were forced to accept the permanence of their bases in the region. They also learned that kindness and leniency were interpreted by the extremists as the hand of God dealing out bitter defeats to His enemies. Americans will come to accept that a permanent military presence in the Middle East is as necessary to the defense of the United

States and its allies as similar deployments in Europe or Asia. It would be better—and safer—to reach that conclusion sooner rather than later.

It is common nowadays to hear that "war never solves anything." (Google the phrase and you will see what I mean.) Nothing could be further from the truth. In fact, war *always* solves something. War occurs when two or more sides disagree on something important. It may be as simple as "We want your property" and "You can't have it," but a disagreement occurs that is ultimately solved by the war. In the case of the War on Terror, the disagreement is centered on a fundamental view of the world. Islamist terrorists want a world of Sharia, in which the Abode of Islam has finally eliminated the Abode of War. In the meantime, they want American troops and culture out of the Middle East. The United States refuses to accept that worldview. Because it is powerful and in the way, the United States is the target of the terrorists' jihad. Yet, just as with the Jewish attacks on Rome, the final outcome is not in doubt. Americans will not accept Osama bin-Laden's invitation to "embrace Islam," even if the Islamic tax rate is "only 2.5 percent." They will not replace their president with a sultan, or cover their women's heads, or give up liquor, or any of the other requirements of Sharia. Like Romans, Americans are willing to be tolerant but not conquered. Since the terrorists have no means to conquer the United States, they must lose. The war, when it someday ends, will have solved something.

Because religious terrorism *is* religious, it cannot be fought only on the battlefield. The Romans were able to contain or quell Jewish terrorism with arms, but they could not stop it. In order to do that, they had to change the religion itself. Judaism was changed. It became a faith, not a kingdom; a system of beliefs, not a government. As such, it was able to take its place among the many religious beliefs of the cosmopolitan Roman Empire. That is how the Romans won their War on Terror. And it is how the Americans will win theirs. Islam must change. Like ancient Judaism, Islam is already modernized in many parts of the world. But the medieval components of Islamic law and culture, where they are still active, must be adapted to the modern world. Islam must become—as it has already become for millions of Muslims worldwide—a personal faith, not a system of government. It must everywhere become tolerant, not just of Christians and Jews, but of all faiths—even of former Muslims who have converted to other religions. Like modern Judaism, Islam must interpret its holy law within a modern, rather than a medieval, context. That will be difficult and painful, just as it was for the Jews. In both cases, the faithful must come to terms with a world not of their making. But it is the only way to bring peace.

No religion changes overnight. Even the Catholic Church, which gave birth to the modern world, took several centuries to adapt to it. But in the end crusades, inquisitions, and the papal monarchy were left behind because, although they made sense in the medieval world, they had no place in the modern. Islam will continue to change under the same sorts of pressures. The Romans attempted to solve the problem by allowing the Jews to integrate their own laws into a semi-independent state under Roman protection. That is not unlike what the United States is currently attempting in Iraq. The system was never very stable and ultimately the Romans scrapped it for direct rule. But Americans might have better success. Americans have certain advantages that Romans lacked. Modern technologies allow them to keep a much closer eye on terrorist activity in the Middle East and around the world. Americans are, therefore, much better able to contain or at least respond to it. Although modern Iraq may be a troubled place, it is nothing compared to Judaea in the first century AD. Perhaps, by responding quickly and efficiently to terrorist and other Islamist activity, the United States can forcibly reduce it to manageable levels. That will not end the problem, but it will curb the bloodshed. And that is a good thing.

Americans have another advantage over the Romans—their culture, which is both innovative and everywhere. It is a consumer culture, to be sure. But it is an attractive one for all that. One of the reasons that Islamist leaders fulminate against Hollywood and American corporations is that they know that they offer something that their people want. As a consumer culture, it is focused above all on the individual, his or her desires, and the gratification of those desires. The Romans had plenty of money and they were good businessmen. But they did not have a culture that was either innovative or particularly attractive to foreigners. Americans do. It may be that with military strength and a heavy dose of American consumerism, Islamist terrorism can be starved to death, cut off from its supply of willing recruits. That will not happen quickly, but it could happen.

If it doesn't, the alternative will be much bloodier. Indeed, if we can draw any lesson from the experience of the Romans, it is that the violence in the war against terrorism may get much worse before it gets better. That will not happen if the United States is able to contain the problem to the Middle East. But that is a tall order. According to a 2007 report of the International Institute for Strategic Studies, al-Qaeda has revived after the conquest of its base in Afghanistan and now has the capacity to launch "large-scale attacks in the western world."

Consider this scenario: Al-Qaeda issues a video on the Internet in which three masked men show off a recently obtained nuclear "suitcase bomb." They demand an immediate withdrawal of all American troops from the Middle East and the release of all Islamist detainees in American military installations. If these demands are not met within seventy-two hours, the terrorists promise to explode their device in a large American city. Experts who study the video confirm that the terrorists probably do have a working nuclear device and that they are probably already in the United States. A comprehensive security crackdown is ordered in all of the nation's major cities. The president addresses the nation and the world but naturally refuses to submit to the terrorist demands. Then, two hours after the presidential address, while the roads out of American cities are still jammed with fleeing cars, the terrorists release a one-word response: "Judgment." A massive explosion goes off in downtown Chicago. Most of the loop is leveled, including the Sears Tower. One million Americans are killed in the initial blast. Another two hundred thousand are critically injured. Deadly radiation necessitates the evacuation of the entire Chicagoland area. As the world looks on with horror, in the streets of Cairo, Damascus, and Tehran there is dancing.

How would Americans respond? If the toppling of the World Trade Center and the attack on the Pentagon brought about the conquest of

Afghanistan and Iraq, what would the elimination of a major American city bring? It is not difficult to guess. The outrage of the American people would be beyond measure. A nuclear retaliation would not be out of the question. Indeed, Americans might well conclude that Islam itself was too dangerous to live with it. What then? The closing of mosques? Internment camps? Perhaps even the conquest of Arabia? We cannot know. But in that sort of atmosphere of fear and rage, anything is possible.

The point of this exercise is this: The ancient Romans were also pushed too far. Thousands of their citizens were killed and whole cities were captured. The result was the destruction of Judaism's most holy places. First the Temple was burned to the ground. Then Jerusalem itself was abolished. That was the sort of demolition and carnage that the Romans ultimately used to change Judaism. We must hope that the same thing will not be necessary to change radical Islam.

A nuclear attack is an extreme example, to be sure. But it illustrates an important point about the future of the War on Terror. If the first strategy is successful—if terrorism can be contained in the Middle East and the culture there liberalized, then Islamist terrorist strikes will gradually cease and the war will be won quietly—with a whimper rather than a bang. If that strategy fails, we will know it when terrorism again hits the homeland. The American response will be outrage, disgust, and a determination to fight the war with even greater vigor. That will necessarily mean the projection of additional American power into the Muslim Middle East. The cycle will repeat with ever greater death tolls, destruction, and misery—just as it did for the Romans. But at some point the scale will tip. Terrorism will decline and finally disappear because Islam will no longer contain the elements necessary to support it. After a very long and painful road, it will have been modernized.

Chapter 11

Crying Over the Fall

On a sunny day in 146 BC the forces of Rome were preparing to take care of some unfinished business. Carthage, their once powerful nemesis, lay prostrate before them. The lonely city was all that was left of a Carthaginian Empire that had once spanned the western Mediterranean, that had put fear into the hearts of the Italians, and had threatened the survival of Rome itself. Just the city, defiant and proud till the end. The might of Rome had descended on this capital, now shorn of its empire, and found that it was still a formidable foe. For more than two years the Carthaginians had held off the Roman advance. But no longer. On this pleasantly warm day the walls of Carthage were finally breached. The city was on fire. The legions were marching in.

From a rocky point not far from the city, the Roman commander, Scipio Aemilianus, stood watching. Standing beside him was his good friend Polybius, the Greek writer whose words we have often listened to in this book. It was a great moment for Scipio and for Rome. Carthage, at last, was gone. Polybius turned to his friend, expecting to see his face aglow with pride. Instead, he found Scipio quietly weeping, his hands covering his face. Surprised, Polybius asked him what was wrong. What could be wrong? He'd been victorious over Rome's greatest enemy. Scipio turned toward Polybius, tears still streaming down his rough cheeks, and said, "A glorious moment, Polybius; but I have a dread foreboding that someday the same doom will be pronounced on my own country." Wise words, Polybius concluded. Because every state, no matter how powerful, must one day fall.

Sixteen centuries later, another commander watched as his soldiers poured into a capital city shorn of its once mighty empire. The commander was Sultan Mehmed II of the Ottoman Turks and the city was Constantinople, the last remnant of Rome. Emperor Constantine XI, the last commander of Roman forces, fought bravely on the walls of the capital. But it was a hopeless struggle. He was killed and then beheaded by the invading soldiers. The last Romans were rounded up by the conquerors and sold into slavery. The event for which Scipio had shed tears had come to pass. Rome, at last, had fallen.

Every empire must fall. Rome did and the United States will too. But there is no sense in joining Scipio in a good cry about it. After all, Scipio's tears were sixteen hundred years early. If the United States can hang on for another thousand years or so, most people would consider that to be a good run. It is natural, though, to wonder how it will all come about. In this book, we have seen many striking similiaries between the rise of Rome's Empire of Trust and America's. Can those similarities also give us some clue about the fall of America's empire? And if so, can we do something now to prevent it?

In a word, no. The dynamics that we have been exploring in this book are related to the means by which Rome and the United States grew large empires. By examining those dynamics we have been able to see how and why these states created a historical rarity, an Empire of Trust. Difficult to build, these sorts of empires are just as difficult to destroy. And even when they are gone, they are still mourned—or at least Rome has been. One would be hard-pressed to think of any empire in history whose ghost has had such a profound effect on later peoples and cultures. But the dynamics that we have been exploring are what led to the empires' rise. They have nothing inherently to do with their decline. The fall of Rome was caused by internal political as well as external factors that were unique to Rome. America is not Rome. Americans are just building their Empire of Trust like the Romans.

That said, there is an understandable tendency to see in Rome's decline and fall lessons for modern America. It happens all the time. To take a random, recent example: in August 2007 the comptroller general of the United States, David Walker, issued a report stating that there were "striking similarities" between America's current situation and the factors that brought down Rome, including "declining moral values and political civility at home, an overconfident and overextended military in foreign lands, and fiscal irresponsibility by the central government." He concluded, "In my view, it's time to learn from history and take steps to ensure the American Republic is the first to stand the test of time."

So, let's explore the fall of Rome a bit—just to make certain that the comptroller general isn't onto something. The first thing to know about the fall of Rome is that it is complicated. Shelves of books and reams of scholarly articles have been written on the subject. To begin with, there was more than one "fall." The first was the fall of the Roman Republic in 27 BC. It was then that the old republican government was largely abolished in favor of the direct rule of one man—an emperor. The Senate still met, but it was a weak artifact of a bygone world. The second "fall" occurred in AD 476 when the last Roman emperor in Italy was deposed and the Germanic barbarians, who had already claimed most of the western portions of the empire, took over. The third and final "fall" was the conquest of Constantinople in 1453, when the last remnant of the Roman Empire was conquered by the Turks.

So, which fall are people worried about? Most recent commentators (including the comptroller general) are looking at the first. Writers like Chalmers Johnson and Robert Harris see President Bush's conquest of Iraq and domestic spying as evidence that he has become an emperor. By waving the bloody toga of 9/11, they argue, Bush has managed to overturn the Republic.

This is hyperbole masquerading as argument. The Roman Republic did not fall because a tricky elected official was able to hoodwink the Roman people. It fell because of an inherent flaw in the republican system. Roman government had been created for a city-state, not an empire. The Romans tweaked and altered it here and there as the empire grew, but their naturally conservative nature kept them from making any widespread changes. In any case, for most of their history the Romans did not believe that they had an empire, so there was no sense in making changes to accommodate something that didn't exist.

The inherent flaw was this—no effective buffer existed between the civilian government and the military. In the Roman system, consuls exercised military command power, known as *imperium*. They were elected for short terms, and when they finished, they became senators (if they weren't already). As the empire grew, the consuls found it impossible to command the far-flung legions of Rome. So they delegated. They would give imperium to men with experience—senators, of course. When the consul's term expired he would usually confirm the continued use of military command for the senator or proconsul in the field.

How was this a problem? At first, it wasn't. But as these senators spent more time with their legions, they became associated with them. Various legions began to look to their senators to support them in Rome. Support usually consisted of nice plum assignments to wealthy areas with plenty of booty. Bonuses were expected too. Imagine if American senators today were simultaneously military commanders in the field. They would naturally bring to their political jobs in Washington an outlook shaped by their experiences abroad as well as their association with their units. Likewise, the men of the units would look to their commanders in Congress as their political supporters. The political enemies of a particular military unit's senator would naturally become the enemies of that unit as well. And that can't be good.

In Rome, as time went on, some of these senators, like Sulla and Pompey, were able to acquire so much support among the Roman military that they could even use the legions as a political tool. So, for example, Julius Caesar (another senator) could report to his troops in Gaul that they were not being treated fairly because of his political enemies in Rome. This would naturally upset the soldiers, who, at Caesar's command, would obligingly march on Rome. Caesar's enemies would then conveniently disappear and everybody was happy—or else.

Because of this flaw, by the mid-first century BC the means to power in Rome was through the military. Nothing else mattered. The men in the legions no longer had confidence in their government. They were professional soldiers who did not like being poorly paid or sent to backwater assignments simply because their commander was politically weak in Rome. They naturally sought out a leader who could deliver the goods. If he took care of them, they would take care of him. Pompey could act almost as the ruler of Rome because everyone knew that a large part of the Roman military would gladly march into the city at his command.

Even with these military strongmen, the Republic died slowly. It took two massive civil wars that spread destruction and turmoil across the empire to finally convince the Romans to accept the rule of one man with sole control over the military. Augustus Caesar was that man. And yet, even he was careful to dress up his rule in republican finery. He rejected a royal title, instead simply calling himself *princeps*, or first citizen. He was also careful to have the Senate vote him all of his powers through legal channels, even though his real power flowed directly from his control of the legions.

Has the American president become a new Augustus? Not even close. The simple fact is that in this regard the Roman and American constitutions just don't work the same way. The Roman Republic broke down because politicians were also generals and they needed to pay off their troops with booty, bonuses, and good assignments. That led the troops to value their loyalty to their politician commanders higher than their loyalty to the Roman constitution. The American situation is very different. Although a professional force, the American military is led by professional generals, not senators or other politicians. American military personnel do not have booty as part of their benefits package, so there is no incentive for them to favor one assignment over another sufficiently to do something about it. In the American system, the military is purposely kept separate from the civilian government. It intersects only with the office of the president, who is the commander in chief. Yet the president is himself restricted by the electorate, term limits, and the Congress's power of the purse.

All of this was done on purpose. As we saw at the beginning of this book, the Founding Fathers were intent on having a Roman republican system without the flaws that led to its demise. They were determined to insert checks and balances between the branches that would keep any one group from acquiring absolute power. John Adams felt so confident about these new adjustments to the Roman model that he proclaimed that if the Romans had had them "it is impossible for any man to prove that the republic would not have remained in vigour and in glory at this hour."

Claiming that President Bush or any other American president is a new Pompey or Augustus is simply the kind of frivolousness to be expected in a time of Pax. It sells books and makes for good talk-show fodder, but it is historically absurd. The men who overturned the Roman Republic did so by wielding raw military power against their own government. Sending the armed forces to Iraq (after a supporting congressional resolution) is one thing, sending them to Washington, D.C., is quite another. If a president—no matter how popular—gave an order to the marines to surround Capitol Hill it would not be obeyed. That is because American troops value their oath to defend the American Constitution higher than their duty to obey their commanding officer. As long as that remains the case, the republic will be safe—at least from the dangers faced by the Roman Republic.

The fall of the republican form of government in Rome did not mean the fall of its Empire of Trust. Indeed, the greatest days of Roman peace, security, and prosperity occurred under the emperors. The period of the "Five Good Emperors" (AD 96–180) is usually considered to be Rome's golden age. Although the new system was bad for senators, most people found it to their liking. Local governments were largely left to themselves, with little interference from the emperor. That changed after AD 285, when the office of the emperor and the imperial administration were codified and expanded. But by that time the empire was already in trouble. The root cause remained the same. The people of Rome had bought internal stability at the expense of allowing one man to control the military. That worked as long as there was one man or dynasty strong enough to hold it. When weaknesses occurred, other men with command over their own legions were tempted to use them to seek the imperial throne. As a result, much of the late third and fourth centuries AD were taken up with civil wars among the Romans themselves.

Yet even that was not enough to kill the empire. In the West, the end came when Germanic tribes invaded, taking advantage of Roman weaknesses. Rome itself fell to the Goths in AD 410, although only temporarily. By AD 476 there was no longer a Roman Empire in Italy at all. It was ruled by a Gothic king. And yet, still, the Roman Empire survived. At its new capital in Constantinople (modern Istanbul) the emperors continued to adminster the eastern half of the empire. It is a striking testament to the nature of an Empire of Trust that even though Rome itself and the entire Latin-speaking world was lost and living under barbarian kings, the Greek East continued to call itself the Roman Empire. It would do so for the next thousand years before it succumbed to Muslim empires.

Rome fell in the West in 476 and in the East in 1453 because it was attacked and defeated from the outside. There were internal weaknesses, to be sure. But it was not an empty shell. Their economy was in shambles by AD 300, but that did not stop the Romans from having the largest and most powerful military in their history. Economic strength is good, but it is not a necessity for the survival of an Empire of Trust. It is sometimes said that moral decay led to the fall of Rome—and that it will do the same to America. All of those orgies and gladiator fights finally took their toll on a Roman people so drunk on hedonism that the Germans easily conquered them. This is an odd argument when we consider that the Rome that fell was Christian. The gladiator fights had been abolished a century earlier and the orgies were noticibly thinner on the ground. Edward Gibbon famously argued that it was Christianity itself that killed the Roman Empire, putting the best and brightest into monasteries and turning the eyes of the Romans from glory in this world to salvation in the next. Yet, this fails to explain why the Christian Roman Empire continued to survive in the East for another millennium.

In any event, all of these are medieval factors with no bearing at all on modern America. In the final analysis, Rome fell because all empires do. By the end of its life it was more than two thousand years old. It had grown, adapted, and changed across the centuries. By the fifteenth century—only a few decades before Columbus discovered America—there was nothing left of the ancient empire that had once spanned the known world. After a desperate show of exhausted valor, it breathed its last.

The United States is at a very different place in its life cycle. Still less than three centuries old, America is a young country and an even younger empire. Driven by the same internal and external dynamics as the youthful Rome, the United States is building an Empire of Trust along the same lines. Like the Romans in the early second century BC, Americans remain optimistic about the future and confident in their abilities. They have reason to be. Although there will always be challenges—more war, more bloodshed, more disunity—the cherished goal of security for themselves and their allies seems within reach. Americans have almost secured their horizon. That is what an Empire of Trust is driven to do. We may not be able to see the end of America's road, but its direction seems clear enough. And, for both Americans and the world, it is a good road to follow.

At least the Romans thought so.

A NOTE ON SOURCES

I am well aware of the problems that can arise from the use of ancient authors. They wrote history from a literary rather than scientific perspective. In a number of instances in this book I have quoted speeches or other dialogues verbatim from their ancient source. It is likely that many of these words were not uttered, although I have tried to avoid obvious fabrications. In most cases, though, I believe that they are accurate or very close to what was said at the time. Livy, for example, had an axe to grind, but he was also a careful scholar with access to records that have long since perished. For their part, Polybius and Josephus were eyewitnesses to many of the events and conversations that they describe. I do not accept, here or elsewhere, a historiographical approach that dismisses all sources as lies or propaganda. Too often this is simply a license for historians to project their own narratives or biases onto a suddenly blank historical slate. Some sources do lie, but a great many do not. I have tried in this study to use the latter.

Translations are usually based on the works listed in the bibliography, which I have in general found to be solid. In some cases I have corrected the translations for errors, emphasis, or to modernize the English.

NOTES

Chapter 1

3 *our children, and our wives:* Livy, 29.17.

3 *and double the amount put back:* Livy, 29.19.

5 *the actual dynamics at work at all:* See, e.g., Mommsen, *History of Rome;* Frank, *Roman Imperialism;* Badian, *Roman Imperialism;* Kallet-Marx, *Hegemony to Empire.*

5 *rejects opportunities for the extension of power:* Badian, *Roman Imperialism,* 1.

7 *the prisoners in Iraq and their families:* Congressional Record: May 10, 2004, S5072.

8 *It is a beginning to set things right:* Ibid., S5069.

8 *We liberate, not torture, and we free, not oppress:* Ibid., S5071.

9 *which is one big reason that they are getting one:* Ferguson, *Colossus,* provides an excellent discussion of America's reluctance to admit to an empire that already exists.

9 *Everything else—internal politics, economics, art—was secondary:* Todd, *After the Empire,* 59.

9 *aftermath of Rome's fall:* Kupchan, *End of the American Era.*

10 *the world of enemies they had created:* Johnson, *Sorrows of Empire,* 15–16.

10 *in the wake of 9/11:* Harris, "Pirates of the Mediterranean."

11 *the ranks of the civilized world:* Walker, "An Empire Unlike Any Other," 135.

11 *our people have gained the whole world:* Cicero, *De re publica,* 3.35.

11 *loyalty to yourself and your family:* BBC, *Rome* Press Pack.

12 *consider the development to be a good thing:* Ferguson, *Colossus;* Lal, *In Praise of Empires.*

12 *down an historical dead end:* Buchanan, *Republic, Not an Empire.*

12 *all of the other countries on the planet:* GlobalSecurity.org, "World Wide Military Expenditures."

13 *exploit foreign raw materials directly:* Lal, "Empire and Order," 18.

14 *imperialism of anti-imperialism:* Ferguson, *Colossus.*

19 *the French took this association with Rome:* Huet, "Napoleon I," 54–61.

19 *It is to be America:* Beard, *Giddy Minds,* 87.

Chapter 2

22 *conquest of the woman's honor:* Livy, 1.58.

23 *adulterer shall not go unpunished:* Ibid.

23 *nor any other to be king in Rome!:* Livy, 1.59.

24 *It was unthinkable:* Even centuries later, when the empire really was ruled by one man, the emperors were careful never to call themselves "king" and covered their power in the trappings of republican ceremony. Although they ruled, they made it appear that they were simply a first among equals.

25 *worn purple as a mark of pride:* 1 Maccabees 8:12, 14.

29 *a rule of laws, not men:* Livy, 2.1.

29 *a fair trial and a clear conviction:* "Twelve Tables," in *Roman Civilization,* 1:107–16.

31 *through many centuries and generations:* Cicero, *De rep.,* ii, 1, 2; see Scullard, *History of the Roman World, 753 to 146 BC,* 124.

31 *by the light of their experience:* Polybius, 6.10.13.

31 *it was the Senate that ruled Rome:* Cineas, an ambassador of Pyrrhus, reported that the Senate was an assembly of kings.

32 *Polybius, who, while not a Roman, was writing about them:* Richard, *Founders and the Classics.*

33 *catch up on their Latin and Greek:* Sellers, *American Republicanism,* 21–23.

33 *God has made this tranquility for us:* Ibid., 12–16.

34 *receives the support of Jupiter:* Aeneid, 9.625.

35 *the greatest power that has ever existed:* Adams, *Defence,* 1:175.

35 *that was what Adams and his associates sought to copy:* Sellers, *American Republicanism,* 38.

36 *simply another way of saying mob rule:* See Chapter 8 for a fuller discussion of this problem.

36 *and in glory at this hour:* Adams, *Defence,* 1:335–36.

36 *unless each in its department is independent and absolute:* Ibid, 1:48.

Chapter 3

39 *their livelihood is most assured:* Cato, *On Agriculture,* preface. See also Petrochilos, *Roman Attitudes,* 55–62.

40 *the state of apprehension of the army:* Livy, 3.26.

42 *They would see to their formation themselves:* Scullard, *A History of the Roman World, 753 to 146 BC,* 359.

43 *insisting that it suited them just fine:* Ibid., 360–61.

44 *to care much about their little farms:* Ibid., 389–93.

45 *while 56 percent did so in the South:* See Kohut and Stokes, *America Against the World,* 95.

47 *to come to terms with their own religions on their own:* Scullard, *A History of the Roman World, 753 to 146 BC,* 393–97.

51 *or submit to their pollution:* Livy, 39.13.

51 *the chastity of your wives and children?:* Livy, 39.15.

52 *to fear them in their united strength:* Livy, 39.16.

52 *but to be punished and put an end to:* Ibid.

52 *seriously upsetting the* pax deorum: For a detailed and perceptive treatment of this event with full citations, see Erich Gruen, *Studies in Greek Culture and Roman Policy,* 34–78.

53 *inadequate to the government of any other:* John Adams, "Letter of October 11, 1798," *Works,* 9: 228.

54 *no better than the builders of Babel: Debates in the Federal Convention,* 181.

54 *but with His wrath?: Writings,* 8:404.

54 *in exclusion of religious principle: Writings,* 13:308.

54 *most Americans believe that it is absolutely necessary for a person to believe in God in order to be moral:* Pew Global Attitudes Project, "Views of a Changing World," June 3, 2003, survey, available at pewglobal.org.

54 *religion should be taught in the home:* Kohut and Stokes, *America Against the World,* 106.

54 *three times as many Americans believe in the virgin birth as in evolution: Economist,* Nov. 6, 2003.

55 *because of their unique national character:* See especially *Anti-Americanism.*

55 *who has been discovered in such conduct:* Polybius 6.56.6.

58 *New York money people:* See Jonah Goldberg, "Leave No Blowhard Behind," *National Review Online,* Feb. 2, 2007.

58 *the United States had better do something about it:* For variations on this theme, see Steyn, *America Alone.*

60 *to whom such things are better than a feast:* Sallust, *Jugurthine War,* 120–21.

61 *self-indulgence and effeminacy:* Livy, 29.19.

Chapter 4

65 *the earliest days of the American republic:* I have read with interest Robert Kagan's recent book, *Dangerous Nation.* In it, he argues that American isolationism is a mirage, that from the beginning of the republic "a grand strategy" can be discerned to build a great empire. As a historian, I am naturally dubious of grand strategies, particularly when they are pursued by a great many people over the course of many decades. However, Kagan is certainly correct that there is something about the American character that can at once embrace the image of isolationism and expand at a rapid rate. Uncovering that "something" is worthwhile, and what this present book is all about.

65 *collisions of her friendships or enmities:* Washington, *Writings,* 13:316.

65 *She is the champion and vindicator only of her own: Abridgment of the Debates of Congress,* 8:435.

65 *we should have nothing to do with conquest: Writings,* 3:275.

66 *with humble and contrite hearts. Amen: Great Short Works,* 221.

69 *so much harder as you are stronger:* See Frank, *Roman Imperialism,* 8.

70 *who have not been bloodthirsty and barbarous in their warfare:* Cicero, *De officiis,* 1: 34–35.

70 *throw themselves upon the mercy of our generals:* Ibid.

71 *all the headaches that come with it:* Veyne, "Y a-t-il eu un impérialisme romain?"

75 *was rejected entirely at Rome:* Frank, *Roman Imperialism,* 32.

77 *as well as to strike and punish:* Ibid.

80 *For long will be the time that you will weep hereafter: Antiquities,* 19.5.

84 *they handed over every gift that they had received:* Ultimately, they were allowed to keep the gifts as rewards for their service. Dionysius of Halicarnassus, *Antiquities,* 20; Cassius Dio, *Roman History,* 10.41.

Chapter 5

88 *governed with wisdom and statecraft: De re publica,* 1, frg. 43.

91 *insistent that no such treaty existed. And they would know:* Polybius, who was later in a position to know, quite adamantly declared that there never was such a treaty. *Hist.,* 3.26.

93 *technology, and Americans, can fix anything:* See Kohut and Stokes, *America Against the World.*

97 *the treaty was ratified by the Senate in 226 BC:* It is sometimes said that Rome also promised in this treaty not to project power south of the Ebro. This is a modern interpretation, though, and not based on ancient sources.

102 *shaken as they were by so many conflicting emotions:* Livy, 21.16.

104 *The Carthaginians accepted the gift:* See Livy, 12.18 and Polybius, 3.20–30.

105 *Americans cannot allow it and neither could the Romans:* See Badian, *Foreign Clientelae,* 51–52.

105 *a sad and emphatic warning against putting any trust in alliances with Rome:* Livy, 21.19.

109 *self-indulgence and effeminacy:* Livy, 29.19. The whole debate can be further explored in Livy, 28.40–45 and Plutarch, *Fabius,* 25–26.

Chapter 6

120 *Philhellenism became a central feature of Roman elite culture:* See Gruen, *Hellenistic World,* 250, with citations.

121 *it all became the rage in the Rome of the second century BC:* Ibid., 255–60.

121 *were "possessed" about philosophy:* Plutarch, *Cato,* 22.2–3.

123 *refined barbarians:* Strabo, 1.4.9.

124 *no distinct Hellenic image of Rome had taken shape:* Gruen, *Hellenistic World,* 325.

126 *it is folly and madness to hope that anything in Greece will remain as it is now:* Livy, 31.29.

127 *that his people had used when wielding power:* Livy, 31.31.

128 *without any hope of reconciliation:* Polybius, 37.1–4.

129 *European thought and politics have become increasingly permeated with anti-Americanism:* See Revel, *Anti-Americanism.*

130 *agreed to arrest and hand over those guilty for the murders:* Livy, 22.29.

130 AND SHALL LIVE UNDER THEIR OWN LAWS: Livy, 33.32.

131 *that right and equity and law may be everywhere supreme:* Livy, 33.33.

133 *Romans were, after all, barbarians:* Petrochilos, *Roman Attitudes,* 108–10.

133 *Why, then, were the Greeks so resentful?:* See Plutarch, *Flamininus,* 11.

135 *But her patience was not inexhaustible:* Scullard, *History of the Roman World, 753 to 146 BC,* 273.

136 *no longer has the military capacity to seriously threaten the United States:* See the fuller discussion in Chapter 7.

137 *Europeans believed that the American military was making the world more dangerous, actually increasing the chance of war:* Kohut and Stokes, *America Against the World,* 24.

137 *anti-Americanism in continental western Europe has not only grown, but has become a standard of discourse:* See Fouad Ajami, "The Anti-Americans," *Wall Street Journal,* July 3, 2003.

137 *calling Royal's accusation "extreme":* Associated Press, "Royal Compares Sarkozy to Bush," by Angela Charlton, May 4, 2007.

137 *leaving McDonald's, Disney, and Coca-Cola in their wake:* See Kohut and Stokes, *America Against the World,* passim; Berman, *Anti-Americanism in Europe.*

138 *for the reason that they are known to oppose your policies:* Polybius, 24.9.

138 *a postmodern world in which all is peaceful and ideas no longer have any real meaning:* See, e.g., Kagan, "Power and Weakness."

138 *that is increasing emissions of carbon dioxide:* Ferguson, "Empire Falls."

138 *Europe is slowly committing suicide:* Ibid.; Steyn, *America Alone.*

138 *the next generation will be one-half the size of the current one:* CIA World Factbook, 2007.

139 *by small degrees cities became resourceless and feeble:* Polybius, 36.17.

140 *a means of securing for Greeks maximum of freedom of action:* Polybius, 24.13.

140 *even lie about the Romans with no repercussions whatsoever:* Pliny, *Natural History,* 34.16; Ovid, *Ex Ponto,* 4.14.

140 *better buildings would arise than those which had gone down in the flames:* Seneca, 91.13. See also Gruen, *Hellenistic World,* 354.

141 *leaves Europe plenty of time to build up this potential if it wants to:* Todd, *After the Empire,* 174, 192–93. See also Bender, *Weltmacht America,* who in an otherwise fine book, argues that the ancient Greeks and their relationship to Rome is not at all analogous to the present relationship of Europe to the United States because, unlike the Greeks, the Europeans could unite and become a military threat to the Americans.

142 *forgot their civilization in the wilds of Italy:* Dionysius of Halicarnassus, 1.4.

142 *had to succeed while still preserving the republican state:* Livy, 9.18.

143 *they were much more favorable toward Communist China than to the United States:* Kohut and Stokes, *America Against the World,* 29.

146 *So deep was the prevailing aversion and hatred of them:* Polybius, 30.29. See also Gruen, *Hellenistic World,* 336.

147 *were rewarded for their country's protection and support with insults and ridicule:* Ibid.

147 *when not living lives of moral decay:* Gruen, *Hellenistic World,* 261; Isaac, *Invention of Racism,* 384.

148 *But of course:* Rob Long, "The Long View," *National Review,* May 28, 2007.

149 *for he lost his wife and son:* Plutarch, *Cato,* 23–24.

149 *but those of the Romans in their hearts:* Ibid., 12.

149 *the Greek spirit questioned everything and settled nothing:* Ibid.

153 *that Mummius not only appreciated Greek culture but generously restored ruined Greek temples, was irrelevant:* Gruen, *Hellenistic World,* 266.

153 *which did nothing to improve the characters of its professors:* Sallust, *Jugurthine War,* 120.

153 *the better one learns Greek the more a scoundrel one becomes:* Cicero, *De oratore,* 2.265.

153 *dished out contempt for Roman elites who affected Greek manners:* Gruen, *Hellenistic World,* 264–65.

154 *while Antonius claimed to be completely unfamiliar with it:* See Petrochilos, *Roman Attitudes,* 30–31.

155 *Romania is no longer a victim looking for a savior, but a partner of the United States:* Associated Press, "Romanian Parliament Approves U.S. Troops," May 2, 2007.

155 *will remain strong allies of the United States for many years to come:* See also, Bugajski and Teleki, *Atlantic Bridges.*

155 *it is not much more prevalent in Britain than it is among America's own elites:* On matters of foreign affairs, British public opinion is astonishingly close to that of the Americans who identify themselves as members of the Democratic Party. Kohut and Stokes, *America Against the World,* 215–16.

155 *has been steadfastly and overwhelmingly pro-American:* From the *Pew Global Attitudes Project.* See the analysis in Michael Mosbacher and Digby Anderson, "Recent Trends in British Anti-Americanism," in *Understanding Anti-Americanism,* 87–88.

157 *polls in Europe continue to show low levels of identification with the EU:* Fergusson, *Colossus,* 251–52.

157 *Predictions of a new European superpower, therefore, are neither convincing, nor borne out by the facts:* See, for example, Kupchan, "The End of the West"; Huntington, "The Lonely Superpower."

157 *used for public works around their countries:* NATO Supreme Allied Commander General James Jones told Congress in 2004 that only 3 to 4 percent of European forces are "expeditionary deployable." See "European Military Might Lacks Numbers," *Fox News,* May 11, 2004.

157 *They consist of two deployable units of fifteen hundred soldiers each:* "New Force Behind EU Foreign Policy," *BBC News,* March 15, 2007.

Chapter 7

161 *and embrace him as their very good friend:* Polybius, 29.27.1–7.

162 *a thing unprecedented in history?:* Ibid., 1.1.5.

162 *everyone in the known world now had to obey them:* See P. S. Derow, "Polybius, Rome, and the East," *JRS* 69 (1979): 1–15; J. S. Richardson, "Polybius' View of the Roman Empire," *Papers of the British School at Rome* 47 (1979): 1–11; A. Lintott, "What Was the *'imperium romanum'?,*" *Greece and Rome* 28 (1981): 53–67.

165 *the way that we speak of Rome today:* Kaplan, *Warrior Politics,* thinks so.

165 *Worldwide supremacy appears first not as a goal but as an accomplishment:* Gruen, *Hellenistic World,* 286. See also 280.

165 *our government could be called more accurately a protectorate of the world rather than an empire:* Cicero, *De officiis,* 2.27.

165 *no more than a first among equals:* Kohut and Stokes, *America Against the World,* 50.

168 *American forces in Iraq currently number around 160,000:* Figures from GlobalSecurity.org.

170 *It was the constant search for an unattainable total security that led both peoples into their Empires of Trust:* As Kurt A. Raaflaub has noted, Roman leaders were "nervous and highly security-conscious, all too willing to take preventive actions whenever they perceived a possible threat, or to accept offers of alliance that to us seem to have entailed more problems than advantages." "Born to be Wolves?", 292.

170 *By defending our allies our people have gained the whole world:* Cicero, *De re publica,* 3.35.

170 *and preceded by a reasonable demand for restitution:* Ibid.

172 *See, senators, how you are bound by this precedent that you yourselves have established?:* Livy, 37.54.

173 *Even Rome's critics admitted that they painstakingly kept their word:* Polybius, 24.13.

175 *we will defend their rights and fight you on sea and land:* This was a standard form of treaty at the time. For other examples, see Lewis and Reinhold, *Roman Civilization,* 1: 355–56.

176 *ordering him to cease attacking their friend or face the consequences:* For more on this, see Chapter 9.

177 *that, you have learned by personal experience:* Sallust, *Jugurthine War,* 138–39.

177 *his accomplices were beaten and decapitated in Rome:* Appian, *Samnite Wars,* 9.1.

178 *was simply un-Roman:* See Chapter 1 above.

178 *Yet it was not the moral code of the Abderans that was on trial—but that of the Romans:* Livy, 43.4.

179 *if not from European slave traders?:* Revel, *Anti-Americanism,* 17–18.

180 *without any hope of reconciliation:* Polybius, 37.4.

183 *and confirm the decision of the Senate:* Livy, 31.7.

184 *our inherent right of self-defense:* See http://www.whitehouse.gov/nsc/nss/2006/.

185 *do not trust the United States to "act responsibly in the world":* WorldPublicOpinion. org.

185 *immune from counterattack:* See the arguments laid out in Chapter 8.

185 *troop strengths have been declining worldwide, not increasing:* Ibid.

186 *American troops simply do not exit:* Boot, *Savage Wars,* 337 and passim.

187 *so will Americans agonize over Vietnam:* A useful guide to the still-vibrant Vietnam debate is provided by Herman, "Who Owns the Vietnam War?"

193 *abandoning America's policy of promoting freedom and democracy in his invasion of Iraq:* See, e.g., Ignatieff, "Who Are Americans to Think That Freedom Is Theirs to Spread?"

194 *all such idealism should be abandoned:* Merry, *Sands of Empire.*

194 *But it is security, not liberation, that drives the progress of the Empire of Trust:* See the excellent analysis of American pursuit of security by James Chace, "In Search of Absolute Security."

194 *a citadel for every nation and people:* See, e.g., *In Catilinam,* 4.11; *Pro Sulla,* 33.

194 *freedom to the enslaved:* Livy, 45.18.

194 *autocrats and tyrants of any sort:* Gruen, *Hellenistic World,* 339.

194 *the cities were freed from serious civil discord and internecine massacres:* Polybius, 36.17.

194 *as many as have heard of their fame have feared them:* 1 Maccabees 8:12.

195 *These are imperial arts, and worthy thee: Aeneid,* 6: 851–53 (John Dryden, trans.).

Chapter 8

197 *and the martial enthusiasm of the people:* Gibbon, *Decline and Fall,* 1: 2.

197 *after Rome had eliminated all of its serious military rivals:* See Cornell, "The End of Roman Imperial Expansion," 157–60.

198 *Primates do it too:* See Sapolsky, "A Natural History of Peace."

198 *could instead be fashioned into peaceful creatures:* See the excellent study by Howard, *The Invention of Peace.*

201 *outright warfare is concentrated in sub-Saharan Africa:* "Human Security Report 2005," Human Security Centre, http://www.humansecurityreport.info/.

202 *limiting rivalries to trade and other pursuits of peace:* George W. Bush, http://www.whitehouse.gov/news/releases/2002/06/20020601-3.html.

202 *of surpassing, or equaling, the power of the United States: National Security Strategy of the United States,* September 2002.

206 *The operative word here is* theoretically: Available at http://www.defenselink.mil/pubs/pdfs/070523–China-Military-Power-final.pdf.

206 *no longer leaves harbor:* Lieber and Press, "The Rise of U.S. Nuclear Primacy."

206 *American satellites and other technological infrastructure: 2007 U.S.-China Economic and Security Review — Report to Congress.* Available at http://www.uscc.gov/annual_report/2007/07_annual_report.php.

208 *and get them flying again that's their decision:* Associated Press, "Russia Sends Long Bombers Back on Patrol," August 17, 2001; Associated Press, "Russian Bombers Intercepted After Breaching NATO Airspace," September 14, 2007.

209 *by 2010 Russia will have only 150 missiles or fewer:* Lieber and Press, "The Rise of U.S. Nuclear Primacy."

210 *MAD no longer exists:* Ibid.

211 *only a fraction of the alliance meets the standard of spending at least 2 percent of GNP on defense:* DOD Transcript 3989.

211 *have militaries too small to meet their treaty obligations: The 2004 Statistical Compendium on Allied Contributions to the Common Defense,* http://www.defenselink.mil/pubs/allied_contrib2004/allied2004.pdf.

211 *among the thirteen remaining allies:* Ibid.

212 *to respond to American requests for help in patrolling the world's oceans:* "All at Sea," *The Guardian,* January 21, 2004.

212 *None were designated for the defense of Germany:* Walker, "The New German Army."

213 *It could also include Roman bases and foreign aid:* Braund, *Rome and the Friendly King,* 182–83.

214 *King Ariarathes IV of Cappadocia sent his son and heir to Rome for his education:* Livy, 42.19.

214 *Charops, the ruler of Epirus:* Polybius, 27.15.

214 *Attalus III and Demetrius II of Syria were in Rome for the same purpose:* Livy, 45.44.

214 *they were taking money from both kings:* Gellius, *Attic Nights,* 11.10.4.
215 *he began to be afraid of the reaction of the Roman people:* Sallust, *Jugurthine War,* 14.
216 *It is you who are insulted in the wrong done to me:* Ibid.
217 *the force that you can bring to bear on him?:* Ibid., 25.
217 *all public resentment had evaporated:* Ibid., 26.
218 *a city for sale and ripe for destruction, if it ever finds a buyer:* Ibid., 37.
219 *numerous members of Congress regularly travel abroad to listen to constituencies:* Nancy Pelosi as Speaker of the House made a much publicized tour of the Middle East in the spring of 2007, shortly after the Democrats took control of Congress. Leaders like Syria's President Bashar Assad welcomed Pelosi as a rival to President George W. Bush, whose policies in the Middle East he opposed.
222 *most of the world will point their fingers at the U.S. government:* Byman and Pollack, *Things Fall Apart,* 2–3.
223 *it was the overseas kingdoms that came to them:* Badian, *Imperialism,* 30–31; Braund, "Royal Wills."
224 *he avoided a flogging and demanded a trial in Rome:* Acts 22:25.
225 *these are the ones that affect my way of life more than anything else:* "Europeans Like Bush Even Less Than Before," by Sarah Lyall, *New York Times,* May 9, 2004.
225 *All you can do is wait and watch: you're powerless:* Available at http://www.guardian.co.uk/uselections2004/story/0,13918,1326033,00.html.
226 *the end of a six-year nightmare for the world:* Associated Press, "World Welcomes Shift in U.S. Politics," by Paul Haven, November 8, 2006.
227 *Europeans are following the U.S. presidential primaries:* "Europeans watch U.S. Elections with Heightened Interest," by Jeffrey Stinson, *USA Today,* January 9, 2008.
228 *even coining new words for new technologies:* Daniels, "Sense of Superiority," 65–67.

Chapter 9

236 *an "evil maniac," a "fuehrer," and a "terrorist":* Jeff Jacoby, "A New Low in Bush Hatred," *Boston Globe,* September 10, 2006.
236 *that I have never seen in forty-four years of campaign watching:* Jonathan Chait, "Mad About You," *The New Republic* (September 2003).
239 *scarcely the germ of the luxury that was still coming:* Livy, 39.6.
240 *Rome would lose her empire when she had become fully infected with Greek culture:* Plutarch, *Cato,* 23.
240 *addicted to the pleasures of Greek life:* Gruen, *Hellenistic World,* 262.
241 *there was a great display of wealth both in public and in private:* Polybius, 31.25.
241 *acquired a taste for vice and obtained a means of gratifying it:* Pliny, *Natural History,* 33.53.
241 *I would not venture to say this of all of them:* Polybius, 18.35.
242 *extravagance and proud displays of personal wealth:* Ibid., 6.57.
243 *will change its nature to the worst thing of all, mob-rule:* Ibid.
243 *their culture, and their way of life were sick and ready to die:* See Gruen, *Hellenistic World,* 340–41.

243 *through self-indulgence and licentiousness:* Livy, Preface.

245 *they preempted their bodies' needs with self-indulgence:* Sallust, *Catiline Conspiracy,* 7–14.

245 *the Republic, which hitherto had been the common interest of all, was torn asunder:* Sallust, *Jugurthine War,* 41.

246 *From heaven to earth: Sibylline Oracles.* Terry, trans., 72–73.

248 *genre of literature that Romans of the Pax had long enjoyed reading:* My analysis here is purely within the literary and cultural context of Rome. The Book of Revelation as Scripture is an entirely different matter outside the scope of this book.

Chapter 10

252 *every man hourly expecting death, as in war:* Josephus, *Jewish War,* 2.266.

253 *The short answer is that the Crusades had nothing at all to do with 9/11:* For a fuller discussion, see my *New Concise History of the Crusades.*

260 *or make alliance with those who war against them:* 1 Maccabees 15:17, 19.

263 *whatever ceremonies were necessary for its purification:* Josephus, *Antiquities,* 14.4.

263 *But outside of Palestine the Jews did not cause trouble, so they were tolerated:* See the excellent analysis of Gruen, "Roman Perspectives on the Jews."

266 *while he was inspecting a new palace construction on the Esquiline Hill:* Philo of Alexandria, *Legatione,* 44–46.

267 *just as the Romans had been tolerant of them:* Grant, *Jews,* 135.

267 *contempt toward the gods of other peoples:* Josephus, *Antiquities,* 19.

267 *with the help of an angel:* Acts 12:1–19.

267 *Christians naturally saw the hand of God in Agrippa's demise:* Acts 12: 23.

268 *Once again, the Roman authorities restored order:* Josephus, *Antiquities,* 20.

268 *many people killed in the trampling:* Josephus, *War,* 2.224.

269 *although they did not stay away for very long:* Acts 18:2; Cassius Dio, 60.6.3; Suetonius, *Claudius,* 25.4.

269 *on the pretense that God would show them signs of approaching freedom:* Josephus, *War,* 2.259.

269 *For many years he, too, remained a rallying point for terrorists and insurgents:* Josephus, *War,* 2: 261; *Antiquities,* 20; Acts 21:38.

272 *since for sparing them up until now they have received no thanks at all:* Josephus, *War,* 2.

273 *massacring many Gentiles:* Grant, *Jews,* 310, n. 7.

274 *who had notoriously mistreated the Jews under his jurisdiction:* Josephus, *War,* 2.558.

277 *just what we should expect from men so depraved!:* Ibid., 6.333ff.

279 *In all 220,000 persons were killed:* Cassius Dio, 68.32; see also Eusebius, *Ecclesiastical History,* 4.2.

279 *the devastation was immense:* Grant, *Jews,* 237.

280 *more than 200,000 Romans and Greeks:* Cassius Dio, 68.32.

284 *Terrorism is not an economic issue:* On this point, see Krueger, *What Makes a Terrorist.*

284 *that further the oppression of women:* St. Petersburg Declaration; http://www
.secularislam.org.

285 *Even the Cold War will seem short by comparison:* Philip H. Gordon makes a convincing case for similarities between the War on Terror and the Cold War. However, Islamism is not simply an ideology, like Marxism or Anarchism. It is a
variety of Islam that, in one form or another, has existed for centuries. See "Can
the War on Terror Be Won?"

286 *even if the Islamic tax rate is "only 2.5 percent":* Osama bin-Laden, video transcript,
Sept. 6, 2007.

288 *large-scale attacks in the western world:* IISS, *Strategic Survey 2007.*

Chapter 11

291 *Because every state, no matter how powerful, must one day fall:* Polybius, 38.21–22.

292 *to ensure the American Republic is the first to stand the test of time:* "Learn From the
Fall of Rome, US Warned," by Jeremy Grant, *Financial Times,* August 14, 2007.

292 *Bush has managed to overturn the Republic:* Johnson, *Nemesis;* Harris, "Pirates of
the Mediterranean." Peter Irons's *War Powers* argues that presidential power to
command the military threatens the republic and is not what was intended by the
framers. He believes that the courts should invalidate presidential military orders
that are not sanctioned by a declaration of war.

293 *Bonuses were expected too:* For examples, see Livy, 30.45; 34.46; 40.59.

295 *have remained in vigour and in glory at this hour:* Adams, *Defence,* 1:335–36.

295 *with little interference from the emperor:* Tacitus, *Annals,* 1.2; see also Lintott, *Imperium Romanum,* 111–28.

296 *people so drunk on hedonism that the Germans easily conquered them:* Vance, "Decadence and the Subversion of Empire."

296 *continued to survive in the East for another millennium:* This argument has recently
been resurrected, at least in part, by Amy Chua, *Day of Empire,* 54–55. Chua believes that Christianity's intolerance, along with Rome's inability to continue to
embrace diverse cultures, led to its fall. As with Gibbon's construction, though,
Chua fails to explain why the Christian Roman East, which had its own share of
Germans, survived for another thousand years.

BIBLIOGRAPHY

Primary Sources

Abridgment of the Debates of Congress from 1789 to 1856, 16 vols. New York: D. Appleton and Co., 1858.

Adams, John. *A Defence of the Constitutions of Government of the United States of America,* 3 vols. London: C. Dilly, 1787–88.

———. *The Works of John Adams, Second President of the United States,* 10 vols. Boston: Little, Brown, and Co., 1850–56.

Appian. *Roman History,* trans. Horace White, Loeb Classical Library, 4 vols. London: W. Heinemann, 1928.

Cassius Dio. *Roman History,* trans. Earnest Carey, Loeb Classical Library, 9 vols. New York: Macmillan Co., 1914–27.

Cato, Marcus Porcius. *On Agriculture,* trans. William Davis Hooper and Harrison Boyd Ash, Loeb Classical Library. Cambridge, Mass.: Harvard University Press, 1934.

Cicero, Marcus Tullius. *De officiis,* trans. Walter Miller, Loeb Classical Library. Cambridge, Mass.: Harvard University Press, 1975.

———. *De oratore,* trans. E. W. Sutton and H. Rackham, Loeb Classical Library, 2 vols. Cambridge, Mass.: Harvard University Press, 1942.

———. *De re publica, De legibus,* trans. Clinton Walker Keyes, Loeb Classical Library. Cambridge, Mass.: Harvard University Press, 1928.

———. *In Catilinam 1–4. Pro Murena. Pro Sulla. Pro Flacco: B. Orations,* trans. C. MacDonald, Loeb Classical Library. Cambridge, Mass.: Harvard University Press, 1977.

The Debates in the Federal Convention of 1787, eds. Gaillard Hunt and James Brown Scott. New York: Oxford University Press, 1920.

Dionysius of Halicarnassus. *The Roman Antiquities,* trans. Earnest Carey and Edward Spelman, Loeb Classical Library, 7 vols. Cambridge, Mass.: Harvard University Press, 1947–60.

Eusebius of Caesarea. *Ecclesiastical History,* trans. Kirsopp Lake, Loeb Classical Library, 2 vols. New York: G. P. Putnam's Sons, 1926–32.

Gellius, Aulus. *The Attic Nights,* trans. John C. Rolfe, Loeb Classical Library, 3 vols. Cambridge, Mass.: Harvard University Press, 1961.

Jefferson, Thomas. *The Writings of Thomas Jefferson,* 9 vols. Washington, D.C.: Taylor and Maury, 1853–54.

Josephus. *Jewish Antiquities,* trans. H. St. J. Thackeray and Ralph Marcus, Loeb Classical Library, 9 vols. Cambridge, Mass.: Harvard University Press, 1998.

———. *The Jewish War,* trans. G. A. Williamson and E. Mary Smallwood. New York: Dorset Press, 1981.

Livy. *History of Rome,* trans. William F. Roberts, Everyman Library, 6 vols. London: E. P. Dutton, 1912–24.

Ovid. *Tristia and Ex Ponto,* trans. Arthur Leslie Wheeler, Loeb Classical Library. Cambridge, Mass.: Harvard University Press, 1988.

Philo of Alexandria. *Works,* trans. F. H. Colson and G. H. Whitaker, Loeb Classical Library, 10 vols. New York: G. P. Putnam's Sons, 1929–62.

Pliny. *Natural History,* trans. H. Rackham, Loeb Classical Library, 10 vols. Cambridge, Mass.: Harvard University Press, 1938–63.

Plutarch. *Lives,* trans. Bernadotte Perrin, Loeb Classical Library, 9 vols. Cambridge, Mass.: Harvard University Press, 1968–84

———. *Lives of Illustrious Men,* trans. J. Langhorne and W. Langhorne, 2 vols. London: Henry G. Bohn, 1855.

Polybius. *Histories,* trans. W. R. Paton, Loeb Classical Library, 6 vols. New York: G. P. Putnam's Sons, 1922–27.

Roman Civilization: Selected Readings, ed. Naphtali Lewis and Meyer Reinhold, 3rd ed., 2 vols. New York: Columbia University Press, 1990.

Sallust. *The Jugurthine War and The Conspiracy of Catiline,* trans. S. A. Handford. Baltimore: Penguin, 1963.

Seneca, Lucius Annaeus. *Ad Lucilium epistulae morales,* trans. Richard M. Gummere, Loeb Classical Library, 3 vols. Cambridge, Mass.: Harvard University Press, 1961–62.

Sibylline Oracles, The, trans. Milton Spenser Terry. New York: Hunt and Eaton, 1890.

Strabo. *Geography,* trans. Horace Leonard Jones, Loeb Classical Library, 8 vols. New York: G. P. Putnam's Sons, 1917–33.

Suetonius. *Works,* trans. J. C. Rolfe, Loeb Classical Library, 2 vols. Cambridge, Mass.: Harvard University Press, 1997–98.

Tacitus, Cornelius. *Works,* trans. John Jackson, Loeb Classical Library, 5 vols. Cambridge, Mass.: Harvard University Press, 1979–86.

Virgil. *Vergil's Aeneid and Fourth ("messianic") Eclogue: in the Dryden translation,* ed. Howard Clarke. University Park: Pennsylvania State University Press, 1988.

Washington, George. *The Writings of George Washington,* ed. Worthington Chauncey Ford, 14 vols. New York: G. P. Putnam's Sons, 1889.

Secondary Works

Aberbach, Moshe, and David Aberbach. *The Roman-Jewish Wars and Hebrew Cultural Nationalism.* New York: St. Martin's Press, 2000.

Bacevich, Andrew J. *American Empire: The Realities and Consequences of U.S. Diplomacy.* Cambridge, Mass.: Harvard University Press, 2002.

Badian, Ernst. *Foreign Clientelae, 264–70 BC.* Oxford: Clarendon Press, 1958.

———. *Roman Imperialism in the Late Republic,* 2nd ed. Ithaca: Cornell University Press, 1968.

Beard, Charles A. *Giddy Minds and Foreign Quarrels.* New York: Macmillan, 1939.

Beecher, Edward. *The Papal Conspiracy Exposed.* Boston: Stearns, 1855.

Beecher, Lyman. *A Plea for the West.* New York: Leavitt, Lord and Co., 1835.

Bello, Walden. *Dilemmas of Domination: The Unmaking of the American Empire.* New York: Metropolitan Books, 2004.

Bender, Peter. *Weltmacht Amerika: Das Neue Rom.* Stuttgart: Klett-Cotta, 2003.

Berman, Russell A. *Anti-Americanism in Europe: A Cultural Problem.* Stanford: Hoover Institution Press, 2004.

Boot, Max. *The Savage Wars of Peace: Small Wars and the Rise of American Power.* New York: Basic Books, 2002.

Braund, David. *Rome and the Friendly King: The Character of the Client Kingship.* New York: St. Martin's Press, 1984.

———. "Royal Wills and Rome," *Papers of the British School at Rome* 51 (1983): 16–57.

Buchanan, Patrick J. *Day of Reckoning: How Hubris, Ideology, and Greed Are Tearing America Apart.* New York: Thomas Dunne Books, 2007.

———. *A Republic, Not an Empire: Reclaiming America's Destiny.* Washington, D.C.: Regnery, 1999.

Bugajski, Janusz, and Ilona Teleki. *Atlantic Bridges: America's New European Allies.* Lanham: Rowman and Littlefield, 2006.

Bunkley, Josephine M. *The Testimony of an Escaped Novice from the Sisterhood of St. Joseph.* New York: Harper and Bros., 1855.

Byman, Daniel L., and Kenneth M. Pollack. *Things Fall Apart: Containing the Spillover From an Iraqi Civil War.* The Saban Center for Middle East Policy at the Brookings Institution, Analysis Paper Number 11, January 2007.

Chace, James. "In Search of Absolute Security." In *The Imperial Tense: Prospects and Problems of American Empire,* ed. Andrew J. Bacevich. Chicago: Ivan R. Dee, 2003, 119–33.

Chomsky, Noam. *Hegemony or Survival: America's Quest for Global Dominance.* New York: Metropolitan Books, 2003.

Chua, Amy. *Day of Empire: How Hyperpowers Rise to Global Dominance—and Why They Fall.* New York: Doubleday, 2007.

Cornell, T. J. "The End of Roman Imperial Expansion." In *War and Society in the Roman World,* ed. John Rich and Graham Shipley. New York: Routledge, 1993, 139–70.

Daniels, Anthony, "Sense of Superiority and Inferiority in French Anti-Americanism." In *Understanding Anti-Americanism: Its Origins and Impact at Home and Abroad,* ed. Paul Hollander. Chicago: Ivan R. Dee, 2004.

Delisser, Richard L. *Pope or President? Startling Disclosures of Romanism as Revealed by its own Writers.* New York: R. L. Delisser, 1859.

Derow, P. S. "Polybius, Rome, and the East," *Journal of Roman Studies* 69 (1979): 1–15.

Eckstein, Arthur M. "Conceptualizing Roman Imperial Expansion under the Republic: An Introduction." In *A Companion to the Roman Republic,* ed. Nathan Rosenstein and Robert Morstein-Marx. Oxford: Blackwell, 2006, 567–89.

Faulkner, Neil. *Apocalypse: The Great Jewish Revolt Against Rome, AD 66–73.* Stroud: Tempus, 2002.

Ferguson, Niall. *Colossus: The Price of America's Empire.* New York: Penguin, 2004.

———. *Empire: The Rise and Demise of the British World Order and the Lessons for Global Power.* New York: Basic Books, 2002.

Frank, Tenney, *Roman Imperialism.* New York: Macmillan Co., 1929.

Fulton, Justin D. *Washington in the Lap of Rome.* Boston: W. Kellaway, 1888.

Gibbon, Edward. *The History of the Decline & Fall of the Roman Empire,* ed. J. B. Bury, 3 vols. New York: Heritage Press, 1946.

Gordon, Philip H. "Can the War on Terror Be Won? How to Fight the Right War." *Foreign Affairs* 86/6 (2007): 53–66.

Grant, Michael. *The Jews in the Roman World.* New York: Charles Scribner's Sons, 1973.

Gruen, Erich S. "The Bacchanalian Affair." In *Studies in Greek Culture and Roman Policy.* Berkeley: University of California Press, 1996.

———. *Culture and National Identity in Republican Rome.* Ithaca: Cornell University Press, 1993.

———. *The Hellenistic World and the Coming of Rome.* Berkeley: University of California Press, 1986.

———. "Roman Perpsectives on the Jews in the Age of the Great Revolt." In *The First Jewish Revolt: Archaeology, History, and Ideology,* eds. Andrea M. Berlin and J. Andrew Overman. New York: Routledge, 2002, 27–42.

———. "Rome and the Greek World." In *The Cambridge Companion to the Roman Republic,* ed. Harriet I. Flower. Cambridge: Cambridge University Press, 2004, 242–67.

Harris, Robert. "Pirates of the Mediterranean," *New York Times,* September 30, 2006.

Harris, William V. *War and Imperialism in Republican Rome, 327–70 BC.* Oxford: Clarendon Press, 1979.

Herman, Arthur. "Who Owns the Vietnam War?" *Commentary* 124/5 (2007): 42–52.

Holleaux, Maurice. *Rome, la Grèce, et les Monarchies Hellénistiques au IIIe Siècle avant J.-C. (273–205).* Paris: E. de Boccard, 1921.

Huet, Valérie. "Napoleon I: A New Augustus?" In *Roman Presences: Receptions of Rome in European Culture, 1789–1945,* ed. Catharine Edwards. Cambridge: Cambridge University Press, 1999, 53–69.

Huntington, Samuel P. "The Lonely Superpower." *Foreign Affairs* (March–April 1999).

Hutton, Will. *A Declaration of Interdependence: Why America Should Join the World.* New York: W. W. Norton and Co., 2004.

Isaac, Benjamin. *The Invention of Racism in Classical Antiquity.* Princeton: Princeton University Press, 2004.

Ignatieff, Michael. "Who Are Americans to Think That Freedom Is Theirs to Spread?," *New York Times Magazine,* June 26, 2005.

Irons, Peter. *War Powers: How the Imperial Presidency Hijacked the Constitution.* New York: Metropolitan Books, 2005.

Johnson, Chalmers. *Nemesis: The Last Days of the American Republic.* New York: Metropolitan Books, 2007.

———. *The Sorrows of Empire: Militarism, Secrecy, and the End of the Republic.* New York: Metropolitan Books, 2004.

Kagan, Robert. *Of Paradise and Power: America and Europe in the New World Order.* New York: Alfred A. Knopf, 2003.

————. "Power and Weakness," *Policy Review,* 113 (2002).

————. *Dangerous Nation.* New York: Alfred A. Knopf, 2006.

Kallet-Marx, Robert Morstein. *Hegemony to Empire: The Development of the Roman Imperium in the East from 148 to 62 BC.* Berkeley: University of California Press, 1995.

Kaplan, Robert D. *Warrior Politics: Why Leadership Demands a Pagan Ethos.* New York: Random House, 2001.

Kohut, Andrew, and Bruce Stokes. *America Against the World: How We are Different and Why We Are Disliked.* New York: Times Books, 2006.

Krueger, Alan B. *What Makes a Terrorist: Economics and the Roots of Terrorism.* Princeton: Princeton University Press, 2007.

Kupchan, Charles A. *The End of the American Era: U.S. Foreign Policy and Geopolitics in the Twenty-first Century.* New York: Knopf, 2002.

————. "The End of the West." *Atlantic Monthly* 290 (November 2002): 42–4.

Lal, Deepak. *In Praise of Empires: Globalization and Order.* New York: Palgrave Macmillan, 2004.

————. "Empire and Order," *Historically Speaking* 8 (2007): 15–18.

Lieber, Keir A., and Daryl G. Press. "The Rise of U.S. Nuclear Primacy." *Foreign Affairs* (March/April 2006).

Lieven, Anatol. *America Right or Wrong: An Anatomy of American Nationalism.* New York: Oxford University Press, 2004.

Lintott, Andrew. "What Was the *'imperium romanum'*?" *Greece and Rome* 28 (1981): 53–67.

————. *Imperium Romanum: Politics and Administration.* New York: Routledge, 1993.

Lomas, Kathryn. "Italy during the Roman Republic, 338–31 BC." In *The Cambridge Companion to the Roman Republic,* ed. Harriet I. Flower. Cambridge: Cambridge University Press, 2004, 199–224.

Madden, Thomas F. *The New Concise History of the Crusades.* Lanham: Rowman and Littlefield, 2005.

Maier, Charles S. *Among Empires: American Ascendancy and Its Predecessors.* Cambridge, Mass.: Harvard University Press, 2006.

Mandelbaum, Michael. *The Case for Goliath: How America Acts as the World's Government in the Twenty-first Century.* New York: Public Affairs, 2005.

Mattern, Susan P. *Rome and the Enemy: Imperial Strategy in the Principate.* Berkeley: University of California Press, 1999.

Merry, Robert W. *Sands of Empire: Missionary Zeal, American Foreign Policy, and the Hazards of Global Ambition.* New York: Simon & Schuster, 2005.

Mommsen, Theodor. *The History of Rome,* trans. W. P. Dickson, 4 vols. London: Dent, 1920–21.

Monk, Maria. *Awful Disclosures of the Hotel Dieu Nunnery of Montreal.* New York: Maria Monk, 1836.

Morse, Samuel F. B. *Foreign Conspiracy Against the Liberties of the United States.* New York: Leavitt, Lord and Co., 1835.

Mosbacher, Michael, and Digby Anderson. "Recent Trends in British Anti-

Americanism." In *Understanding Anti-Americanism: Its Origins and Impact at Home and Abroad*. Chicago: Ivan R. Dee, 2004.

Murphy, Cullen. *Are We Rome? The Fall of an Empire and the Fate of America*. New York: Houghton Mifflin, 2007.

Ogilvie, R. M. *Early Rome and the Etruscans*. Atlantic Highlands: Humanities Press, 1976.

Petrochilos, Nicholas. *Roman Attitudes to the Greeks*. Athens: University of Athens, 1974.

Potts, William S. *Dangers of Jesuit Instruction*. St. Louis: Keith and Woods, 1846.

Raaflaub, Kurt A. "Born to be Wolves? Origins of Roman Imperialism." In *Transitions to Empire: Essays in Greco-Roman History, 360–146 BC, in Honor of E. Badian*, ed. R. W. Wallace and Edward Monroe Harris. Norman: University of Oklahoma Press, 1996, 271–314.

Revel, Jean-François. *Anti-Americanism*. San Francisco: Encounter Books, 2003.

Rich, John. "Fear, Greed, and Glory: The Causes of Roman War-Making in the Middle Republic." In *War and Society in the Roman World*, ed. John Rich and Graham Shipley. New York: Routledge, 1993, 38–68.

Richard, Carl J. *The Founders and the Classics: Greece, Rome, and the American Enlightenment*. Cambridge, Mass.: Harvard University Press, 1994.

Richardson, J. S. "Polybius' View of the Roman Empire," *Papers of the British School at Rome* 47 (1979): 1–11.

Sapolsky, Robert M. "A Natural History of Peace." *Foreign Affairs* (January/February 2006).

Schäfer, Peter. *The History of the Jews in the Greco-Roman World*. London: Routledge, 2003.

Scullard, H. H. *From the Gracchi to Nero: A History of Rome from 133 BC to AD 68*, 5th ed. New York: Routledge, 1982.

———. *A History of the Roman World, 753 to 146 BC*, 4th ed. New York: Methuen, 1980.

Sellers, Mortimer N. S. *American Republicanism: Roman Ideology in the United States Constitution*. New York: New York University Press, 1994.

———. "The Roman Republic and the French and American Revolutions." In *The Cambridge Companion to the Roman Republic*, ed. Harriet I. Flower. Cambridge: Cambridge University Press, 2004, 347–64.

Shipley, Graham. *The Greek World after Alexander, 323–30 BC*. New York: Routledge, 2000.

Steyn, Mark. *America Alone: The End of the World as We Know It*. Washington, D.C.: Regnery Publishing, 2006.

Todd, Emmanuel. *After the Empire: The Breakdown of the American Order*, trans. C. Jon Delogu. New York: Columbia University Press, 2003.

Veyne, Paul. "Y a-t-il eu un impérialisme romain?" *Mélanges d'Archéologie et d'Histoire de l'École Française de Rome* 87 (1975): 793–855.

Twain, Mark, *Great Short Works of Mark Twain*, ed. Justin Kaplan. New York: HarperCollins, 2004.

Vance, Norman. "Decadence and the Subversion of Empire." In *Roman Presences:*

Receptions of Rome in European Culture, 1789–1945, ed. Catharine Edwards. Cambridge: Cambridge University Press, 1999, 110–24.

Walker, Martin. "An Empire Unlike Any Other." In *The Imperial Tense: Prospects and Problems of American Empire,* ed. Andrew J. Bacevich. Chicago: Ivan R. Dee, 2003.

———. "The New German Army." *In the National Interest,* Jan. 22, 2004.

ACKNOWLEDGMENTS

This book has benefited from the help, patience, and good humor of many people. Thanks are due to John F. Thornton, my agent, who offered many suggestions when my ideas were only just forming and plenty of support along the way. I am grateful to John Alexander of Recorded Books, who listened to and challenged those ideas before I put them on paper. Stephen Morrow of Dutton/Penguin has been an unfailing support, patiently and diplomatically helping an author trained for the scholarly world to write for the real one. Finally, I thank my wife, Page Ettle, who with her trusty scissors and a steady supply of *The New York Times,* kept the head of an ancient historian still grounded in the present. I could not have written this book without her loving support.

INDEX

ABOUT THE AUTHOR

Thomas F. Madden is Professor of History and Director of the Center for Medieval and Renaissance Studies at Saint Louis University. A prolific author, he is also a respected media expert, appearing in such venues as *The New York Times, Washington Post, USA Today,* the History Channel, the Discovery Channel, and others.

His books include the *New Concise History of the Crusades* (2005) and the award-winning *Enrico Dandolo and the Rise of Venice* (2003). He has also published extensively on the ancient and medieval Mediterranean as well as the history of Christianity. Awards for his scholarship include the 2005 Otto Gründler Prize, awarded by the Medieval Institute, and the 2007 Haskins Medal, awarded by the Medieval Academy of America.

Madden served for eight years as Chair of the Department of History at Saint Louis University. He received his B.A. from the University of New Mexico and his M.A. and Ph.D. from the University of Illinois with research specialties in Medieval Europe, Ancient Rome, and Islamic History. Today he divides his time between teaching, producing scholarly studies, and writing other things that people will actually read.

He lives in St. Louis, Missouri with his wife and two daughters.